Schriftenreihe der Bet Tfila – Forschungsstelle für jüdische Architektur in Europa
herausgegeben von Aliza Cohen-Mushlin, Vladimir Levin und Alexander von Kienlin
Band 13

Publications of Bet Tfila – Research Unit for Jewish Architecture in Europe
edited by Aliza Cohen-Mushlin, Vladimir Levin, and Alexander von Kienlin
volume 13

Galka Scheyer – A Jewish Woman in International Art Business

edited by Katrin Keßler

Michael Imhof Verlag

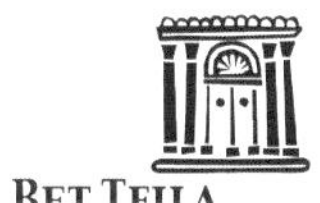

Cover images:
front: Galka Scheyer at Kings Road, early 1930s (from: The Architecture of R. M. Schindler, MOCA, Los Angeles 2001)
back (f. l.): Emmy E. Scheyer, "Footbridge" (Private Collection Braunschweig), and "Prophetess of the Blue Four" (The San Francisco Examiner, Nov. 1, 1925)

Katrin Keßler (Hrg.):
Galka Scheyer – A Jewish Woman in International Art Business
Schriftenreihe der Bet Tfila – Forschungsstelle für jüdische Architektur in Europa,
hrg. v. Aliza Cohen-Mushlin, Vladimir Levin und Alexander von Kienlin, Band 13
Michael Imhof Verlag, Petersberg 2021

Compilation: Andéol Bellec
Layout: Bet Tfila – Research Unit, Braunschweig
Reproduction: Michael Imhof Verlag, Petersberg
Print: Druckerei Rindt GmbH & Co. KG, Fulda

© 2021
Michael Imhof Verlag GmbH & Co. KG
Stettiner Straße 25
D-36100 Petersberg
Tel. 06 61/29 19 166 0, Fax 06 61/29 19 166 9
https://www.imhofverlag.de

ISBN 978-3-7319-1206-4

Gedruckt mit freundlicher Unterstützung / Published with the generous support of

321 – 1700 Jahre jüdisches Leben in Deutschland
Bürgerstiftung Braunschweig
Stadt Braunschweig, Dezernat für Kultur und Wissenschaft
US-Generalkonsulat Hamburg

Gefördert durch:

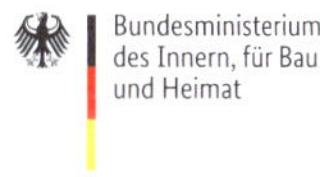

aufgrund eines Beschlusses
des Deutschen Bundestages

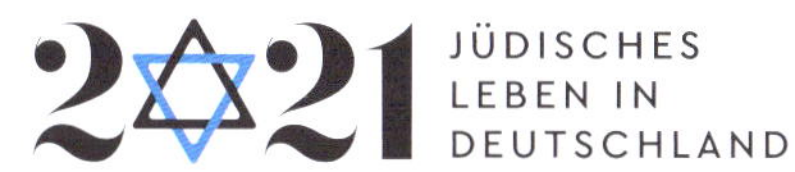

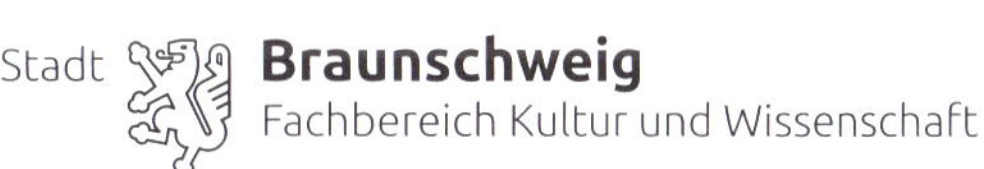

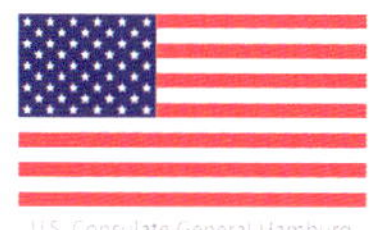

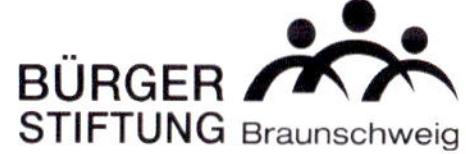

The content of the articles as well as the authorization for photo publishing rights are the sole responsibility of the authors.

It has not proven possible to locate or contact copyright holders in all instances. Naturally, legitimate claims will be satisfied in the framework of the usual arrangements.

Table of Contents

Introduction

It was at a reception given by the Municipality of Braunschweig for the guests of a conference of the Bet Tfila – Research Unit for History of Jewish Architecture in Europe that Dr. Anja Hesse, head of the Cultural Department of the Municipality of Braunschweig, came up with the idea of making the former Braunschweig resident Galka Scheyer better known in the city and beyond. This idea then developed into the concept for an international conference, which took place in Braunschweig from November 26 to 27, 2019, and we were glad that the most significant scholars working on this topic came to present their results which are now available here in printed form.

Some of the authors have been dealing with the life and work of this amazing woman, painter, collector, art dealer, and art manager, for many years. During the conference, a fascinating panorama of art, society, and history of the twentieth century emerged in the synopsis – thus serving as a background for Galka Scheyer's vibrant personality. This volume is another contribution to a series of events and publications that will bring Galka Scheyer as a personality to the attention of the city and the region to learn more about her life and about the people of her time. During the conference, the unveiling of a commemorative and information plaque donated by the Braunschweig Civic Foundation (Bürgerstiftung Braunschweig) took place, which now indicates Galka Scheyer's birthplace in the cityscape – an important step towards giving her a place in public memory. With the (German) tour brochure "Galka Scheyer in Braunschweig. On the trail of the Jewish art mediator" (Katrin Keßler & Gilbert Holz-gang, *Galka Scheyer in Braunschweig. Auf den Spuren der jüdischen Kunstvermittlerin*, Braunschweig 2021), which the Bet Tfila – Research Unit developed along with Gilbert Holzgang of the Galka Emmy Scheyer Zentrum e.V., residents and their guests can now discover places that were important to Galka Scheyer in the city and where her love of art developed.

One hundred and thirty years ago, in 1889, Emilie Esther Scheyer, who later called herself Galka, was born as the daughter of Henriette and Leopold Scheyer. She thus belongs to that generation of people born in the 1880s who – as artists, architects, writers, or musicians – had a decisive influence on the development of modernism in the twentieth century. Emilie Esther Scheyer's father was an entrepreneur, first a leather wholesaler and later the owner of Braunschweig's largest canning factory of the time – canning was a real Braunschweig specialty! The wealthy family belonged to the Jewish community of Braunschweig. The new synagogue in the Steinstraße, built as a symbol of the Jewish community's participation in German society, was only fourteen years old when Emilie Scheyer was born. Artistically gifted and blessed with great curiosity, the young woman left Braunschweig for Oxford, Paris, Munich, and Brussels. On her way, she encountered the latest trends in modern art and its artistic personalities. Of particular importance was her encounter with Alexej von Jawlensky in Switzerland. Galka Scheyer took over the task of distribution and sale of his works in 1919. From then on, she devoted herself to art management and the art trade. In 1924, Scheyer founded the "Blue Four" with Jawlensky, Klee, Kandinsky, and Feininger, the latter of whom she had met at the Bauhaus in Weimar. She organized exhibitions and promoted their works with some success – although women as art agents were probably even more unusual than painters or sculptors in the 1920s. To open up new markets for "her" artists, she finally went to the USA in 1924. In California, having obtained American citizenship in 1931, she continued her work with her own gallery. She once again made herself the center of a broad artistic-cultural network that became of existential importance for the survival of many Jewish Germans in the USA – especially after the immigration of those persecuted by National Socialism from 1933 onwards.

Scheyer's fate changed from being a migrant to an exile as a result of the anti-Semitic policies in Germany – her Braunschweig relatives became victims of National Socialist Germans in various ways. Her brothers had to sell the business and with her help were able to emigrate in time. Her mother died in 1942 at the age of 81 in a so-called Judenhaus; these were houses in which Jews were crammed into before being deported to concentration camps. Galka Scheyer died in Hollywood in 1945, a few months after the end of the war and the Holocaust.

Whether, when, and to what extent Galka Scheyer saw herself as part of a German-Jewish or, more generally, Jewish culture or religion, remains unclear. Her life path and personality seem too individual, too extraordinary, to be easily classified – and in too many ways she is the exception and not the rule.

Nevertheless, with her family, artistic and cultural networks, she stands for many who, in retrospect, we consider to belong to the environment of German-Jewish culture of the late nineteenth and first half of the twentieth centuries. But what does this Jewish culture mean today, what traces have the German-Jewish emigrants and exiles left behind in the countries they went to after fleeing from National Socialist Germany?

Many people worked together on this publication, and we would like to thank all of them: Suzan Meves, Stade, for editing the texts; Andéol Bellec and Mirko Przystawik, Bet Tfila – Research Unit, for the layout, and – of course – all the authors for their efforts. The editing and printing were made possible through the financial support of the society "321–2021. 1700 Years of Jewish Life in Germany," the City of Braunschweig, the Bürgerstiftung Braunschweig (Braunschweig Civic Foundation), and the US Consulate General in Hamburg. To all of them, we would like to extend our warmest thanks! And we are convinced that our efforts have laid a foundation for the remembrance of Galka Emmy Scheyer.

Katrin Keßler, Ulrich Knufinke

GALKA SCHEYER'S LIFE
AND SOCIAL BACKGROUND IN EUROPE

Gilbert Holzgang

During the thirty five years Galka Scheyer spent in Europe, she changed her social background some five times. She was a woman who made friends easily and thus became acquainted with many persons. Based on archive material, I will mention about eighty of them.

The First Phase of Her Life

Emilie Esther Scheyer, called Emmy or Galka Scheyer, grew up in the old residential city of Braunschweig with its 120,000 residents, its castle and churches, half-timbered and Wilhelminian manor houses, workshops and factories.

Leopold Scheyer, Emmy's father, was born in the small-town of Bleicherode in the southern part of the Harz Mountains. In 1881, he opened a leather business for shoemakers in Braunschweig. Four years later, he married Henriette Katzenstein, who had grown up in Kassel, the capital of the electorate of Hesse.

In 1886 and 1887, two sons, Paul and Erich, were born. The family lived at Okerstraße 10, when Emilie Esther Scheyer was born on April 15, 1889. Three years, later the family moved to a new domicile, centrally located at the Monumentsplatz (today's Löwenwall).[1]

Valeska Heynemann, later known as Lette Valeska, sought to write a biography of her schoolmate Emmy. From it we learn that Henriette Scheyer was a person "showing a distinguished bourgeois manner with its set of upper-class prejudice typical of the small duchy residence."[2] In her book, Lette Valeska does not mention the fact that both the Scheyer and the Heynemann families were of Jewish faith – this seemed to be irrelevant up until 1933. Valeska and Emmy are likely to have attended the urban secondary school for girls ("Kleine Burg"). Unfortunately, proven evidence is missing.

1 Emmy, Erich, and Paul Scheyer, February 23, 1891 (Courtesy of the Getty Research Institute, Los Angeles (980065)).

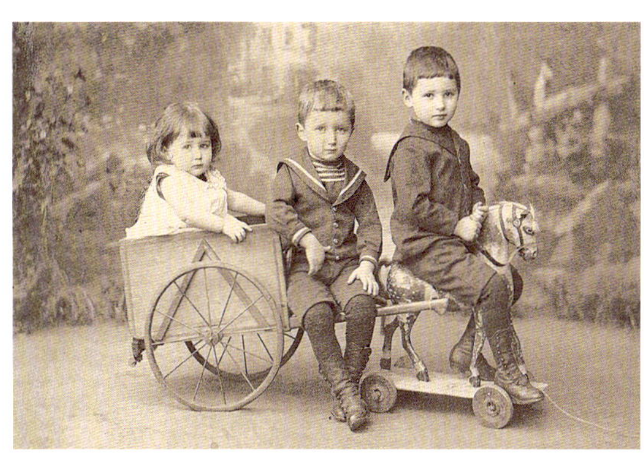

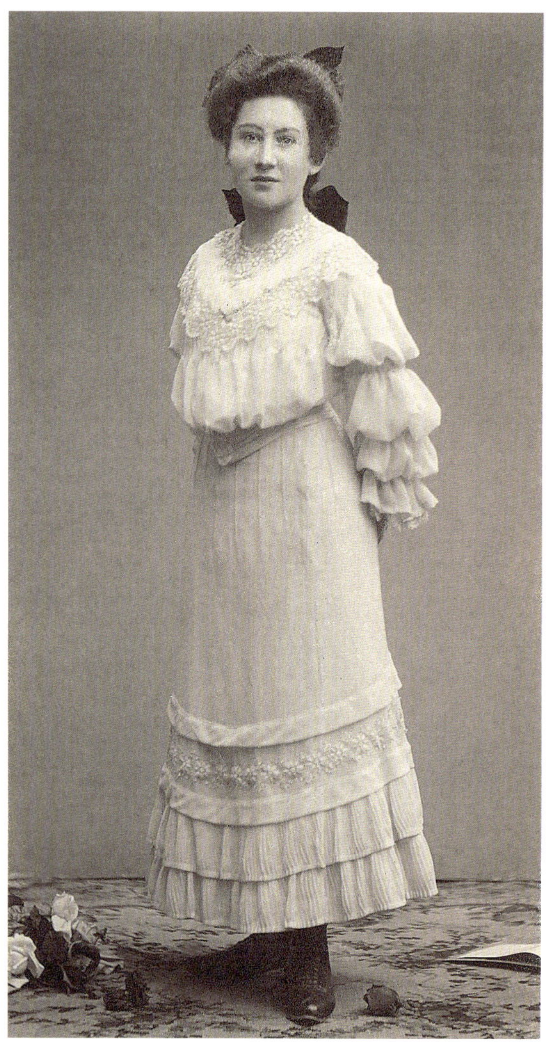

2 Portrait of Emmy Scheyer, 1905 (Courtesy of the Getty Research Institute, Los Angeles (980065)).

After ten years of compulsory education, Emmy Scheyer became a student at a boarding school for young ladies in Dornholzhausen in the Taunus region (Rhineland).[3] English was an obligatory subject.[4] According to the social standards of their class her friends did as well. Käte, the daughter of lumber merchant Wilhelm Brachvogel and his wife Erna, enrolled at the Hölterhoffstift in Bad Honnef, not far from the Rhine and the city of Bonn[5] and later married Otto Ralfs.[6]

Emmy's friend Elsa Daubert, daughter of the can manufacturing industrialist Wilhelm Daubert and his wife Margarete grew up in Braunschweig's historic town center, at the Marstall, along with her parents and her brother. Emmy and Elsa were close friends with Käthe Evers, daughter of grammar school teacher Robert Evers and his wife Margarete, who lived in a three-story house in the Ottmerstraße that had a veranda, a bay window and art-nouveau furniture.[7] Scheyer's family had a huge renaissance style sideboard topped by a paper flower bouquet à la Hans Makart, which greatly impressed Valeska Heynemann.[8]

In 1906, Emmy's father sold his shares in the leather trade company and bought the can manufacturing factory W. Maseberg in Braunschweig's Wiesenstraße.[9]

At that time, cultural life of the urban middle-class mainly consisted of going to opera and theater performances at the ducal court theatre and to the concerts of regimental bands held in front of the castle. The annual exhibitions of the local art association "Kunstverein" not only presented traditional works of art but also modern ones by Charles J. Palmié and his pupil Anna Löhr, who adopted the French style of pointillist painting which scandalized many critics and visitors. The headquarters of "Dörbandt Art Trade" were located on the Bohlweg. As early as 1906, and later on as well, it showed a great deal of courage by exhibiting works by such "Brücke" artists as Schmidt-Rottluff and Heckel, who were then completely unknown.

The Ducal Museum (today's Herzog Anton Ulrich-Museum) occasionally organized alternate exhibitions of old and new masters (e. g., Dürer, Rembrandt, Böcklin, Menzel) and – at least three to four times a year – also contemporary artists, such as Hans Herse,[10] Emmy Scheyer's art teacher at school, and Gustav Lehmann, the son of a local businessman, graduate of the Munich Academy of

Art, who studied under Franz Stuck and Charles J. Palmié. In November 1907, he succeeded in presenting a selection of his oeuvre at the Ducal Museum. During the next years, he sold many of his works to local industrialists and members of the educated class. The customers' identity is known but the question whether or not they belonged to Emmy Scheyer's acquaintances remains unanswered.[11] Lehmann, however, played an important role in …

the Second Phase of Her Life

Emmy Scheyer enjoyed painting. She probably took private lessons in oil painting at the studio of a well known flower painter, Anna Pricelius.[12] A flower still life still exists and is signed "E. E. Scheyer" on the stretcher frame, with a "7" indicating the year 1907. Emmy's desire to become an artist caused considerable problems. Painting from time to time – even in oil – was just barely accepted by the social standards of her well-off class. Becoming a professional artist – how shocking – was absolutely out of the question!

In 1907, Brunswick grammar school teacher Karl Hildebrandt held a lecture on "Understanding Modern Painting."[13] Possibly Emmy Scheyer heard it or read his articles on impressionism, pointillism and the "Brücke" artists' group.[14]

It is also quite likely that she participated in a course on plein air painting held by Charles J. Palmié in autum 1908 in Braunschweig-Riddagshausen.[15] Gustav Lehmann was probably one of the participants as well as a young Austrian painter named Fritz Krčal. However, we are sure that Albert Hamburger, son of a wealthy local store owner, did. He painted the same small bridge as Palmié did.

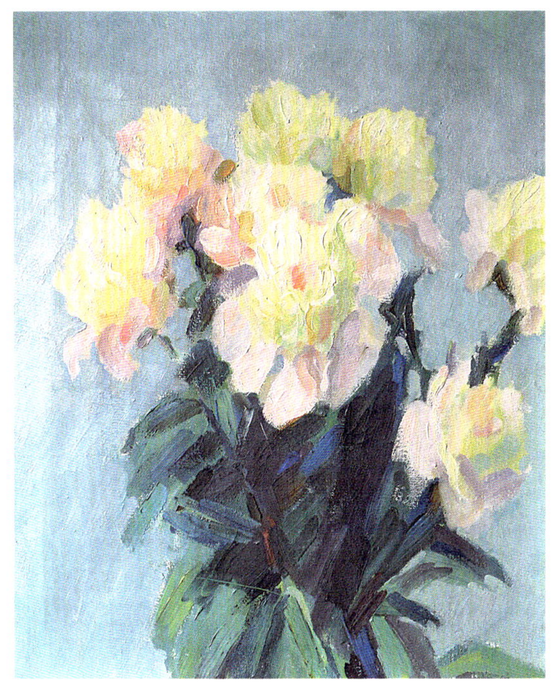

Emmy E. Scheyer, Peonies, oil on canvas, 1907 (Private collection, Munich).

In the spring 1909, a sales exhibit of Palmié's works was held in the Ducal Museum.[16] The parents of Emmy Scheyer's school friend Käte Brachvogel are said to have bought one of the paintings.[17] At that time, Emmy Scheyer lived in Braunschweig in the splendid Kaiser Wilhelmstraße. Later, the entire family moved to a villa located in front of the can factory W. Maseberg, which had moved to the Goslarschestraße.[18]

In April 1909, Emmy Scheyer celebrated her twentieth birthday. Five days later, her father died during a stay in Berlin at the age of fifty seven "after a short serious illness" according to the obituary notice.[19] Paul, Erich and Emmy Scheyer, his three children, were officially registered as the new owners of the above mentioned factory.[20]

In August 1909, Emmy Scheyer visited Gustav Lehmann in Munich, accompanied by Albert Hamburger. Lehmann started working on a portrait of him and also created an ex libris for Emmy Scheyer. Shortly hereafter, Emmy left for England where she had found a job as a nanny, according to Lette Valeska.[21] In Oxford, she participated in an English language course and gained her diploma.[22]

Back in Braunschweig, Emmy Scheyer was able to view the latest works by her teacher Gustav Lehmann, first exhibited in the salon of Ottilie Witting, a department store heiress, and later in the Ducal Museum.[23] Assumptions were made somewhat later of a serious conflict that had broken out between Emmy Scheyer and her family. In July 1910, Paul Scheyer informed the municipal authorities that his sister, Miss Emilie Scheyer, had resigned from the W. Maseberg company.[24] As far as the reasons for this step are concerned, it is quite possible that Emmy's decision to continue her education as an artist had been the trigger.

Her relationship towards her mother and her brothers remained strained for years. In her letters, we find such remarks as "their world isn't mine" or her assertion that her family "only holds material goods in high esteem." The relationship with her brother Paul seemed to have been particularly oppressive. However, communication with her younger brother Erich, an art collector, was somewhat better. His wife Margrit was the only person with whom Emmy was on friendly terms.[25]

During the summer of 1910, Emmy and Gustav Lehmann travelled to Italy – a courageous step for a young unmarried lady in those days! In Viareggio, they painted quite similar subjects, namely sailboats. Emmy created an oil sketch and a larger painting signed and dated on the stretcher frame, as she had done with the flower still life in 1907. Scheyer made an oil painting of Viareggio, as seen from the mole. Whether this work originated in 1910 or 1911, when both Lehmann and Scheyer

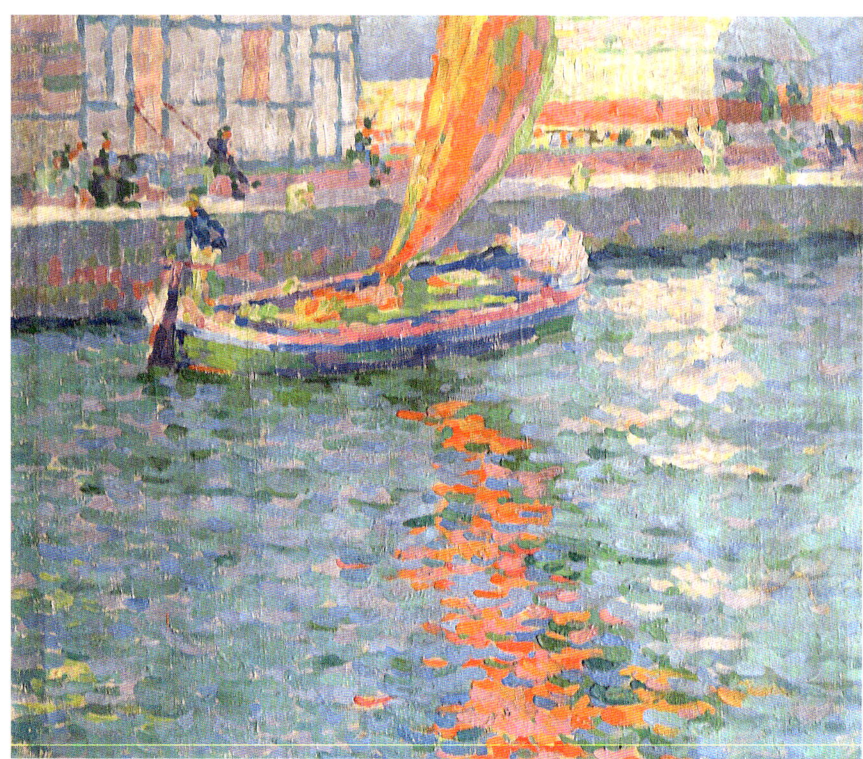

4 Emmy E. Scheyer, Boat in Viareggio, oil on canvas, 1910 (Private collection, Braunschweig).

were once again in Italy, is not certain. In 1911, they produced further subjects in and around Pisa, the paintings *Field Full of Flowers* for example, and *Ponte di Mezzo*.

I have no knowledge why Emmy Scheyer began signing her works with the French pseudonym Renée – literally meaning "being reincarnated" – preferring it to the German equivalent "Renate."

Hardly any valid information is available on Emmy Scheyer's acquaintances in 1912. According to Lette Valeska, Emmy Scheyer stayed in Paris, where she visited museums and took language courses. Two diplomas show that Emmy Scheyer successfully attended a summer school in Saint-Valéry-en-Caux (Normandy).[26] In 1913, she produced an interior painting, very much in Gustav Lehmann's style.

In her draft version for a scholarship application in 1939, Emmy Scheyer states that she had lived in Munich for a whole year – as Lehmann did – attending lectures by Heinrich Wölfflin,[27] but she was not officially immatriculated at the university.

In 1914, Emmy Scheyer (alias Renée) tried her hand at portrait painting. She depicted a redheaded girl and a young man but we do not know who they were. Apparently her friends Käthe Evers and Elsa Daubert also attended Lehmann's studio in Munich, practising portrait art. In 1914, Käthe Evers painted Lehmann and an elderly woman. Elsa Daubert portrayed Emmy Scheyer. Albert Hamburger also frequented the studio and created a portrait of Lehmann as well as a self-portrait and several other studies.

The available evidence of photos and written documents confirm: all members of the set of artists from Braunschweig used to meet in Munich and went on trips to upper Bavaria.[28] Lehmann unexpectedly died after an appendectomy in July,

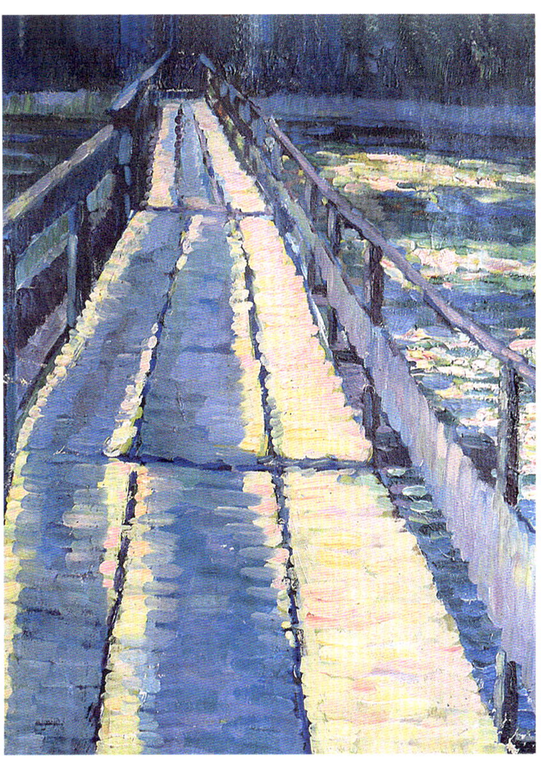

5 Emmy E. Scheyer (Renée), Footbridge, oil on canvas, 1914 (Private collection, Braunschweig).

1914[29] and on the outbreak of the First World War, Elsa Daubert immediately returned to Braunschweig. Emmy Scheyer and Käthe Evers followed.[30]

Here they painted a footbridge across the river Oker, only 150 meters away from Emmy's birthplace. By January 1915, most of Emmy Scheyer's important social contacts had died: Her father Leopold Scheyer, Charles Palmié and Gustav Lehmann. Albert Hamburger was killed at the front in France during WWI.

Emmy decided to move to Brussels, then a capital of the arts, where her friend Valeska Heyneman had been working as a secretary for four years.[31] This was the beginning of Emmy Scheyer's third phase of her life.

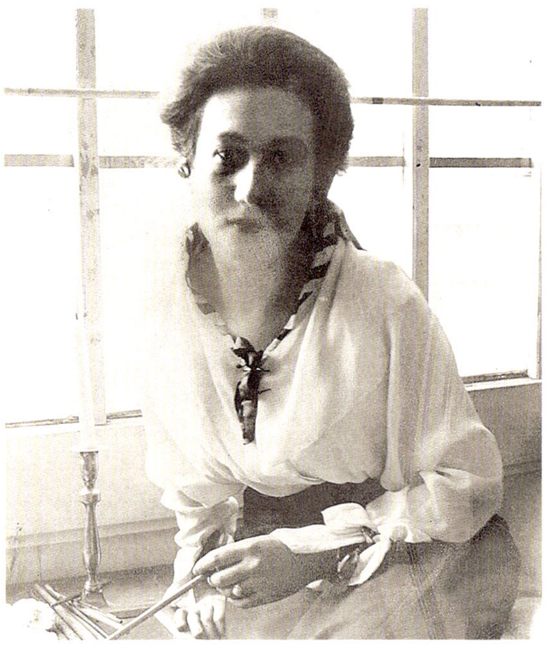

6 Emmy E. Scheyer, Brussels, photo as painter in front of atelier window, 1916 (Courtesy of the Norton Simon Museum, The Blue Four Galka Scheyer Collection Archives, Pasadena, CA).

7 Emmy E. Scheyer (Renée), Self-Portrait, oil on canvas, 1916 (Courtesy of Julia Hammid and the Estate of Tino Hammid).

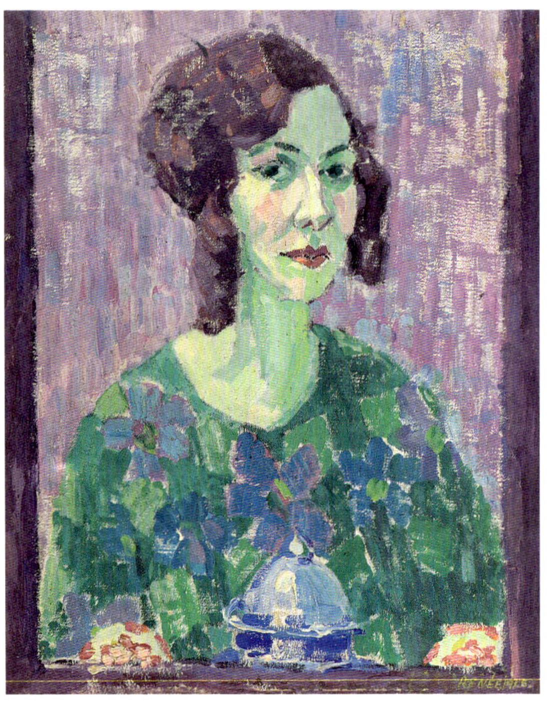

Third Phase of Her Life

In Brussels she made friends with Jos Albert (1886–1981), a poor painter who became her teacher.[32] Several works were created here: A self-portrait signed *Renée* and a small painting titled *In the Nursery* verso and *Brussels 1916* on the front by unknown hand in America, presumably showing Louise Albert, her teachers wife, and their son Émile with a gun, playing as a cowboy or a cavalryman. A similarly structured work portrays Valeska Heynemann, mending stockings. There are also larger paintings: *Lady and Her Mirror Image*, a self portrait as *Lady on Balcony* and a still life, the only work by Scheyer to be deposited in a museum. Emmy Scheyer painted *In the Morning Room* in Brussels. The person in the background is wearing the jersey of Eintracht Braunschweig, a successful soccer team in those days; verso is an unfinished painting *Two Ladies* of unknown identity.

The painting *Snow-Covered Pine-Tree* carries a double signature by "E. Sch." and "Renée." Gustav Lehmann had created similar winter subjects. In her apartment, Emmy Scheyer also painted a still life with flowers on a round arched window sill, dome and portico of the Belgian Palace of Justice in the background. The painting *Sunflowers* is neither signed nor dated. Emmy Scheyer's US relatives have always considered it one of her works. Verso is an unfinished painting of a lady with a hat. The same painter model can be seen in Emmy Scheyer's painting *Lady in an Easy Chair*. She bears a certain resemblance to ladies and cocottes painted by Ernst Ludwig Kirchner in Berlin, but here she opens her coat and blouse in front of the viewer with a seductive gesture.

Last but not least, Emmy Scheyer painted strange portraits with yellow and green faces, and at the studio of sculptor Louis van der Meulen, she created busts made of plaster or clay of Valeska Heynemann and other persons.[33] The *Head of a Girl* originated in 1916 according to Isabel Wünsche.[34]

In 1921, van der Meulen surprised Emmy with a letter after a long period of silence.[35] The reason he thought she could be in the artist's colony of Laren in Northern Holland was that she had recently stayed there, trying to sell a painting by Vincent van Gogh, property of Marianne Werefkin, Alexej Jawlensky and Bernhard Mayer, a very successful international fur trader. Along with his wife Auguste, he founded a cultural association, inviting Thomas Mann and other important figures to Brussels. He financed a branch of Ovide Decroly's reform school without further ado. He also supported anarchists with considerable sums of money.[36]

Another significant acquaintance from Emmy Scheyer's wealthy background were Paul Bachrach, a successful shoe industrialist and velvet and silk trader, and his wife Elvira Bachrach, born in Elberfeld (now a suburb of Wuppertal). Elvira was a former classmate of Else Schüler, later Else Lasker-Schüler.[37] The Bachrach couple had a daughter named Charlotte, then aged fifteen. She had studied free dance under Alexander Sacharoff in Lausanne (Switzerland) since 1915. In her unpublished memoirs, she wrote that she became acquainted with Alexej Jawlensky via Sacharoff who had recommended to her father that he should collect works by Jawlensky.[38] Indeed, Paul Bachrach became a great sponsor of this painter. He also bought at least three works by Emmy Scheyer, of which only the titles still exist.[39]

In April 1916, Emmy Scheyer celebrated her twenty-seventh birthday in Braunschweig and presumably visited an exhibition in memory of

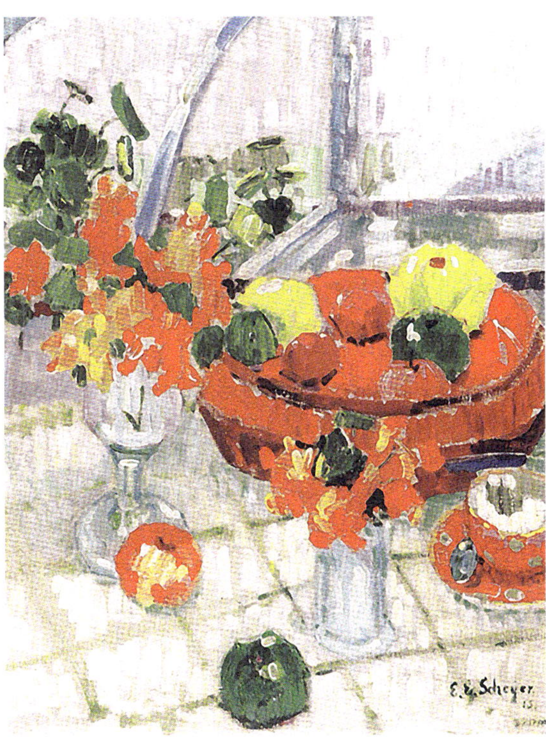

8 Emmy E. Scheyer (Renée), *Still Life*, oil on canvas, 1915 (Courtesy of the Museum of Art, Bern).

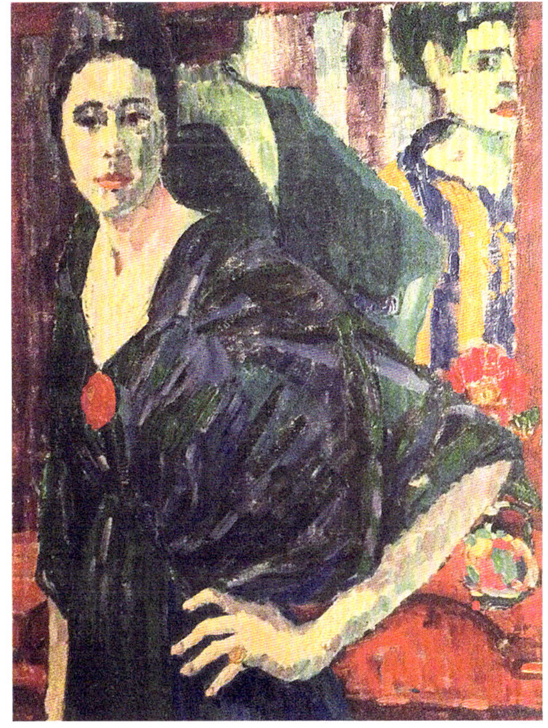

9 Emmy E. Scheyer (Renée), *In the Morning Room*, oil on canvas, 1915 (Private collection, London).

Gustav Lehmann, Albert Hamburger and Günter Brakebusch. On that occasion, many of their works were sold to well-known Brunswick citizens. Marianne Kanter wrote an enthusiastic review.[40] She and her husband Hugo Kanter were collectors of classical modern art – Toulouse-Lautrec for example.[41] It is quite possible, though not proven that the Kanters belonged to Emmy Scheyer's social background.

During her stay in Braunschweig, Emmy could have visited an exhibition of the Berlin gallery Der

Sturm in the Ducal Museum, which had merely provided the location without any conceptional involvement. Herwarth Walden held a speech. He presented works by Albert Bloch (an American painter, member of the group Der Blaue Reiter), Heinrich Campendonk, Franz Marc, Paul Klee and others.[42]

Five days after her birthday, Emmy Scheyer traveled back to Brussels and – according to Lette Valeska's biography draft – gave up her flat, saying that she wanted to go to Switzerland where

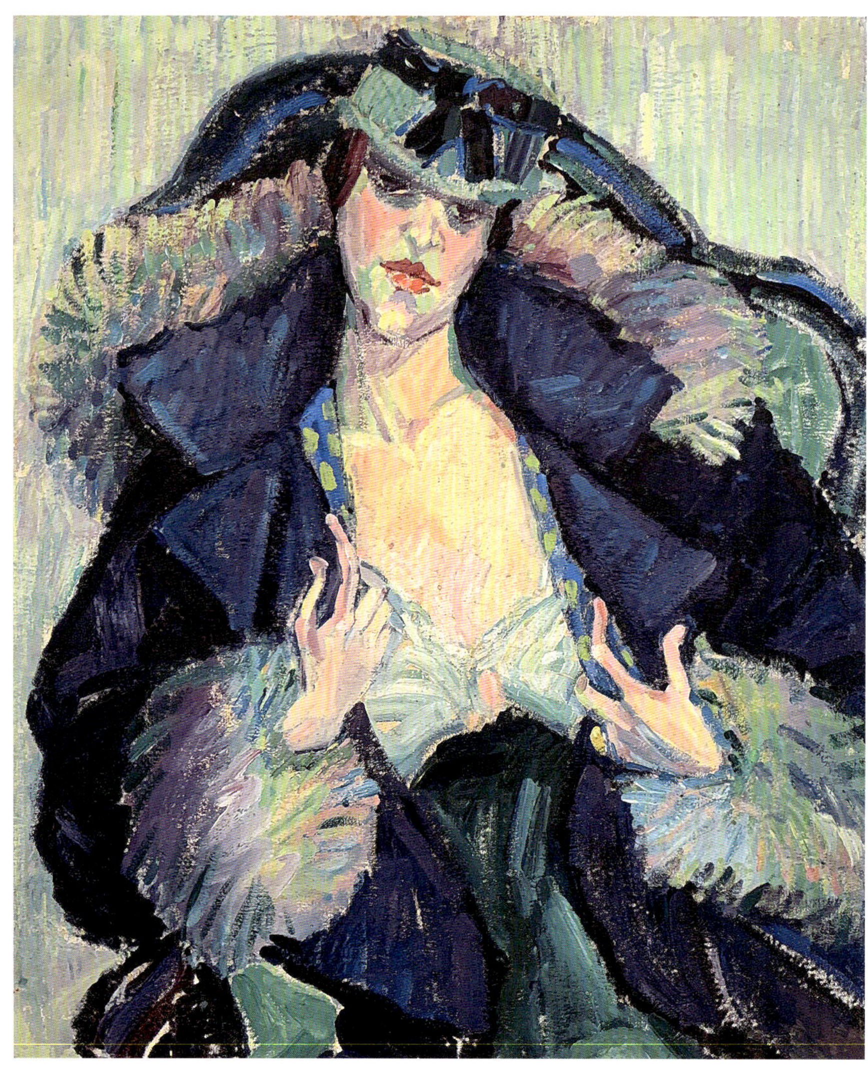

10 Emmy E. Scheyer (Renée), Lady in Easy Chair, oil on canvas, 1916 (Private collection, Braunschweig).

many leading artists lived due to the war.[43] In Lausanne at Lake Geneva, a small exhibition of works by Russian and Polish artists was held between October 20 and November 5, 1916.[44] There are grounds for my assumption that Paul Bachrach recommended Emmy Scheyer to visit the show. Shortly thereafter, she met Jawlensky, Helene Nesnakomoff and her son Andrej in their exile Saint Prex near Lausanne, most probably also Marianne Werefkin.[45]

In Basel or Zurich she met gallery owner Han Coray and/or Edwin Wolfensberger, the director of the art salon Wolfsberg, which presented works by Jawlensky. Emmy Scheyer succeeded in winning collectors who bought several paintings by Jawlensky.[46]

The Galerie Dada organized exhibitions of the gallery Der Sturm and displayed works by Werefkin, Jawlensky, Kandinsky, Feininger, Klee, Albert Bloch and many others, in addition to children's drawings from the collection of painter Arthur Segal. It has been hinted that Werefkin and Jawlensky participated in Dada soirées – possibly Emmy Scheyer was among the guests.[47] Jawlensky was very creative during those months, portraying Emmy Scheyer or being inspired by her countenance. In the autum of 1917, Jawlensky found a new domicile in Zurich.[48] Thanks to this connection, Emmy Scheyer became acquainted with Alexander Sacharoff's partner Clotilde von Derp.

In November, 1917, Emmy Scheyer moved to Zurich, sharing the same guest house as Charlotte Bachrach.[49] From here she sent a letter to Paul Jonas Meier, the director of the Ducal Museum in Braunschweig, asking him for approval to exhibit her works (paintings and sculptures). The names of her sponsors Gustav Lehmann, Ottilie Wit-

ting and Karl Hildebrandt are given as reference. Although Emmy Scheyer received a positive answer, the show did not take place.[50]

The Fourth Phase in Her Life

started early in 1918, when Jawlensky expressed his thanks to Paul Bachrach for the opportunity to make Emmy's acquaintance.[51] He then settled in Ascona (Swiss canton Tessin) with his family.[52] Emmy Scheyer followed them.[53]

Her social background changed once again, but now in a very radical way. It can be proven that she contacted the following persons:

a. Karl Vester, the estate manager of Monte Verità;
b. Peter Groß, a son of Otto Groß, the psychiatrist surrounded by scandal;

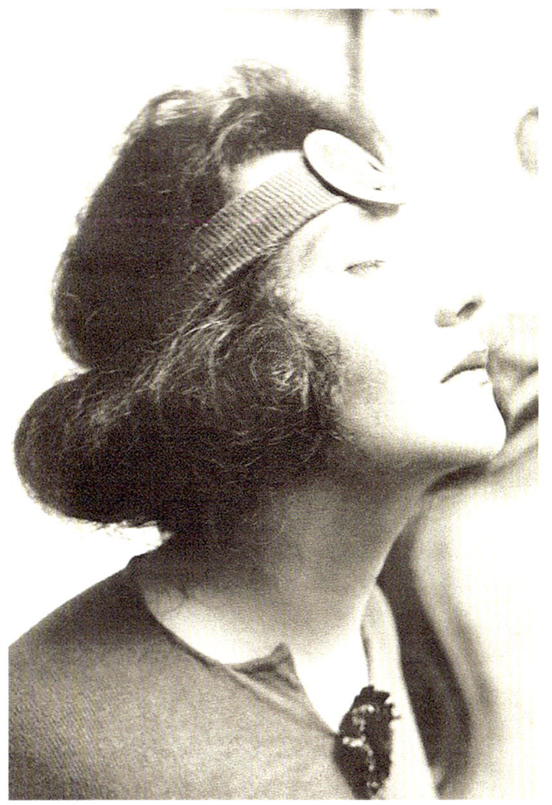

11 Emmy Scheyer, Ascona, in profile, looking towards the right, photo: ca. 1918. (Courtesy of the Norton Simon Museum, Pasadena, California).

c. dancers Mary Wigman, Katja Wulff, Anica Jan and Raja Belensson;

d. poetess and illustrator Else Lasker-Schüler;

e. Allander, a son of Elisabeth Streng, the long-time companion of Gusto Gräser who founded the artist colony Monte Verità;

f. painters Ernst Frick, Hans Looser and Richard Seewald.

As early as 1919, Allander Streng and Hans Looser liked to call Emmy Scheyer "Galka," as Jawlensky did, using the Russian word for jackdaw as her nickname.[54] Another aspect of utmost importance: Emmy Scheyer succeeded in Ascona in cultivating connections with Arthur Segal, Bernhard Mayer and Paul Bachrach, who all lived temporarily with their families in the little town. And her contact with Jawlensky gained in intensity. In 1919, he repeatedly spent time drawing and painting from a higher area above Lago Maggiore, accompanied by Emmy Scheyer painting the same scenery beside him in her specific manner.

Her relationship with Marianne Werefkin, however, deteriorated increasingly in Ascona. Loud quarrels occurred. Marianne Werefkin and Hans Looser mention hearing Emmy's penetrating voice and her "yelling" at the top of it.[55] Karl Vester characterized "the Scheyer" in his unpublished diaries as "an emotionalized, hysterical female" (ein überspanntes hysterisches Frauenzimmer).[56]

Clotilde von Derp's unpublished memoirs express sheer contempt. She even makes an ambiguous remark on the length of Emmy Scheyer's nose.[57] It's still an open question whether Emmy Scheyer's passion to encourage children and teenagers to develop their talents to the full was a natural gift or if the exchange of views between her, Arthur Segal and Albert Bloch during their joint time in Ascona had such a productive effect.

In 1919, Emmy Scheyer modeled a clay bust and scratched the title *Solveig* and the year of origin on it. There are reasons to believe that Charlotte Bachrach alias Charlotte Bara is portrayed.

Lette Valeska mentioned that Paul and Erich Scheyer had asked her in autumn 1919 to help Emmy with her departure from Ascona and return to Braunschweig.[58] Possibly Henriette Scheyer had also urged her daughter to immediately end living with freethinking and impoverished bohemians in Ascona. Some of whom, Else Lasker-Schüler for instance, had been suspected of spying[59] or had even been in prison, such as Ernst Frick.[60]

On her trip back to Braunschweig, Emmy Scheyer met a Dr. Erler in Zurich. In their correspon-

12 Emmy E. Scheyer, Solveig, clay, Photo: 1919 (Private collection, Brussels).

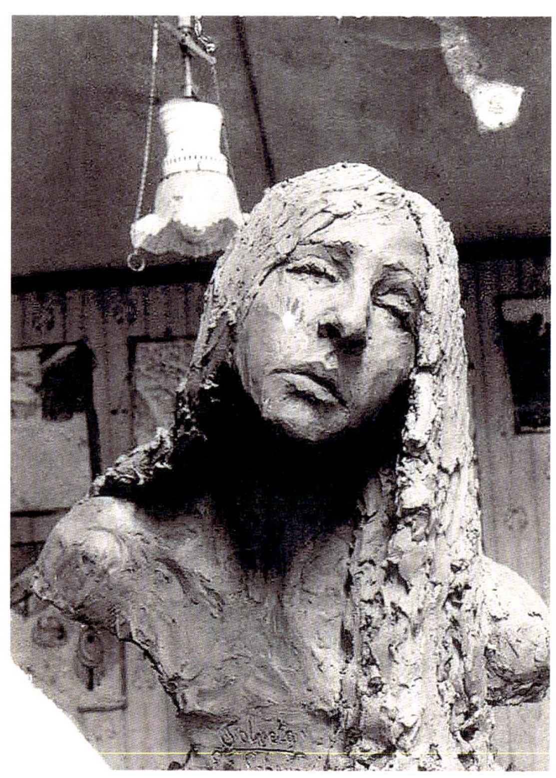

dence she and Jawlensky only used this name – it was Dr. Erich Katzenstein's cover name.[61] He supported socialists and anarchists and he gave Emmy Scheyer and Jawlensky his support by approaching Paul Erich Küppers in Hannover.[62] In Munich Emmy Scheyer fetched a couple of paintings from Jawlensky's and Werefkin's flat which she needed to have at her disposal at home. The painter had earlier given her a letter of recommendation to Paul Klee.[63] This was to enable her to make his acquaintance. Later on, she discussed matters concerning Braunschweig with Paul Klee's wife Lily Klee, whose uncle, aunt and cousin lived in Braunschweig.[64]

On arrival in her home town, Emmy Scheyer was surprised to be given the chance of realizing an exhibition of her own paintings, which had been approved two years earlier. On November 30, 1919 her exhibition was opened.[65] She received a positive review in the local press and sold at least seven works.[66] Unfortunately, the collectors' names remain unknown.

Emmy Scheyer later paid a visit to her cousin Änne Mosbacher in Kassel, who had made a name of herself as an experimental portrait and nature photographer. But then Emmy fell into a deep depression. Her brother Erich proved to be a reliable support in this crisis. They talked about her situation, but also about such topics as the mechanism of the art market or Jawlensky's prospects in view of galloping inflation in Germany. As a result, she made up her mind to organize new exhibitions of his works.

In the Fifth Phase of Her Life

Emmy Scheyer's social milieu changed totally. In Berlin she stayed at a jeweller's named Bloch and with an unidentified aunt who owned a painting by Jawlensky. She was also successful in gaining Wolfgang Gurlitt for a first Jawlensky exhibit. She then concluded contracts with the Commeter Gallery in Hamburg and with Paul Erich Küppers, director of the Kestner Society in Hanover. Even years later, patron Käte Steinitz remembered how vividly she spoke.[67] In addition, Emmy met gallerist Herbert von Garvens and industrialist Fritz Beindorff in Hanover. In Berlin, she was in touch with Urban Kauth, a collector of Paul Klee's and Jawlensky's work. Kauth had previously worked as a jurist in Braunschweig.[68]

At the Fraueninsel on the Chiemsee (Bavaria), she visited the Mielziner family from Braunschweig, who owned several works by Jawlensky.[69] And she met with Jawlensky collectors in her hometown of Braunschweig, including factory owners Hermann Querner and Albert Hoffmeister; Gustav-Elias Forstenzer, businessman and honorary member of the trade jury; presumably Herman Flesche, municipal architect as well.

There is a long list of museum directors, galerists and collectors Emmy Scheyer was associated with. Named in her letters are Hans Goltz, Richard Reiche, Emil Richter, Edmund Fabry, Ludwig Schames, Israel Ber Neumann, Walter Dexel, and many others. A countless number of journalists should be mentioned whom Emmy Scheyer tried to fill with enthusiasm for Jawlensky.

In Weimar, Emmy Scheyer met Bauhaus stars Walter Gropius, Lyonel Feininger and his wife Julia, and Wassily Kandinsky and his wife Nina.[70] She visited their studios, especially Paul Klee's. Steel wholesaler Otto Ralfs was enthusiastic about his art and visited the Bauhaus Jubilee Exhibition in the summer of 1923.[71]

With Emmy Scheyer's help, Otto Ralfs succeeded in purchasing works by Jawlensky and Feininger. But it did not take long time before she became outraged at his financial practices towards herself and both artists[72] and the conflict between the two art enthusiasts escalated.

However, Emmy Scheyer had already been considering plans stretching out beyond Braunschweig and Europe. She received an invitation from a nearly unknown painter named Rajah von Rubio, who asked her to be her guest in Ossining, north of New York.[73]

Before Emmy Scheyer left for the USA, she gave four lectures in Braunschweig on her Blue Four at the home of Dr. Richard Spanjer-Herford.[74] She sold several original works of the Blue Four in Braunschweig.[75]

Emmy Scheyer's passage to New York was made possible by an advance of $950 for works by Feininger, Jawlensky, Kandinsky and Klee, granted by an editor named Alfred Rose.[76] On May 8, 1924, she boarded the steamship "Deutschland," accompanied by Dr. Eric A. Fennel, who had invited her to his home in Honolulu.[77] Before she could make use of the offer, she once again had to create a new social background.

To find out more about this young unmarried woman who held her ground against the male domain of the art market, is the purpose of a registered association, the Galka Emmy Scheyer Zentrum.[78]

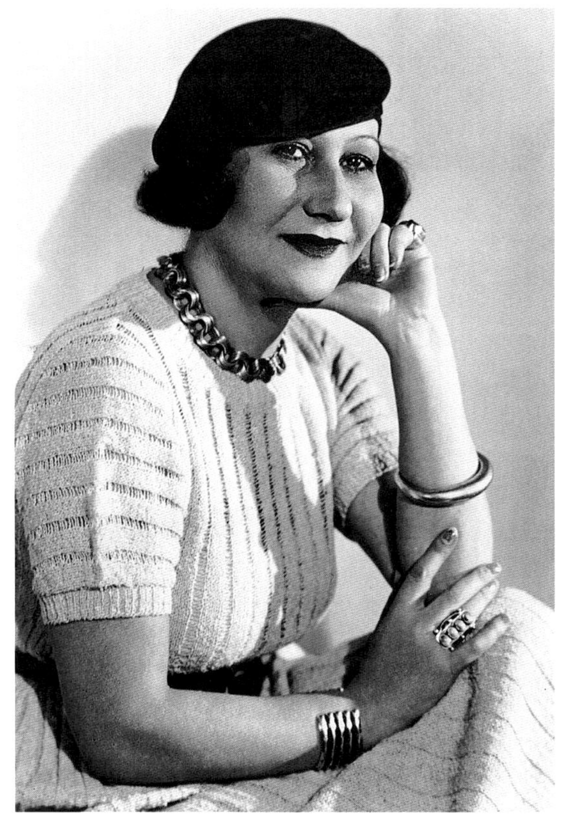

13 Galka E. Scheyer, Los Angeles, ca. 1930 (Courtesy of Courtesy of the Norton Simon Museum, Pasadena, California).

1 Stadtarchiv Braunschweig, D I 12 (Meldekartei), box 632, fols. 452, 456, 458.

2 Lette Valeska, Hans Steiner, "Galka und die Blaue Vier. Der Lebensroman der Galka Scheyer und der Blauen Vier Jawlensky, Feininger, Kandinsky, Paul Klee" (unpublished, ca. 1960), p. 9, The Getty Research Institute, Research Library, Special Collections, *Peg Weiss Papers regarding the Blue Four*, accn. no. 980065, box 82.

3 Stadtarchiv Braunschweig, D I 12, box 632, fol. 458.

4 Ismene Deter, "Ein Prachtbau in Dornholzhausen. Vom 'Viktoria-Pensionat' zur Notunterkunft," *Mitteilungen des Vereins für Geschichte und Landeskunder zu Bad Homburg vor der Höhe* 50 (2001), p. 69.

5 Doris Bartels, "Aus der Schule geplaudert. Eine Ehemalige berichtet," in *Festschrift zur 125-Jahr-Feier Gymnasium Kleine Burg*, ed. by Brigitte Birkholz, and Rainer Engelhard (Braunschweig, 1988), pp. 128–30, especially: p. 130.

6 Stadtarchiv Braunschweig, D I 12, box 93, fol. 55.

7 Stadtarchiv Braunschweig, D I 12, box 171, fol. 291. Private collection, Munich.

8 Valeska, *Galka und die Blaue Vier* (see note 2), p. 11.

9 *Braunschweigisches Adressbuch für das Jahr 1907*. Braunschweig, 1907, p. IV, 252.

10 Archiv Herzog Anton Ulrich-Museum Braunschweig (HAUM), Neu 306.

11 HAUM, Neu 658.

12 *Jahrbuch der bildenden Kunst*, ed. by Max Martersteig (Berlin, 1903), Verzeichnisse, III. Ausübende Künstler, col. 204.

13 *Braunschweigische Landeszeitung* (*LAN*), April 11 and April 16, 1909.

14 *LAN*, July 8, 1906, and April 16, 1907.

15 HAUM, Neu 658.

16 *Neueste Nachrichten Braunschweig*, March 14, 1909.

17 Peter Lufft, "Das Gästebuch Otto Ralfs," in *Arbeitsberichte aus dem Städtischen Museum Braunschweig* 48 (Braunschweig, 1985), p. 7.

18 Stadtarchiv Braunschweig, D I 12, box 632, fols. 452, 458.

19 *LAN*, April 22, 1909.

20 Stadtarchiv Braunschweig, D II 5 (Gewerbesteuer- bzw. Domizilakte), 219.

21 Valeska, "Galka und die Blaue Vier" (see note 2), p. 13.

22 Isabel Wünsche, *Galka E. Scheyer und Die Blaue Vier. Briefwechsel, 1924–1945* (Wabern, 2006), p. 3.

23 HAUM, Neu 658. *LAN*, April 9, 1910.

24 Stadtarchiv Braunschweig, D II 5, 219.

25 The Getty Research Institute, *Peg Weiss Papers regarding the Blue Four*, Box 138.

26 The Getty Research Institute, *Peg Weiss Papers regarding the Blue Four*, Box 127. Wünsche, *Galka E. Scheyer und Die Blaue Vier* (see note 22), p. 3.

27 The Getty Research Institute, *Peg Weiss Papers regarding the Blue Four*, box 127.

28 Elsa Daubert, *Erinnerungsbüchlein*. Private Collection Moringen.

29 Markt Prien a. Chiemsee, Sterbe-Bucheintrag 1914, no. 33; Pfarramt Großkarolinenfeld, Kirchenbuch 1914, Reg. Nr. 12/32/1914.

30 Daubert: D I 12:130, n. p. Scheyer: D I 12: 632, fol. 458. Evers: D I 12: 171, fol. 291.

31 Archives de la Ville de Bruxelles, fonds Bureau des Etrangers, nr. 88010.

32 Valeska, "Galka und die Blaue Vier" (see note 2), p. 14. Philippe Roberts-Jones et la Fondation Jos Albert, *Jos Albert* (Bruxelles, 1986).

33 Valeska, "Galka und die Blaue Vier" (see note 2), p. 16.

34 Wünsche, *Galka E. Scheyer und Die Blaue Vier* (see note 22), pp. 3 and 25.

35 Emmy Scheyer in an unpublished letter to Jawlensky, Mannheim, October, 1921. Alexej von Jawlensky Archive, Muralto.

36 Bernhard Mayer, *Interessante Zeitgenossen. Interesting Contemporaries. Lebenserinnerungen eines jüdischen Kaufmanns und Weltbürgers. Memoirs of a Jewish merchant and cosmopolitan. 1866–1946*, edited by Erhard Roy Wiehn (Konstanz, 1998), pp. 45–47, 61, 63.

37 Charlotte Bara, "Erinnerungen," Museo Ascona, FCB 23-9-118/1-17, p. 14.

38 Charlotte Bara, "Erinnerungen," pp. 10–11.

39 Ville de Bruxelles, ed., "Liquidation des biens sous séquestre. Catalogue d'une importante et très belle…collection Bachrach…Salle Delgay…Lundi 29 Décembre 1924…," p. 12. The titles are: "Portrait d'enfant," "Femme couchée dans un fauteuil," and "Nature morte," their whereabouts today are unknown.

40 *Braunschweiger Allgemeiner Anzeiger*, March 13, 1916.

41 Julia M. Nauhaus, *Die Gemäldesammlung des Städtischen Museums Braunschweig. Vollständiges Bestandsverzeichnis und Verlustdokumentation*, with contributions by Justus Lange (Hildesheim, 2009), p. 575.

42 HAUM Neu 720.

43 Valeska, "Galka und die Blaue Vier" (see note 2), p. 17.

44 *Tribune de Lausanne*, October 19, October 22, and November 4, 1916. *Gazette de Lausanne*, October, 22, 1916.

45 Alexej von Jawlensky, "Lebenserinnerungen," in *Alexej von Jawlensky, Reisen, Freunde, Wandlungen*, ed. by Tayfun Belgin (Heidelberg, 1998), pp. 104–19, especially: p. 117.

46 Angelica Jawlensky, "Ich habe meine Kunst in Ihre Hände gelegt: Emmy Scheyer und Alexej von Jawlensky – eine Freundschaft," in *Die Blaue Vier – Feininger, Jawlensky, Kandinsky Klee in der Neuen Welt*, ed. by Vivian Endicott Barnett, and Josef Helfenstein (Köln, 1997), pp. 63–78, especially: p. 66.

47 Raoul Schrott, *Dada 15/25. Dokumentation und chronologischer Überblick zu TZARA & Co.* (Köln, 2004), pp. 10–11, 73, 90, 95–96. Hugo Ball, *Briefe 1911–1927* (Einsiedeln, 1957), p. 80. Hugo Ball, *Die Flucht aus der Zeit* (Zürich, 1992), p. 158. Hans Arp, *Unsern täglichen Traum…Erinnerungen, Dichtungen und Betrachtungen aus den Jahren 1914–1954* (Zürich, 1955), p. 59.

48 Stadt Zürich, Bevölkerungsamt, Personenregister, "Javlensky, Alexis."

49 Stadt Zürich, Bevölkerungsamt, Personenregister 1901–1933, fol. 656, "Scheyer, Emilie." Postcard Charlotte Bachrach, December 17, 1917, private collection, Brussels.

50 Archiv HAUM Neu 307, Luise Blumenthal und Emmy Scheyer (1917).

51 Alexej von Jawlensky, letter to Paul Bachrach, March 7, 1918, Alexej von Jawlensky Archiv, Locarno.

52 Jawlensky, "Lebenserinnerungen" (see note 45), p. 118.

53 Stadt Zürich, Bevölkerungsamt, Personenregister 1901–1933, fol. 656, "Scheyer, Emilie."

54 Hans Looser, Autobiografical Notes, Private Collection, Emmenbrücke.

55 Zentrum Paul Klee, Bern, and Stefan Frey, eds., *"In inniger Freundschaft." Alexej Jawlensky, Paul und Lily Klee, Marianne Werefkin. Der Briefwechsel* (Zürich, 2013), p. 112. Hans Looser, Autobiografical Notes.

56 Karl Vester, Unpublished Diaries, diary no. 3, Getty Research Institute, Collection Harald Szeemann. Friendly message of Andreas Schwab, Bern.

57 Clotilde Sakharoff, "Les Sakharoff. La vie que nous avons dansée," unpublished typescript, Tanzarchiv Köln, pp. 82–83.

58 Valeska, "Galka und die Blaue Vier" (see note 2), p. 35.

59 Else Lasker-Schüler, *Werke und Briefe, Kritische Ausgabe*, vol. 7: *Briefe 1914–1924* (Frankfurt, 2004), p. 163.

60 Gabriella Borsano, *Harald Szeemann, Monte Verità. Berg der Wahrheit. Lokale Anthropologie als Beitrag zur Wiederentdeckung einer neuzeitlichen sakralen Topographie* (Milano, 1978), pp. 44, 158.

61 Mayer, *Interessante Zeitgenossen* (see note 36), p. 78.

62 Niedersächsisches Landesarchiv Hannover, NLA HA, Dep. 100, no. 10, section J, Erich Katzenstein to Paul Erich Küppers, Munich, n. d.

63 Zentrum Paul Klee, Bern, and Stefan Frey, eds., "In inniger Freundschaft" (see note 55), p. 98.

64 Stadtarchiv Braunschweig, D I 12, box 640, fol. 423.

65 *LAN*, November 30, 1919, and December 13, 1919.

66 Angelica Jawlensky, "Ich habe meine Kunst in Ihre Hände gelegt," pp. 66–67, fn. 12, letter of December (not November) 12, 1919.

67 Kate Steinitz Traumann, *Kurt Schwitters. Erinnerungen aus den Jahren 1918–1930* (Zurich, 1965), p. 127 (with faulty year).

68 Stadtarchiv Braunschweig, D I 12, box 348, fol. 232.

69 Interview Gilbert Holzgang with Ruth Mielziner, September, 2016.

70 Archives of American Art, Galka Scheyer papers 1917–1945, ca. 1,200 items on five microfilm reels.

71 Käte Ralfs in an interview with Ernst-August Roloff, December, 1986. Private collection.

72 Wünsche, *Galka E. Scheyer und Die Blaue Vier* (see note 22), p. 44. Archives of American Art, Galka Scheyer papers 1917–1945, reel 2031/00569 Scheyer's letter to Jawlensky, January 12, 1924.

73 Wünsche, *Galka E. Scheyer und Die Blaue Vier* (see note 22), pp. 37, 70.

74 *Der Cicerone* 16, no. 8 (1924), p. 385.

75 Archives of American Art, Galka Scheyer papers, reel 1644, no. 22; reel 1905, no. 00296 and no. 00300.

76 Wünsche, *Galka E. Scheyer und Die Blaue Vier* (see note 22), p. 36.

77 Hamburger Passagierlisten 1850–1934, p. 58, May 8, 1924.

78 www.galka-scheyer.de; info@galka-scheyer.de

Provenance Research –
Galka Scheyer, Erich Scheyer and the Gesellschaft der Freunde Junger Kunst[1]

Hansjörg Pötzsch

Galka Emmy Scheyer (1889–1945) is undoubtedly one of the most fascinating women in the history of modernism in art, an icon for whom the love of art was both passion and profession. However, the following article approaches the subject of Galka Scheyer not from the perspective of art history, but from that of provenance research.

The research began with two questions raised by the donation of the art collection of the Gesellschaft der Freunde Junger Kunst (Association of Friends of Young Art) to the Herzog Anton Ulrich-Museum in Braunschweig, in 1933.

First of all, was Galka Scheyer an active or passive member of the Gesellschaft der Freunde Junger Kunst? And related to this: was Galka Scheyer one of the owners of the art collection of the Gesellschaft der Freunde Junger Kunst?

The Gesellschaft der Freunde Junger Kunst was founded in Braunschweig in September 1924 on the initiative of the merchant and art lover Otto Ralfs (1892–1955), under the imprimatur of a signet designed by Kandinsky. While Galka Scheyer promoted the "Blue Four" (Feininger, Kandinsky, Klee, and Jawlensky) in the USA from May 1924 on, Ralfs campaigned for modernism in Braunschweig and beyond, starting in September 1924.

After the end of the Bauhaus in Weimar in 1925, he founded the "Klee-Gesellschaft," the "Kandinsky-Gesellschaft" and the "Feininger-Gesellschaft," to secure the artists a livelihood through membership fees. Ralfs owned an art collection of modernism known far beyond Braunschweig's borders that comprised 121 works of art in May 1931, including 54 works by Klee alone.[2]

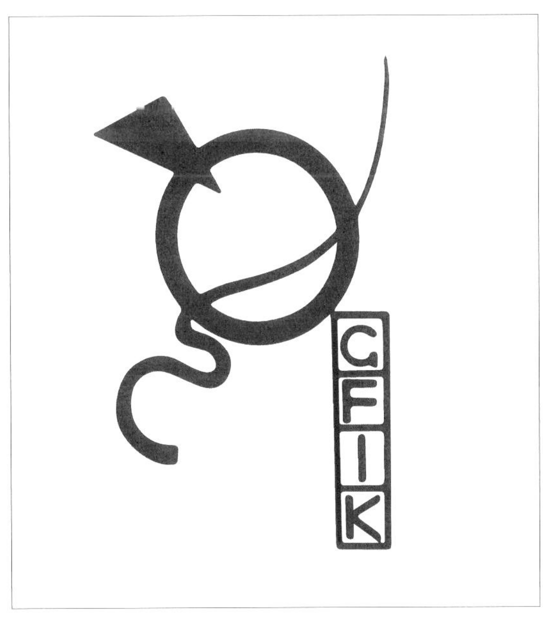

1 Signet of the Gesellschaft der Freunde Junger Kunst (Association of Friends of Young Art), designed by Wassily Kandinsky, 1924 (Letterhead of the Gesellschaft der Freunde Junger Kunst).

Wassily Kandinsky:	4 oil paintings, 6 watercolors
Emil Nolde:	1 oil painting, 5 watercolors
Pablo Picasso:	1 oil painting
Paula Modersohn:	1 oil painting
Alexej von Jawlensky:	2 oil paintings
Jacoba van Heemskerck:	1 oil painting
Otto Gleichmann:	2 watercolors
Christian Rohlfs:	2 watercolors
Lyonel Feininger:	1 oil painting, 3 watercolors
Otto Dix:	3 watercolors
Erich Heckel:	? watercolors ["Aquarelle"]
Piet Mondrian:	1 oil painting
Franz Radziwill:	2 watercolors
Fritz Ohse:	1 pastel
Thilo Maatsch:	2 oil paintings
Emil Maetzel ["E. Maetzel-Johannsen"]	1 oil painting, 4 watercolors
Walter Dexel:	1 oil painting
Willi Meyer ["Willi Meier"]:	4 oil paintings, 10 watercolors
Alfred Kollmar ["Kolmar-Worpswede"]:	5 oil paintings
Gustav Lehmann:	1 oil painting
"Funk-Düsseldorf" [Theodor Funck?]:	1 oil painting
Paul Klee:	4 oil paintings, 14 watercolors, 36 drawings

Works of Art from the Art Collection of Otto Ralfs, Mai, 1931

Niedersächsisches Landesarchiv Hannover, NLA HA, Dep. 100 Nr. 47

Tab. 1 Works of Art from the Art Collection of Otto Ralfs, May 1931 (Niedersächsisches Landesarchiv Hannover, NLA HA, Dep. 100 Nr. 47).

In 1935, Galka Scheyer referred to the fact that she had saved Otto Ralfs "vor dem Schlimmsten" (from the worst) – and his art collection from being auctioned off – by selling two of his paintings, one by Picasso (*Vue d'Avignon*, 1913) and the other Kandinsky's *Vertiefte Regung* (Deepened Impulse, 1928) in Mexico, after he had gone bankrupt in 1931.[3]

The purpose of the Gesellschaft der Freunde Junger Kunst was to arouse the interest of the public in modernism through exhibitions and events and to purchase works of art for a gallery of modernism yet to be founded. The list of the artists whose works were shown at exhibitions of the Gesellschaft der Freunde Junger Kunst in Braunschweig from November 1924 to March 1933 reads like a "who's who" of modernism. The names range from Beckmann and Dix, through the artists of the "Blue Four," to Pechstein and Schmidt-Rottluff.[4]

With the National Socialist "Machtergreifung" (seizure of power) in January 1933, the Gesellschaft der Freunde Junger Kunst knew its days were numbered. There was no longer any possibility of exhibiting or even owning modern art. Modernism had been denounced by the National Socialists as "entartet" (degenerate). Not only was the existence of the Gesellschaft der Freunde Junger Kunst under threat, its members were also personally threatened as a result. Therefore, the group dissolved itself at an extraordinary general meeting on July 6, 1933. Its valuable art collection of more than 20 works of modernism was donated to the Herzog Anton Ulrich-Museum. After the confiscations during the National Socialist "Entartete Kunst" (degenerate art) action in 1937, seven graphics and one sculpture from the collection remained in the Herzog Anton Ulrich-Museum.[5]

Solo and Group Exhibitions
(Selection)

Beckmann (1929)	Kandinsky (1924, 1926)	Munch (1924)
Cavael (1933)	Kirchner (1928)	Nolde (1926)
Chagall (1924)	Klee (1926, 1928)	Pechstein (1928)
Delaunay (1926)	Kokoschka (1924, 1925)	Picabia (1926)
Dexel (1924)	Kollwitz (1930)	Radziwill (1924, 1927)
Dix (1924, 1927)	Kubin (1931)	Schmidt-Rottluff (1924, 1925,
Ensor (1924, 1928)	Lissitzky (1924)	1928, 1932)
Feininger (1926)	Macke (1925, 1931)	Segal (1924, 1925, 1930)
Felixmüller (1927)	Marc (1924, 1931)	
Fraenkel (1932)	Masereel (1931)	
Gleichmann (1924)	Modersohn-Becker (1924)	*Events*
Grosz (1924, 1927)	Moholy-Nagy (1924, 1927)	*(Selection)*
Heckel (1924, 1927)	Mondrian (1924)	
Hofer (1927)	Mueller (1929)	Kandinsky Lecture (1924)
Jawlensky (1924, 1925)	Münter (1926)	Palucca at the State Theatre
		(1927, 1929)
		Gropius Lecture (1929)

Exhibitions and Events of the Gesellschaft der Freunde Junger Kunst
(Association of Friends of Young Art) 1924 – 1933 (Selection)

Stadtarchiv Braunschweig, G XI 19, 1-2

Tab. 2 Exhibitions and Events of the Gesellschaft der Freunde Junger Kunst (Association of Friends of Young Art) 1924–1933 (Selection) (Stadtarchiv Braunschweig, G XI 19, 1-2).

Since only 11 of the remaining 18 members were present at the vote on both the dissolution of the Gesellschaft der Freunde Junger Kunst and the donation to the Herzog Anton-Ulrich Museum, questions about legality arose then as now, because it was not a registered association. For this reason it would have been preferable for all members to have voted and agreed. Linked to this, the self-dissolution of the Gesellschaft as a result of Nazi persecution, gives rise to the question of whether it had any Jewish members. And as the membership lists have been lost, this is not easy to answer. So far, only one Jewish member of the association can be proven beyond doubt: the canned food manufacturer Erich Scheyer (1887–1982), treasurer of the Gesellschaft der Freunde Junger Kunst and Galka Scheyer's youngest brother.[6]

Together with Erich Scheyer and Otto Ralfs, plus Hermann Querner Jr. (1893–1979, also a canned food manufacturer), the architect and university professor Hermann Flesche (1886–1972) and an unknown person named Alb(ert) Hoffmeister, Galka Scheyer was one of the initiators of the exhibition of modern art with works by Klee and Nolde from private collections which opened at the Landesmuseum (renamed Herzog Anton Ulrich-Museum in 1927) on March 16, 1924. This exhibition can be regarded as the initial spark for the founding of the Gesellschaft der Freunde Junger Kunst.[7] Therefore, Galka Scheyer might in principle be counted among those who could have been members – even if one would have to assume a rather passive membership on account of her emigration in May 1924. However, from the written records of her estate there is no statement about any such membership. Nevertheless, both before and after her emigration, connecting lines can be drawn to people in the city of Braunschweig and the region, who were associated with the

Alexej von Jawlensky:	1 oil painting
Arthur Segal:	1 oil painting
Karl Sommer:	1 oil painting
Karl Hofer:	1 oil painting
Karl Christoph Hartig:	1 oil painting
Josef Albers:	1 glass painting
Else Fraenkel:	1 bronze sculpture
Otto Mueller:	1 watercolor
Karl Schmidt-Rottluff:	1 watercolor
Franz Marc:	1 watercolor
August Macke:	1 watercolor
Max Kaus:	1 watercolor
Ellen Passow:	1 watercolor
Kurt Mohr:	1 watercolor
Alfred Kubin:	1 watercolored drawing, 2 lithographs, *(1 pen drawing or lithograph*)*
Frans Masereel:	1 ink drawing
Carl S. Nolde:	1 charcoal drawing
George Grosz:	1 lithograph
Käthe Kollwitz:	1 lithograph, 1 woodcut

** The pen drawing or lithograph by Alfred Kubin was not in the list of the Gesellschaft der Freunde Junger Kunst dated July 6, 1933, but it was documented and confiscated as "entartete Kunst" ("degenerate art") in 1937 in the Herzog Anton-Ulrich Museum.*

Works of Art from the Art Collection of the Gesellschaft der Freunde Junger Kunst (Association of Friends of Young Art), July 6, 1933

Niedersächsisches Landesarchiv Wolfenbüttel, NLA WO, 12 Neu 13 Nr. 19236

Tab. 3 Works of Art from the Art Collection of the Gesellschaft der Freunde Junger Kunst (Association of Friends of Young Art), July 6, 1933 (Niedersächsisches Landesarchiv Wolfenbüttel, NLA WO, 12 NEU 13, Nr. 19236).

Gesellschaft der Freunde Junger Kunst or at the very least with modernism.

First there are her brothers Erich and Paul (1886–1956). Through Galka Scheyer they came in contact with both modern art and its artists. This applies above all to Jawlensky, who was one of Galka Scheyer's first protégés. Jawlensky especially appreciated Erich and his wife Margarete or "Margrit" (1896–1983). He visited them in Braunschweig and painted a portrait of Margrit in the style of his famous heads in early 1924. She was more than revered by him. A sketch in a letter from Jawlensky to Galka Scheyer dated January 1924 refers to this painting. In exchange for his works of art, Jawlensky received from Erich and Paul Scheyer food cans from their own cannery.[8]

Whether Paul Scheyer was like his brother Erich a member of the Gesellschaft der Freunde Junger Kunst remains open to question. It is, however,

very likely. As did Erich, Paul Scheyer also owned an art collection. But little is known either about its size and or what it contained. Paul Scheyer definitely owned the painting *Asketische Landschaft* (Ascetic Landscape) by Arthur Segal, but he does not seem to have liked the work very much, so Segal consequently offered to exchange it.[9] In addition, there were probably works by Jawlensky in his collection. In December 1938, however, Paul Scheyer attached a list of "Umzugsgut" (removal goods) to a questionnaire on his planned emigration to the USA after the "Reichspogromnacht" (the November Pogrom), in which six small pictures, four pictures and an oil painting were mentioned without a more detailed description. It is unclear whether he was given permission to take the works of art he owned with him when he emigrated to the USA in 1939. What is certain is that his "Umzugsgut" was auctioned off "im Auftrag der Gestapo Hamburg" (by order of the Gestapo Hamburg) in March 1941.[10]

Alexej von Jawlensky:	3 variations, 5 oil paintings, 1 ink drawing, 1 folder with 5 lithographs and 1 photo
Andreas Jawlensky:	1 oil painting, 2 drawings, 2 linocuts
Paul Klee:	1 watercolor, 1 etching
Franz Marc:	1 woodcut and 1 linocut
Max Kaus:	1 lithograph
László Moholy Nagy:	1 lithograph
Hans Reichel:	1 oil painting, 1 lithograph, 1 drawing
Arthur Segal:	2 oil paintings, 1 ink drawing
Emmy Esther Scheyer:	1 oil painting
Wassily Kandinsky:	1 lithograph
Jesekiel David Kirszenbaum:	1 etching, 1 ink drawing
Robert Petschow:	9 photos
Lyonel Feininger:	1 etching, 5 linocuts
Marie Laurencin:	1 watercolor, 1 drawing, 2 lithographs
"Munk" (probably Edvard Munch):	1 etching
Marc Chagall:	3 etchings, 1 lithograph
Oskar Kokoschka:	2 lithographs
Alexander Kanoldt:	1 lithograph
Karl Hofer:	1 lithograph
Max Beckmann:	1 etching
Alfred Kubin:	1 pen drawing
Ludwig Meidner:	1 etching
Henri Matisse:	1 etching
Georg Philipp Wörlen:	1 etching
Hans Hartig:	1 watercolor
(No artist specified):	2 Japanese prints
Aenne Mosbacher:	2 photos
Josef Vinecky:	1 wooden figure

20 books about "Junge Kunst" ("young art")

Works of Art from the Art Collection of Erich Scheyer, December 1, 1938

Niedersächsisches Landesarchiv Wolfenbüttel, 18 R Zg. 17/2003 Nr. 32

Tab. 4   Works of Art from the Art Collection of Erich Scheyer, December 1, 1938 (Niedersächsisches Landesarchiv Wolfenbüttel, NLA WO, 18 R Zg. 17/2003 Nr. 32).

More is known about the art collection of his brother Erich. Also in December 1938, Erich Scheyer presented the "Devisenstelle" (foreign exchange board) Braunschweig with a list of works of modernist art which, according to his statements, had been in his possession "seit über 10 Jahren" (for more than 10 years).[11] He applied for permission to send these works to his sister Galka in Hollywood prior to his emigration to Great Britain or the USA. In addition to 20 books and some photographs, the list attached to the application includes 63 artworks – mostly oil paintings, etchings, watercolors, lithographs and drawings – by figures such as Beckmann, Chagall, Matisse, the artists of the "Blue Four" and Galka Scheyer. His application was rejected with an advisory note that he should include the objects in a list of removal goods still to be submitted.

In March 1939, Erich Scheyer emigrated to the UK.[12] He was in fact able to save his art collection and take it with him. However, he soon had to part with some of it in order to finance his new start in Britain. Most of the remainder of his collection was sold after his death in 1982.[13]

His extensive art collection, his personal closeness to artists like Jawlensky, who often visited him and valued and cultivated the contact he had with Erich and his wife Margrit; his correspondence with Segal on the occasion of the Braunschweig exhibition in October 1925; and his correspondence with the Kestner Gesellschaft (Kestner Society) in Hannover concerning the Ensor exhibition in Braunschweig in March/April 1928; all these indicate that Erich Scheyer's role both as an art collector in Braunschweig and as a board member of the Gesellschaft der Freunde Junger Kunst should not be underestimated.[14] Like the group's chairman Otto Ralfs, Erich Scheyer also kept a guest book. Within its pages Feininger, Jawlensky, Klee and Kandinsky are said to have immortalized themselves with about five works of art. However, in contrast to the well-known guest book of Otto Ralfs, which is kept in the Städtisches Museum Braunschweig,[15] the previously unknown guest book of Erich Scheyer is no longer preserved in its original form. The works of art are said to have been taken from the book and framed separately.[16]

Without knowing that her brother Erich's emigration was imminent, Galka Scheyer wrote a letter to him from Hollywood on February 9, 1939. The letter, which deals with art sales, states:

> Ich habe die Rolle von Annie [Who is Annie?] erhalten und sende Dir fuer eine Chagall Radierung $ 12. Ich halte den Preis nicht fuer schlecht. Willst Du mir selber Preise angeben oder soll ich die Preise nach meinem Verstaendnis selber ansetzen?
> Es ist schade dass Du nicht soviel wie moeglich dieser Sachen aufgekauft hast[,] denn wenn es auch nicht leicht ist, so kann man dennoch dafuer Geld bekommen. Also[,] solltest Du noch je Gelegenheit haben[,] billig an sowas zu geraten, so rate ich Dir zu. […][17]

The text leaves a lot of room for interpretation, for example with regard to "aufgekauft" (bought up) and "billig an sowas zu geraten" (get such things cheaply) – that could of course mean that Erich Scheyer bought up works of modernism from third parties after 1933 and before his emigration in 1939, perhaps from Jewish owners before their own emigration … But maybe this is seeing the letter too much from the perspective of a provenance researcher. Erich Scheyer probably tried to sell his extensive collection of modern art, or at least parts of it, through his sister, in order to finance his emigration and subsequent life in exile.

Galka Scheyer knew that Jewish people were not allowed to take their capital along with them when they emigrated from Germany. That is why she probably recommended her brother to invest his capital in modern art in order to circumvent the export ban on foreign exchange, and to have money for survival in exile by selling his art investments after emigration. A letter from Galka Scheyer written in 1935 to the merchant, publisher and art collector Alfred Rose in Hannover, who had financially supported her emigration to the USA and was at that time probably already considering emigration himself,[18] suggests that this could have been meant in this way:

> Ich würde Dir raten[,] Bilder drüben [in Germany] zu kaufen[,] da Du ja kein Geld heraus nehmen kannst. Blaue Vier und Franzosen. Picasso, Braque. Ich denke mir[,] wenn man weiss wo[,] kann man in Deutschland Franzosen billig kaufen, Picasso, Braque sind die teuersten hier. Leger, wenn Du einen Duchamps finden kannst, die gibt es kaum. Er malt nicht mehr (Marcel Duchamps)[.] Von den jüngeren Arp, Miro, Mondrian, billig aber selten. Wenn möglich frühe Chagalls, bekannte Bilder von vor dem Krieg. Kokoschka (früh)[.] Skulptur von Brancusi –. Ro[u]ault. Gemälde sind am besten, kleine Lit[h]os und Radierungen sind weniger wertvoll. Skulptur von Lembruck. Wenn möglich van Gogh, Cezanne, Rousseau, Renoir, Gaugain, die Meister vor den jetzigen Meistern. Die sind natürlich teuer[,] aber ein Investment. Wenn ich jetzt drüben wäre, könnte ich Dir sehr gut helfen. Aber was Du auch immer bezahlst, ist immer besser wie Dein Geld drüben lassen[,] wenn Du [die] absicht [sic] hast[,] auszuwandern. Der kunstmarkt [sic] ist schlecht hier[,] wie überall[,] und ein Überangebot, deshalb wenn Du willst[,] könnte ich die ganze Sammlung übernehmen und erst mal annonym [sic] an die mir bekannten Sammler anbieten. Nicht wie ich das mit meiner Blauen Vier tue, die ich von einem kulturellen Standpunkt hier habe[,] weil mich diese Seite der Kunst erfüllt, deswegen bin ich aber nicht dagegen[,] meine langjährigen Erfahrungen in einer rein geschäftlichen Weise zu gebrauchen. […][19]

With regard to the "Fluchtgut" (flight assets) problem in provenance research, and possible Nazi-persecuted previous owners, new questions are raised by the recommendation given by Galka Scheyer to Alfred Rose and her brother Erich to purchase modern art in Nazi Germany. It's clear she herself was only endeavoring to help family members and friends as much as possible, with both advice and practical action, with their process of emigrating. In this way she made affidavits for her brothers Erich and Paul and their families, and also tried to do the same for her mother Henriette (1861–1941).[20] Her mother still had more than 50 works of art in her possession, mostly by her daughter, but probably also an oil painting by Segal and some works by Galka Scheyer's Braunschweig painter friend Albert Hamburger (1893–1915). In early 1939, Henriette Scheyer received permission from the "Devisenstelle" Braunschweig to send these works of art to her daughter in Hollywood. However, unlike her sons Erich and Paul, Henriette Scheyer herself had no opportunity to emigrate. She died on February 24, 1941, at the Minna-James-Heinemann-Stiftung, a Jewish retirement home in Hannover.[21]

Shortly before her own emigration, Galka Scheyer had said farewell to the friends of modernism in Braunschweig with four slideshow evenings on works of art by Feininger, Kandinsky, Klee and Jawlensky. The cycle, which was to be understood as a kind of dress rehearsal for her planned lectures in the USA on the artists of the "Blue Four," took place between April 13 and April 25, 1924, in the apartment of the Braunschweig doctor Richard Spanjer-Herford (1888–1964) in Wolfenbütteler Straße 2.[22]

Among the possible participants of those four April lecture evenings, tinged by the sadness of farewell, might have been later members of the Gesellschaft der Freunde Junger Kunst: people like Otto Ralfs or Hermann Querner, or others from Braunschweig and its surrounding region mentioned in Kandinsky's address book, such as Thilo Maatsch (1900–83), a painter whose works were later shown in group exhibitions of the Gesellschaft in 1925 and 1930, or the chamber singer Alfred Paulus (1893–1967), or Alexander Boecking (1897–1946), a garden architect.[23] First and foremost, though, one should think of Galka Scheyer's own circle of friends, relatives and acquaintances: like her brothers Erich and Paul, her cousin Gertrud Scheyer (born in 1901), the merchant Gustav Forstenzer (1888–1970) and his wife Lucie (1893–1988), known to have had possessed works of art by Jawlensky;[24] and possibly also her childhood friend Lette Valeska (1885–1985), who followed Galka Scheyer to Los Angeles in 1938.

Perhaps the teacher Charlotte Lange (1890–1977), later to be secretary and the only known female member of the Gesellschaft der Freunde Junger Kunst, was also present. She had little success with trying to follow in Galka Scheyer's footsteps in Hollywood. In 1927, *Das Kunstblatt* mentioned that a Charlotte Lange from Braunschweig was advertising in Hollywood for Picasso, Marc, Brancusi, Archipenko, and younger artists.[25] It's not known if this amounted to anything concrete, however. Perhaps Lange's marriage to the American painter and illustrator Harold Miles (1887–1963), meant she no longer needed this course of action. Whether she and Galka Scheyer met in Los Angeles, remains a mystery.

1 For proofreading my English manuscript, I thank Christopher Terry, Bettina Gierke – and Bertie.

2 Niedersächsisches Landesarchiv Hannover, NLA HA, Dep. 100 Nr. 47 (Bilderaufstellung der Sammlung Otto Ralfs, Mai 1931). Hansjörg Pötzsch, "Freunde der Kunst und der Künstler. Galka Scheyer, Otto Ralfs und die Gesellschaft der Freunde Junger Kunst," in *Beiträge zur Kunst der Moderne. Niederdeutsche Beiträge zur Kunstgeschichte,* ed. by Rainer Stamm, Gloria Köpnick, new series, vol. 3 (Petersberg, 2018), pp. 195, 198.

3 Getty Research Institute Library, GRI, Acc. No. 980065, 136, 5 (Galka Scheyer to Alfred and Edith [Rose], [January or October] 20, 1935).

4 Pötzsch, "Freunde der Kunst und der Künstler" (see note 2), pp. 195–96.

5 Ibid., pp. 206–7.

6 Stadtarchiv Braunschweig, G XI 19, 1 (Rundschreiben an die Mitglieder und ehemaligen Mitglieder der Gesellschaft der Freunde Junger Kunst, October 7, 1933). Pötzsch, "Freunde der Kunst und der Künstler" (see note 2), pp. 206–7.

7 Eckart von Sydow, "Braunschweig: Klee und Nolde im Landesmuseum," *Der Cicerone* 16, no. 8 (1924), p. 378 (with n. 1). Pötzsch, "Freunde der Kunst und der Künstler" (see note 2), p. 192.

8 Pötzsch, "Freunde der Kunst und der Künstler" (see note 2), pp. 189–90.

9 GRI, Acc. No. 880279, 4 (Arthur Segal to Erich Scheyer, September 17, 1927). Pötzsch, "Freunde der Kunst und der Künstler" (see note 1), p. 208.

10 Niedersächsisches Landesarchiv Wolfenbüttel, NLA WO, 18 R Zg. 17/2003 Nr. 32 (Umzugsgut von Paul Scheyer, List, December 10, 1938). NLA WO, 18 R Zg. 17/2003 Nr. 575 (Zollfahndungsstelle Hamburg to Devisenstelle Braunschweig, August 7, 1941). Pötzsch, "Freunde der Kunst und der Künstler" (see note 1), p. 208. Note from Kathrin Kleibl to the author, April 8, 2021.

11 NLA WO, 18 R Zg. 17/2003 Nr. 32 (Erich Scheyer to Devisenstelle, December 1, 1938).

12 Ibid. (with attached "Aufstellung"). Pötzsch, "Freunde der Kunst und der Künstler" (see note 1), p. 208.

13 Note from E. V. to the author, May 21, 2018.

14 GRI, Acc. No. 880279, 4 (Arthur Segal to Erich Scheyer, 28.9.1925). NLA HA, Dep. 100 Nr. 35 (Erich Scheyer to Hanns Krenz, April 4., 1928). Pötzsch, "Freunde der Kunst und der Künstler" (see note 1), pp. 190, 206, 208.

15 See Peter Lufft, *Das Gästebuch Otto Ralfs* (Braunschweig, 1985).

16 Note from E. V. to the author, August 31, 2018.

17 GRI, Acc. No. 880279, 3 (Galka Scheyer to Erich Scheyer, February 9, 1939): "I have received the scroll from Annie [Who is Annie?] and send you for a Chagall etching $12. I think the price is not bad. Do you want to give me prices yourself or should I set the prices myself according to my understanding?
It is a pity that you have not bought as many of these things as possible, because even if it is not easy, you can still get money for them. So, if you ever have the opportunity to get such things cheaply, I advise you to do so."

18 Rose emigrated with his art collection to England in 1939 and to New York in 1943. Isabel Wünsche, ed., *Galka E. Scheyer & Die Blaue Vier. Briefwechsel 1924–1945* (Wabern, 2006), p. 304 (with n. 280).

19 GRI, Acc. No. 980065, 136, 5 (Galka Scheyer to Alfred and Edith [Rose], [January or October] 20, 1935). The umlauts missing from the original text have been added: "I would advise you to buy pictures over there (that means in Germany), since you can't take any money out. Blue Four and French. Picasso, Braque. I think, if you know where, you can buy French cheap in Germany, Picasso, Braque are the most expensive here. Leger, if you can find a Duchamps, they are hard to find. He no longer paints (Marcel Duchamps). Of the younger Arp, Miro, Mondrian, cheap but rare. If possible early Chagalls, known paintings from before the war. Kokoschka (early). Sculpture by Brancusi –. Ro[u]ault. Paintings are best, small lithos and etchings are less valuable. Sculpture by Lembruck. If possible van Gogh, Cezanne, Rousseau, Renoir, Gaugin, the masters before the present masters. They're expensive, of course, but an investment. If I were over there now, I could help you very well. But whatever you pay is always better than leaving your money over there if you have the intention to emigrate. The art market is bad here, like everywhere, and an oversupply, so if you want, I could take over the whole collection and offer it to the collectors I know anonymously first. Not like I do with my Blue Four, which I have here from a cultural point of view, because this side of art fulfills me, but because of that I am not against using my long experience in a purely business way …"

20 Wünsche, *Galka E. Scheyer & Die Blaue Vier* (see note 18), p. 287.

21 Pötzsch, "Freunde der Kunst und der Künstler" (see note 2), p. 208. GRI, Acc. No. 880279, 3 (Galka Scheyer to Erich Scheyer, February 9, 1939). Frank Ehrhardt, Kirsten Bergemann, Jonathan Voges, *Zwischen Erfolg und Ablehnung. Jüdische Braunschweiger und ihr Engagement in der Gesellschaft. Eine Spurensuche* (Braunschweig, 2013), p. 62. Arolsen Achives, Signatur 12410013, 12672161 – Henriette Scheyer (Zählkarte Synagogen-Gemeinde Hannover, 1941), https://collections.arolsen-archives.org/archive/12672161/?p=1&s=henriette%20scheyer&doc_id=12672161 (accessed April 13, 2021).

22 Galka Scheyer to Alexej von Jawlensky, April 10, 1924, quoted from Wünsche, *Galka E. Scheyer & Die Blaue Vier* (see note 18), p. 49.

23 Centre Pompidou, Bibliothèque Kandinsky, Fonds Kandinsky, VK 39 (Répertoire [ca. 1930]), https://archivesetdocumentation.centrepompidou.fr/img-viewer/BK/VK/VK_39/viewer.html?&ns=M5050_X0031_BKEAD_VK_39_001_P.jpg, figs. 8, 37, 45 (accessed April 14, 2021).

24 Pötzsch, "Freunde der Kunst und der Künstler" (see note 2), p. 194. Note from R. F.r to the author, January 9, 2019.

25 J. B. Neumann, "Die neue deutsche Kunst in New York", *Das Kunstblatt* 11 (1927), p. 379.

THE ART OF LETTE VALESKA –
STUDENT AND LIFELONG FRIEND OF GALKA SCHEYER
FROM BRAUNSCHWEIG TO HOLLYWOOD

Renate Evers[1] & Julia Hammid[2]

Lette Valeska (1885–1985)[3] was a close and life-long friend of the artist and avant-garde art patron Galka Scheyer (1889–1945).

Lette Valeska's story is intricately intertwined with Galka Scheyer's life. Their friendship was rooted in their shared childhood in Braunschweig. They maintained close bonds throughout their lives, redefining them at important crossroads. They both used art as their primary medium for communicating internal perspectives and emotions. Both were inspired by their connections to leading artists and the art world of their time. On a more personal level, the lives of both Lette Valeska and Galka Scheyer were notable in escaping societal boundaries and overcoming conventions for women.

After her flight from Nazi Germany and eventual emigration to the US in 1938, Lette Valeska reconnected with her friend Galka in Hollywood, became Galka's art student, and remained a close loyal friend until Galka's untimely death in 1945. Lette Valeska became the archivist of Galka Scheyer's estate as it connected to the Blue Four.[4] But Lette Valeska also embarked on a successful late-life career as a Hollywood photographer, painter and sculptor in her own right. Lette Valeska's artwork depicts her memories of home, youth and childhood. Its subject matter ranges from Biblical, mystical, and Jewish themes, to portraits, couples, and family groups. Her work often expresses abstract topics such as grief, loss, mourning, nurturing, and life. While her early style reminds one of folk art, her later mature style is noted for its sophisticated use of colors and brown-green tonalities, often depicting elongated figures, with long faces, and somber and sad eyes.[5]

1 Misery, 1946/47 (Figs. 1–26 Courtesy of Julia Hammid and Petra Hammid, estate of Lette Valeska).

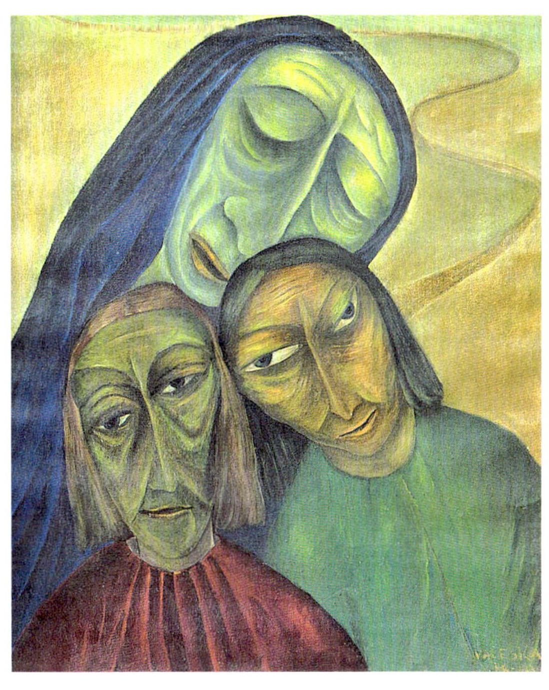

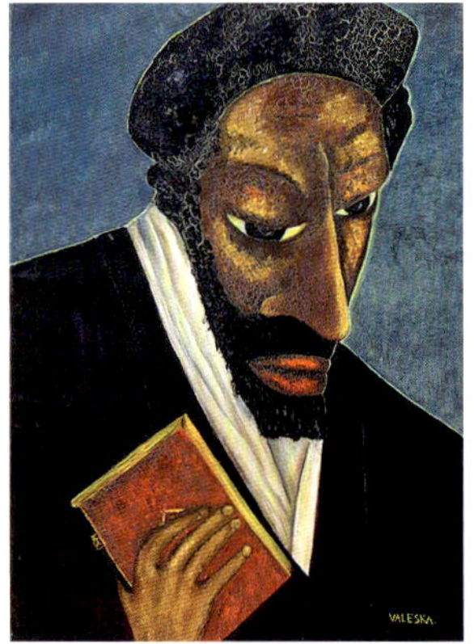

2 Talmudic Student.

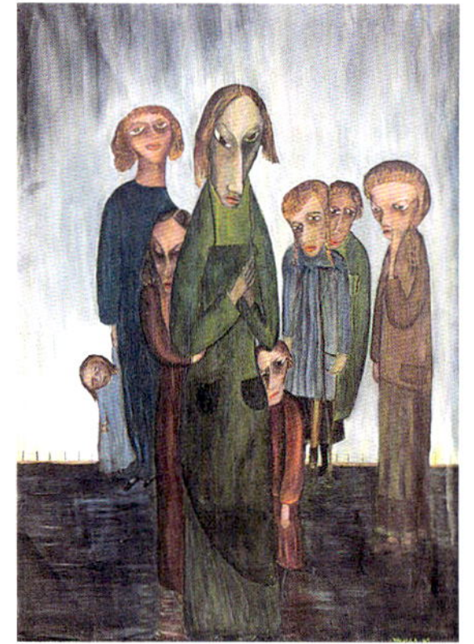

3 Still Waiting, 1945.

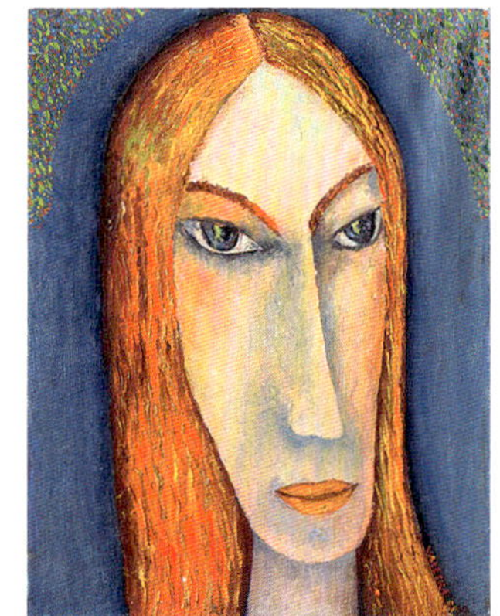

4 Red Head.

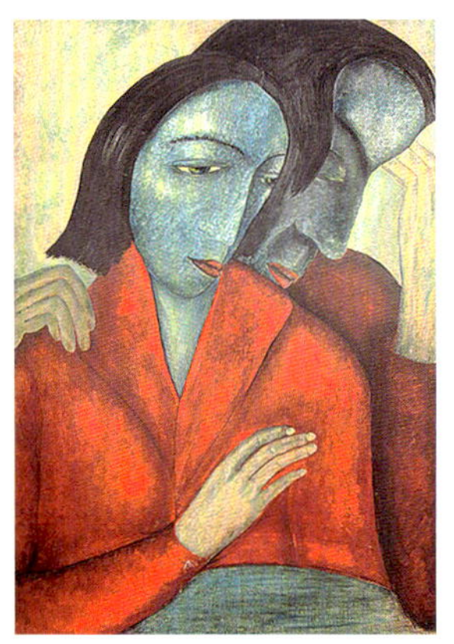

5 The Couple, 1954.

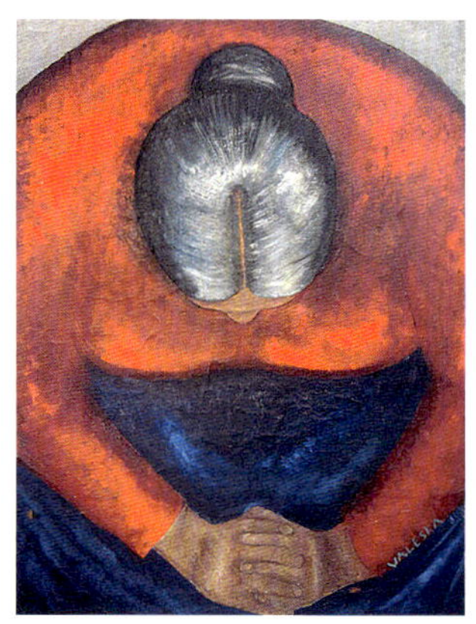

6 Despair 1, 1954.

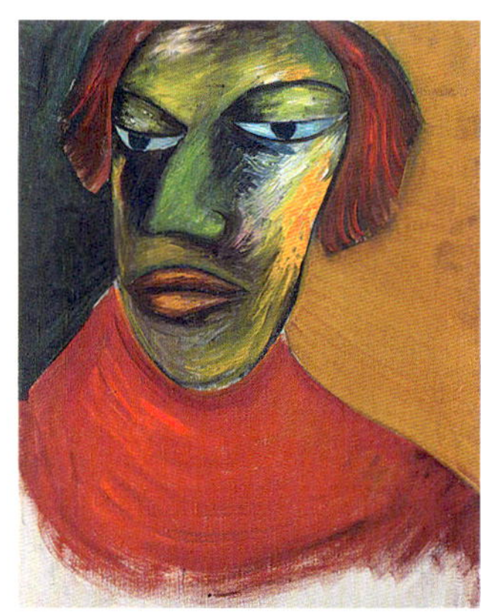

7 Red Dress, unfinished.

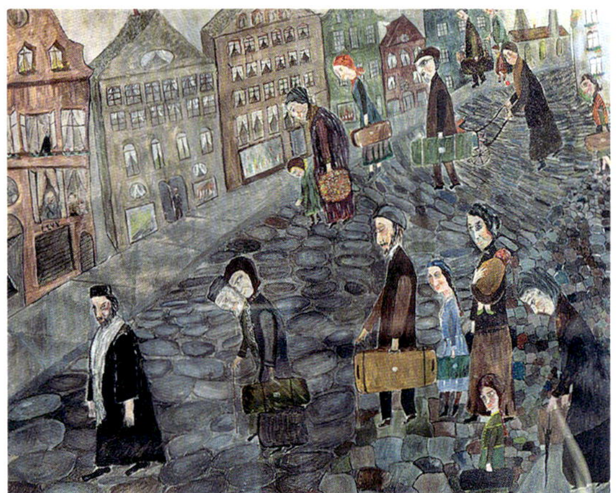

8 Exodus.

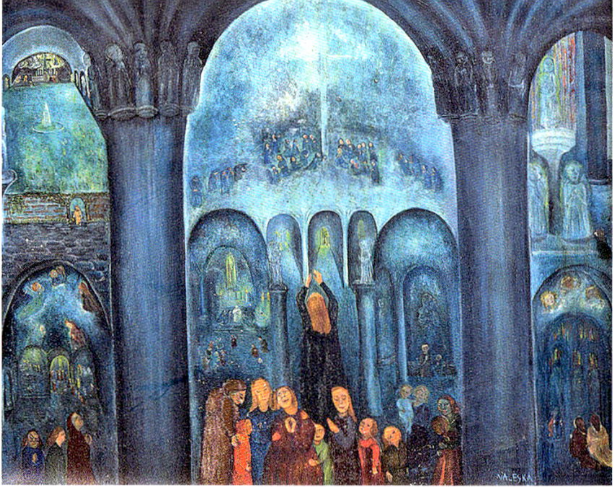

9 In Church, Adoration, 1954.

Lette Valeska – Her Life Story 1885–1985[6]

Lette Valeska was born in Braunschweig in 1885 as Valeska Heinemann. Her parents were Jewish businessman Berthold Heinemann / Heynemann (1852–1930) and his wife Fanny (née Kunstmann, 1854–1942) who lived in Braunschweig.[7] The family ran a successful branch of a large department store chain.[8]

Valeska was one of four siblings.[9] She received a conventional "Höhere Töchter"-Ausbildung in the spirit of the time, attending the Höhere Töchterschule (today Gymnasium Kleine Burg) in Braunschweig from 1891 to 1901.

She received additional lessons in French, English, and Italian from private tutors. She had many female friends, among them Emmy Scheyer (Galka Scheyer's childhood name) who was four years younger. Valeska started photographing at the age of 12. As a young adult she stayed for two years in Berlin and studied at the Berliner Lette-Verein for women[10] which also had a training facility for photography. It is this organization which inspired her later to take her professional name of Lette Valeska. Between 1911 and 1915 she worked as a secretary for foreign languages for a technical newspaper in Brussels. In 1915/16, she studied at the École des Beaux Arts in Brussels along with Galka Scheyer.

After her time being educated abroad, she returned to Braunschweig. In 1920, she married the businessman Ernst Heymann who owned a pharmaceutical chemical company in Frankfurt.

Their daughter Hella was born in 1921. The family lived comfortably in a suburb close to Frankfurt.[11] In 1932, they moved to Paris where Ernst Heymann opened a branch of his business.

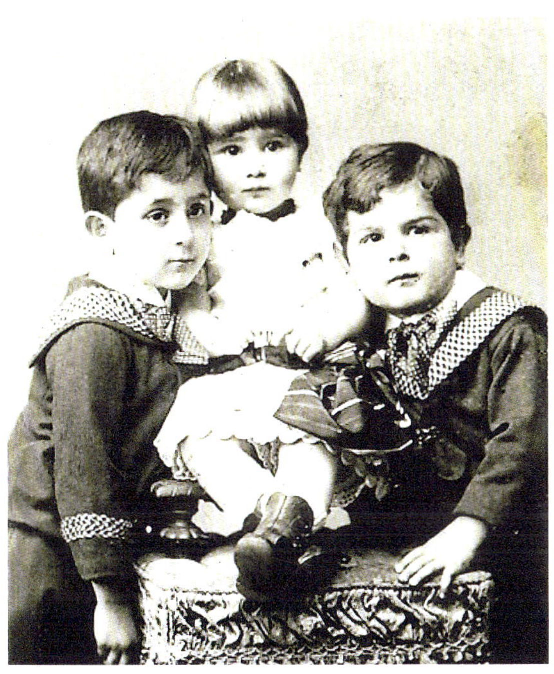

10 Valeska and her brothers Walter and Ludwig Heinemann, Braunschweig, 1880s.

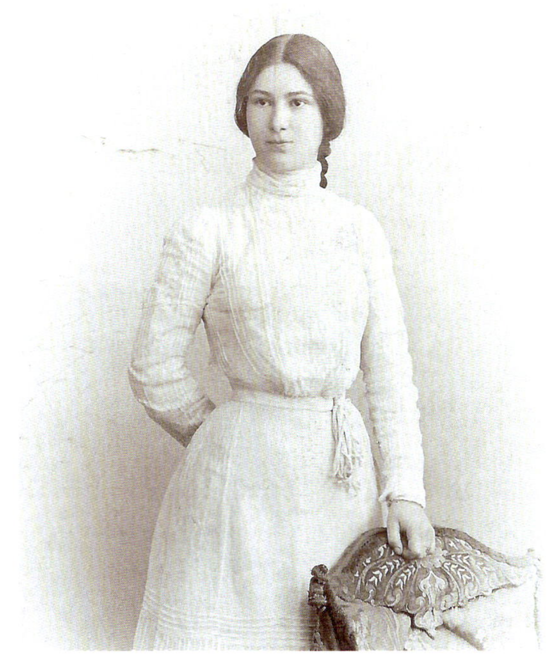

11 Lette Valeska, then Valeska Heinemann, 1901.

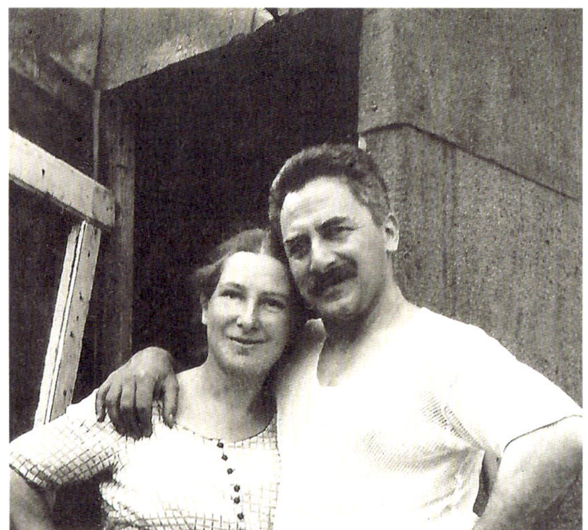

12 Valeska & Ernst Heymann, 1930.

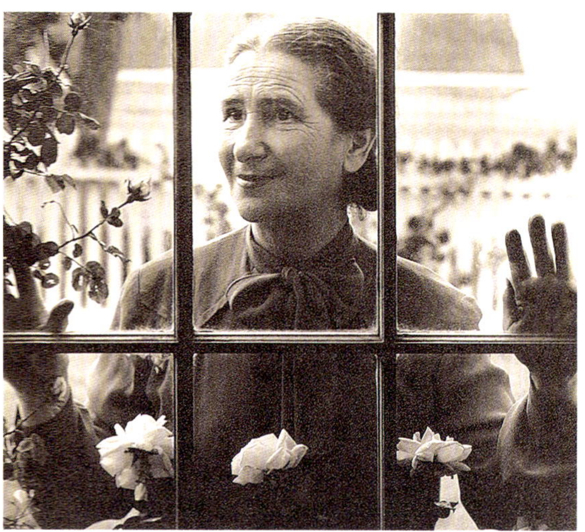

14 Valeska in Los Angeles.

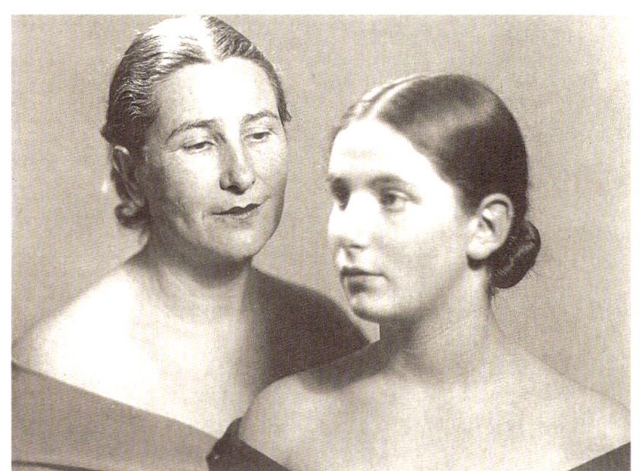

13 Valeska & her daughter Hella, Paris, 1934.

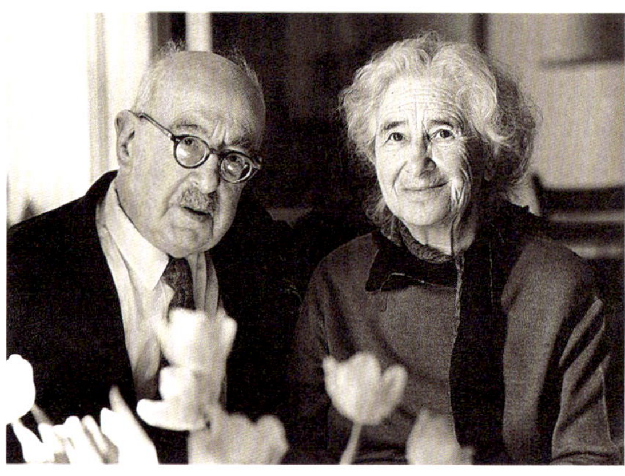

15 Valeska & her brother Walter Heinemann, probably 1960s in the United States.

The family intended to return to Frankfurt in 1933 but an uprising of anti-Semitic employees prevented them from doing so. They remained in France until 1937 when the Nazis confiscated the chemical factory in Frankfurt. The business was dissolved in 1939. Deprived of home and livelihood, the Heymanns emigrated to the United States, first to New York City where Valeska's brother Walter Heinemann (1883–1968) lived with his family, having established himself as a physician again after his emigration in 1935. In 1938, Valeska separated from Ernst and moved with her daughter Hella to Los Angeles on the advice of her old friend Galka Scheyer. Ernst Heymann stayed in New York City where he tragically committed suicide in 1948.

Lette Valeska – The Hollywood Photographer

Faced with the necessity of earning a living in America, Valeska turned to photography.[12] She chose the professional name Lette Valeska instead of Valeska Heymann (née Heinemann). Her photo series of elementary school children opened the door to a career in photographing prominent Hollywood actors.[13] She became highly sought after and photographed Hollywood stars such as Rhonda Fleming, Gregory Peck, Gene Kelly, Ingrid Bergmann, Doris Day, James Stewart, Elizabeth Taylor, Rita Haywood, and Ava Gardner, just to name a few. Valeska preferred not to work in a studio but instead took photos in the natural environment of the subject or sitter of a photograph. She described her style in an interview in 1970: "I have no photographic style. I just talked to the children to relax them. They were never posed." She considered her photos "arrested moments," not portraits. "An arrested moment is living. They are action pictures." She was undis-

mayed that her pictures were not always technically perfect or sharply in focus. "They would be dead if they were technically perfect!"[14]

With the attack on Pearl Harbor and the formal entry of America into World War II in 1941, her career as a photographer came to a halt. Due to wartime restrictions, she was no longer allowed to work as a photographer due to her status as a foreigner from Germany. Thanks to the intervention of friends and supporters her camera equipment was eventually returned to her and she went on to do a new series of children for the California Department of Education.

In 1945, she organized help for children in the Netherlands through the local chapter of Haddasah[15] and the Jewish community in Los Angeles. She especially provided the children of the Dutch town of Rykswick with food parcels in appreciation for a temporary asylum that she had received during her flight from Germany.[16]

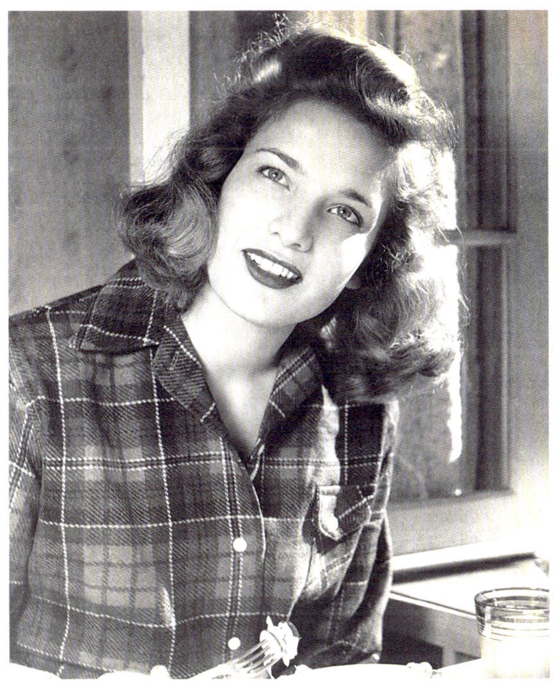

16 Deborah Alden, photographed by Lette Valeska, 1940s.

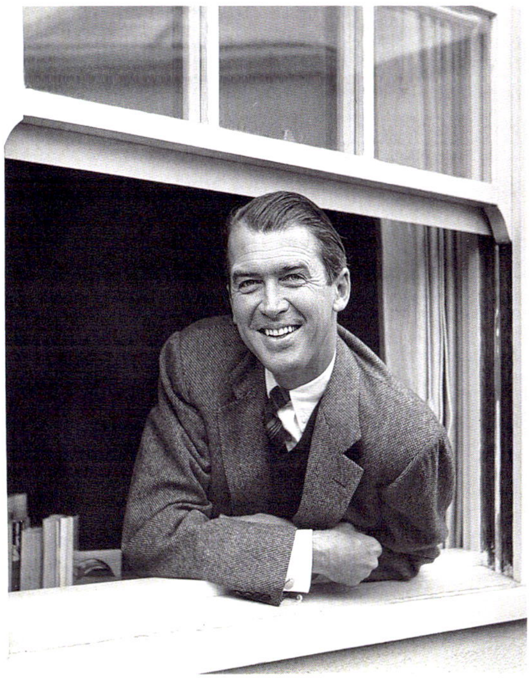

17 James Stewart, photographed by Lette Valeska, 1940s.

Lette Valeska – The Artist

When Valeska came to Los Angeles she was urged by her childhood friend Galka Scheyer to take up painting. Valeska was still in a state of mental travail over starting a new life in another country and separating from her husband. Galka assured her that she would find peace of mind through painting. Valeska recalls that she resisted, saying: "But I've never had a brush in my hands," Galka replied: "You don't know how lucky you are."[17]

In her 1947 memoirs, Valeska writes:

> Then I came to LA to a friend of my youth, Galka Scheyer. The inspiration of this women has changed my whole life. I started to paint, to be refreshed in art, in nonmaterial things and new doors in life opened up for me and I can say that my life has never been richer and more beautiful than it is now.[18]

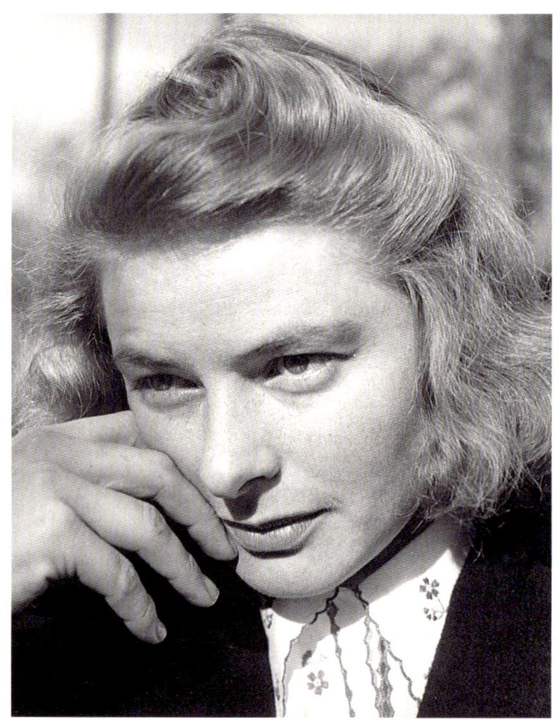

18 Ingrid Bergmann, photographed by Lette Valeska, 1940s.

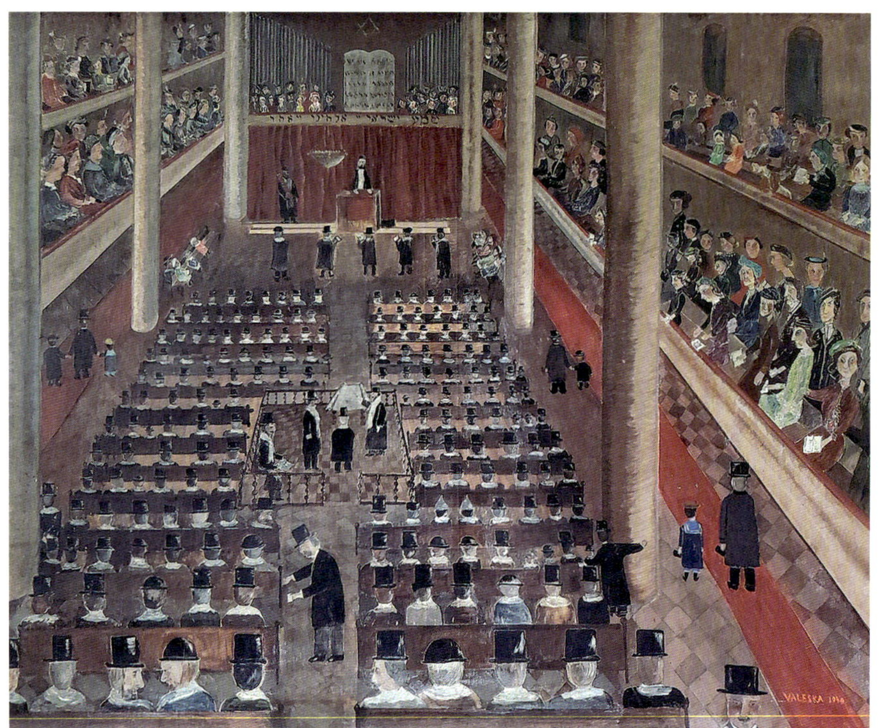

19 Our Synagogue, 1940.

In a later interview, Lette Valeska said:

> Galka Scheyer had the power of bringing some-
> thing out of you. On her deathbed she urged
> me not to go to an academy because it would
> take away my originality.[19]

Her earliest paintings took their subjects from her childhood in Braunschweig as well as family relationships. These images are still very simple, in a charming folk-art style, before her style mature.

An early painting is Valeska's recollection of the interior of the Braunschweig Synagogue (Fig. 19) which was destroyed during the November Pogrom in 1938 and demolished in 1940.[20]

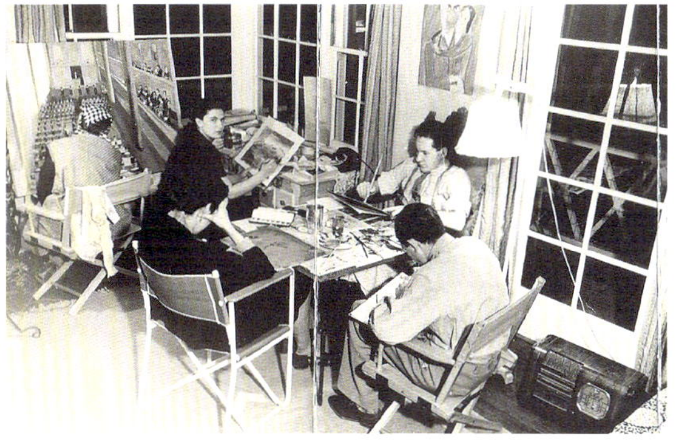

20 Valeska at the easel working on Our Synagogue while her daughter is looking at the camera, in Galka Scheyer's studio, 1940s.

21 Family History, 1940s.

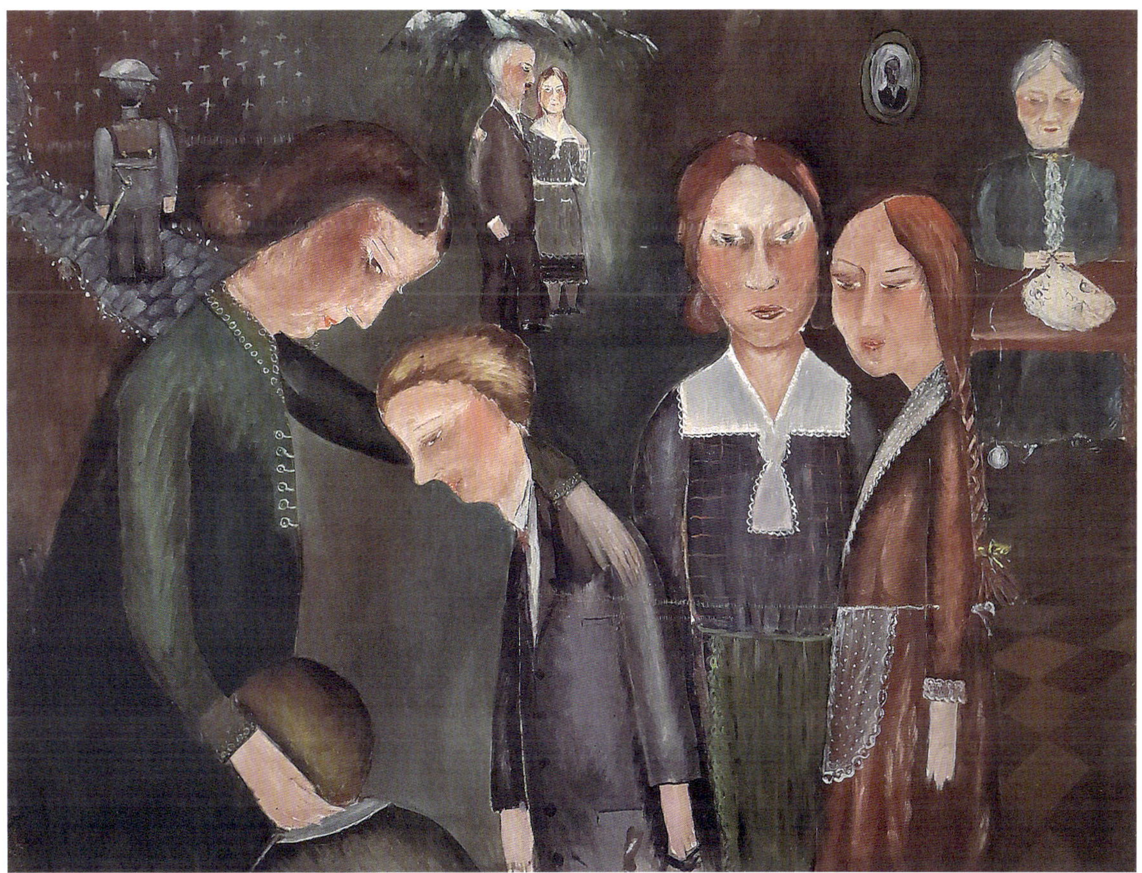

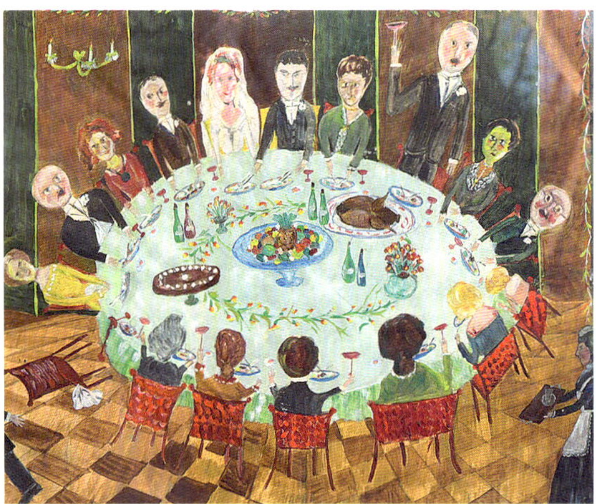

22 My Wedding 1920, painted probably around 1938.

Valeska's painting *Family history* is a simple and slightly crude picture probably from the beginning of her artistic career but a key to her family story and the family conflicts. She writes in her 1947 memoirs:

> I was born 20 July 1885 (couldn't you have made it 1895?) in Braunschweig. My father was happy indeed that his third child was finally a girl and we both were great friends all through my life and his. He was the only one of my whole family (perhaps with the exception of my younger brother who was born eight years later) who understood all I did and valued and thought and told me of all the ideal things in life … my mother, a realistic woman, much more attached to her boys, who did take wonderful care of her family, especially when somebody was sick she sacrificed herself day and night. But I don't remember a single tenderness from her towards me and I suffered so much under her saying and thinking when I wanted another life as she would for me and which was to be free to learn whatever I wanted, to go wherever I wanted … Growing older I understand my own mother better and out of pity for her for her life which was not easy. My sympathy and love for her did grow out of this understanding and I suffered when she died so suddenly in the war. I would have loved to show her all my love and sympathy. And my brothers. Well, I loved them,

and they always were nice to me. I was especially the friend of my brother Walter but not one of them really understood me …[21]

My wedding might be one of Valeska's earliest paintings. She comments in her memoirs:

> Then the time came when I was in love. It is so long ago so we better skip that, and then I got married and from the overpowering of my mother I came under the power of my husband. Also that we better skip … My wedding: The only scene I remembered was the toast my father brought out for me, and that I painted.[22]

Valeska remembers how she learned to ride a bicycle in Braunschweig, and the joy of the memory is reflected in one of her early paintings.

> When I was 12, we were among the first of our town to learn bicycling on the modern two wheel bicycle and went out together very early in the morning into the woods just to lie under the trees and hear the birds singing.[23]

Other early pictures also depict themes connected to her childhood in Braunschweig, e. g., *Skating* (probably depicting the skating rink at Bürgerpark in Braunschweig), *Vacation Time*, *Washday*, *The Market Place*, *Coffee Garden*, *Opera House*, *Sleepy Little Town in Germany*.

Other parts of her work are dedicated to Jewish themes. Biblical and Talmudic themes as well as Jewish mysticism reveal her search for and her embrace of her Jewish identity as well as her religious side. Paintings addressing the Holocaust, emigration, and Jewish suffering mirror her own experiences. In Valeska's words:

> From the first I discovered an almost frightening motivation. My work took the form of religious motifs depicting rabbis, Talmudists and congregants. Secularly there was the ghetto Jew, the concentration camp Jew and the long-suffering Jew.[24]

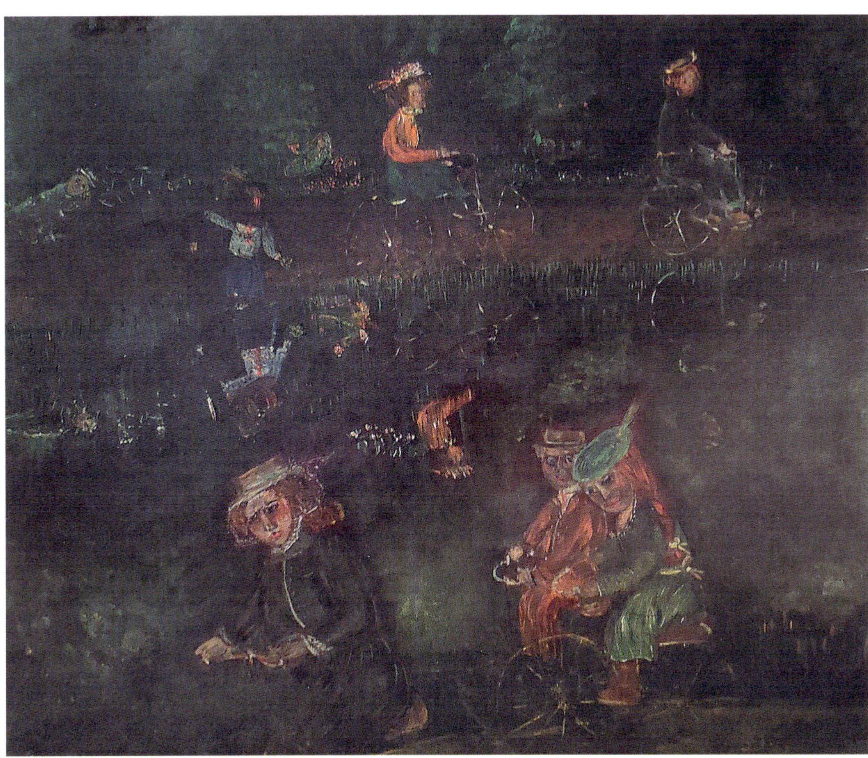

23 Bicycling, 1940s.

Valeska considers her motivation to come from a force greater than herself because her life had previously been removed from Jewish religious and cultural expressions. She depicted Jewish suffering with deep understanding and religious fervor based on her own experience and the experience of her relatives under the Nazi regime.

> I was among the assimilated German-Jews in Germany. And I was little interested in Zionism but with the emergence of the National Socialistic State I became increasingly aware of my Jewish roots. In Los Angeles I joined Hadassah.[25]

"Themes for my paintings are born unconsciously," she says attempting to describe how she creates.

> It is always a mystery to me. A higher source made me do it. A power I cannot explain ... A friend once said that I am the best proof of the collective unconsciousness which comes from the suffering of Jews of thousands of years.[26]

Valeska describes this painting in detail in her 1947 memoirs:

> *Thou Shalt Live*: (Deuteronomy; Chapter 30)
> The father of my friends, a Rabbi in for 38 years, Dr. Rulf (called Dr. Hulf) who always helped the persecuted Jews of Poland & Russia. Once he went to Russia after a pogrom which had burnt down the synagogue and found in the ashes of the synagogue one little bit of paper, a tiny little piece of the Torah which was not burnt and he took it out of the ashes and read the unburnt words in Hebrew from the Torah Thou shall live. He took it home and when he died many years later we would not find any will but in opening his little iron box this piece of the Torah was in it and some words in his handwriting, 'please put this into my grave.' So, my picture is in memory of this great rabbi.[27]

The painting *Der Bucklige* (The Hunchback) from 1954 might be a reference to a painting of one of the artists of the Blue Four – Lette Vales-

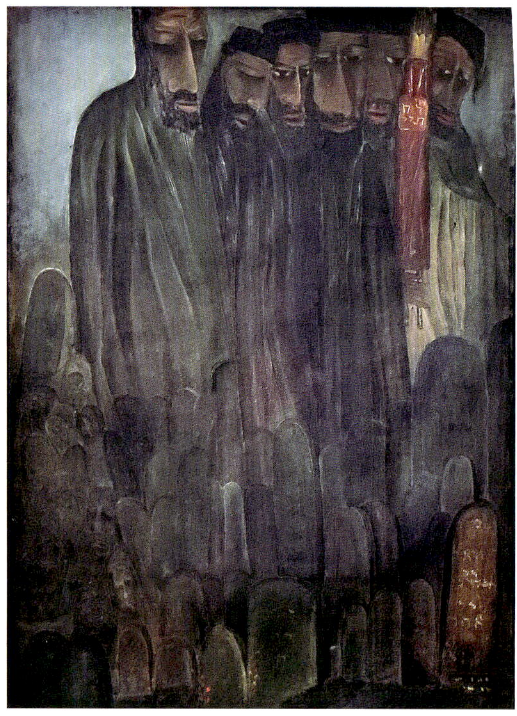

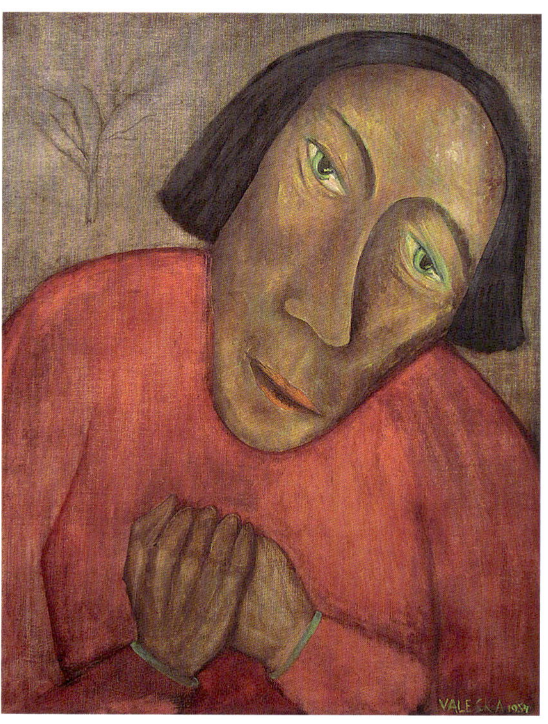

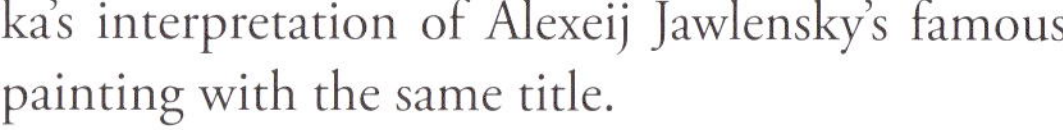

24 Thou Shalt Live, 1946/47.

25 Der Bucklige (The Hunchback), 1954.

ka's interpretation of Alexeij Jawlensky's famous painting with the same title.

Lette Valeska – The Sculptor

Valeska discovered sculpting in 1955 when she was 70 years old. Again, she was told by her teacher, the sculptor Jane Ullman (1908–91) that she needed no training.

Conclusion

Lette Valeska's art works have been shown in a variety of venues, an early exhibition of her paintings related to the Jewish Ghetto themes and Israel subjects at the Bezalel Museum in Israel,[28] in gallery exhibitions including her own one-woman show at the La Tortue Gallery in Santa Monica in 1970, as well in an exhibition of her photos, paintings, and sculptures in 1980 at the Los Angeles Jewish Community Center. During the latter exhibition Valeska was filmed commenting on her art and her connection to the famous Blue Four.[29] Lette Valeska passed away at home in Los Angeles in 1985.

Lette Valeska's work does not belong to any particular school or genre of art. She was influenced by her teacher Galka Scheyer, the Blue Four and other artists of her time, but she has her own unique, genuine style that was revealed and encouraged by Galka Scheyer. Lette Valeska's artwork is a dialog with her past, a dialog with suffering, and especially Jewish suffering. She fully embraced creativity as an expression of life that should not be suppressed or restricted. She found it in the children and actors who she photographed and expressed it in the images that she painted and sculpted.

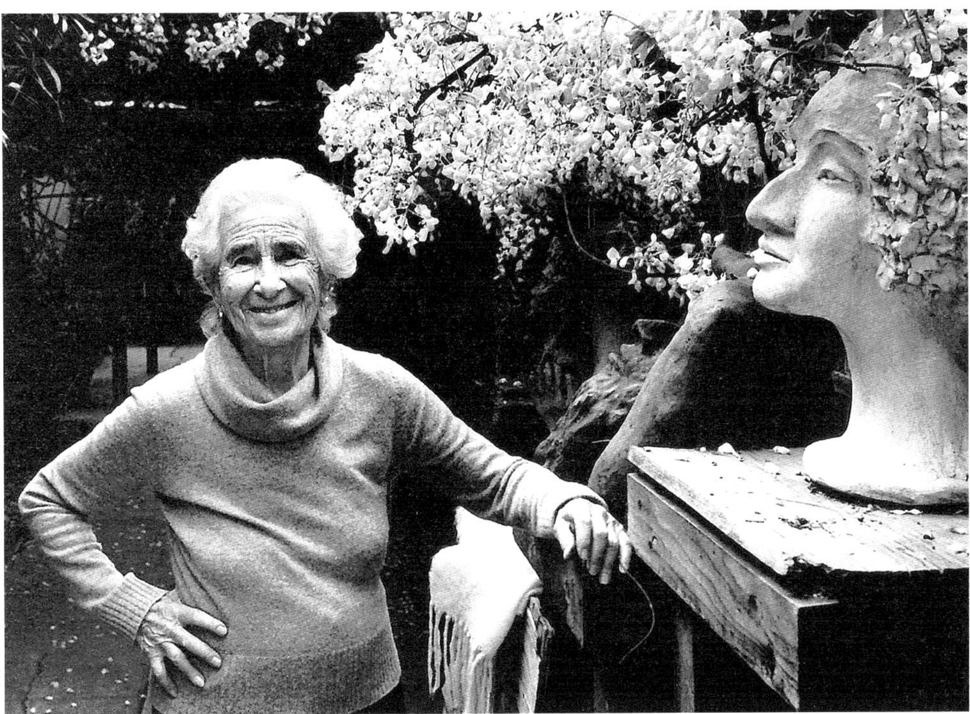

26 Lette Valeska with a sculpture, 1970s.

*Creative power is in each human being … when you paint
you paint with your soul. I do what children do. I play when
I paint. What they paint is truth. It's what they feel.*

— Lette Valeska, 1965[30]

1 Renate Evers is Director of Collections at the Leo Baeck Institute New York | Berlin, a research institute for the history and culture of German-speaking Jews and has built an extensive archive and library collection since its founding in 1955.

2 The article was developed together with Julia Hammid, Lette Valeska's granddaughter, Petra Hammid, the widow of Lette Valeska's grandson, the photographer Tino Hammid (1952–2015).

3 Lette Valeska is her artistic name. She was born as Valeska Heinemann, her married name was Valeska Heymann, in the main part of this article she is referred to as "Valeska."

4 The Blue Four: Paul Klee (Switzerland, 1879–1940); Alexej von Jawlensky (Russia, 1864–1941); Wassily Kandinsky (Russia, 1866–1944); Lyonel Feininger (US, NY, 1871–1956).

5 William Wilson, "Mme. Lette Valeska debuts at 85 with paintings, sculpture and woodcuts at La Torture Gallery (1607 Montana Ave, Santa Monica)," *The Los Angeles Times*, August 17, 1970, p. 8.

6 Biographical details are based on information from her family and the work of Reinhard Bein, a Braunschweig historian, especially: Reinhard Bein, *Sie lebten in Braunschweig: Biographische Notizen zu den in Braunschweig bestatteten Juden (1797 bis 1983)* (Braunschweig, 2009); idem, *Lebensgeschichten von Braunschweiger Juden* (Braunschweig, 2016).

7 Petritorwall 2 & 30 according to Reinhard Bein.

8 "Hamburg Engros-Lager" between 1880–1903 in Schuhstraße 28 as Berthold Heynemann & Co., in 1903 sold to Anna Kleimann, continued as Nuchim Heiber (Texta Handelsgesellschaft) until 1937.

9 Lette Valeska's youngest brother Fritz (1893–1918) died in the 1918 flu epidemic, her oldest brother Ludwig (1882–1942), a ship builder, died with their mother and his wife during a bombing raid in Holland, her older brother Walter (1883–1968) became a physician, was the president of the Braunschweig Jewish community, and also emigrated with his family to the United States, via Palestine, already in 1935. The Leo Baeck Institute preserves Walter Heinemann's papers as well as his memoirs "Braunschweiger Erinnerungen."

10 Founded by Wilhelm Adolf Lette in 1866.

11 Kronberg am Taunus.

12 Art Ronnie, "Say what you want but please … don't compare her to Grandma Moses," *California Living*, August 23, 1970, pp. 22–27.

13 Valeska got permission from Corinne A. Seeds, the principal of UCLA's elementary school to take photographs of children at an elementary school. She wanted to take photographs of the spontaneous activities of children. The photos were exhibited for parents and educators in Los Angeles and later turned into a permanent exhibition, touring the state of California for viewing by educators more widely. She became known and caught the eye of movie actors who hired her to take pictures of their children and later of themselves. Kolma Flake, "Arrested Moments," *Minicam Photography*, no. September (1945), pp. 50–54, especially: p. 50.

14 Art Ronnie, "Say what you want" (see note 12), p. 26.

15 Hadassah: Zionist Jewish women organization.

16 Mira Hamermesh, Otto Zarek, and Lette Valeska, "Paintings of the Ghetto," *Zionist Review*, July 31 (1950), pp. 13–15, especially: p. 15.

17 Interview with Lette Valeska, 1980, as featured in a short untitled video clip on the occasion of the exhibition of her photos, paintings, and sculptures at the Los Angeles Jewish Community Center in 1980, Access: courtesy of the Lette Valeska Estate, VHS tape, 14:40 min., production company: Horizon, in German. Parts of this clip were shown at the 2019 Galka Scheyer Conference with added English subtitles.

18 Lette Valeska, *My life story: Lette Valeska*, unpublished manuscript, written around 1947, three pages, courtesy of the Lette Valeska Estate.

19 Art Ronnie, "Say what you want" (see note 12), p. 27.

20 The New Synagogue in Braunschweig was consecrated in 1875 and located on the Alte Knochenhauerstraße. It was destroyed in 1938 during the November Pogrom (Kristallnacht). After the building was demolished in 1940, it was replaced with a concrete bunker. In 1983, a synagogue was established in the community building next to the bunker. In 2006, a third synagogue, designed by architect Klaus Zugermeyer, was inaugurated in Braunschweig. Harold Slutzkin, "Braunschweig," Destroyed German Synagogues and Communities, https://synagoguesgermany.anumuseum.org.il/index.php/index.php/synagogues-and-communities?pid=59&sid=289:Braunschweig, accessed February 22, 2021.

21 Lette Valeska, *My life story* (see note 18), p. 1.

22 Ibid., p. 3.

23 Ibid., p. 1.

24 Art Ronnie, "Say what you want" (see note 12), p. 27.

25 Ibid.

26 Ibid.

27 Lette Valeska, *My life story* (see note 18), p. 3. probably refers to Isaac (Yitzhak) Rülf (1831, Hesse – 1902, Bonn) a Jewish teacher, journalist, and philosopher, and early Zionist who was rabbi of Memel, East Prussia between 1865–98 and widely known for his aid work.

28 Mira Hamermesh, "Paintings of the Ghetto" (see note 16), p. 15.

29 Lette Valeska Estate (see note 15).

30 Virginia Horn, "Lette Valeska – Richness of Creativity," *The Los Angeles Times*, August 20, 1965, pt. V, p. 3.

Images 1–26: Courtesy of Julia Hammid and Petra Hammid, estate of Lette Valeska.

The Jewish Art Dealer
Galka Scheyer in Paris – A Search for Traces

Gitta Ho

In December 1939, Galka Scheyer applied for a Guggenheim fellowship.[1] Part of the application that the art dealer, collector and art mediator submitted was a detailed curriculum vitæ in which she presented herself as a restless woman. This was especially true for her early years, when she was trained as an artist and never stayed in one place for long. The one typed page of the fellowship application on which Scheyer summarized her training almost reads like a travelogue. For the decade that she considered as her years of education she mentioned no less than seven countries: Belgium, England, The Netherlands, Italy, Switzerland, Germany, and France. Among others, she took up residence for several months in Brussels, Amsterdam, and Paris. About the latter stay, which according to a handwritten note on the application took place from 1912 to 1913,[2] she wrote:

> Residence in Paris for 2 years for Art Studies at the Ecole des Beaux Arts. Piano Studies at the Conservatory of Paris where I held a fellowship. Graduated from the Alliance Française with the Diplôme Elémentaire et supérieure in French.[3]

The application contains few details about Scheyer's first stay in Paris. The following article aims to verify these details, to investigate the motivation of her stay in France, and to discuss aspects of her later interest in French art.

In Paris, Still as an Artist

When Galka Scheyer first traveled to France at the age of twenty-three, she had not yet abandoned her plan to become a painter. One of her works, created just shortly before her departure to Paris in 1912, is the painting *Flower Field* (Fig. 1). Signed by Scheyer with the pseudonym 'Renée,' it shows a landscape depicted in vivid colors with a high horizon and blue mountains forming the background. Considerable place is given to the play of light on the meadow in the foreground. Visible, short brush strokes, sometimes juxtaposed, sometimes overlapping, are reminiscent of post-impressionist works, whose exponents include Paul Signac, Henri-Edmond Cross, and Georges Seurat. Post-impressionism, as well as impressionism from which it emerged, had its roots in France. Whether this influenced Scheyer decision to study in Paris, we do not know today.

In her Guggenheim application Scheyer referred to the fact that her teacher, the painter Gustav Lehmann, had once studied with the impressionist painter Claude Monet. Although this is probably not true, she was certainly aware that a period of training in Paris was part of the career of numerous art students in the 19th century and that her training period in the French capital followed a long tradition. However, her decision to study at the École des Beaux-Arts (Fig. 2) in 1912 was a conservative choice as many young students favored private academies like the Académie Julian, the Académie Colarossi or, from 1908 on, the Académie Matisse. It remains unclear how exactly Scheyer – who does not mention the name of a teacher in whose studio she trained – studied at the École des Beaux-Arts as her name cannot be found in the school's enrollment records.[4] It appears most likely that Scheyer attended the school's classes only occasionally, possibly as a guest student, whose names were not always reliably recorded in the school's administrative records.

A similar situation presents itself for the Conservatoire de Paris at which Scheyer, according to the curriculum vitæ she wrote for the Guggenheim Foundation, studied piano and was supported with a fellowship.[5] The name Emmy Scheyer that she used at that time does not appear in the enrollment lists (Fig. 3). Like at the École des Beaux-Arts it was, however, possible to attend classes at the Conservatoire as a guest student. It can therefore be assumed that Scheyer, as probably also at the École des Beaux-Arts, was not a regular student, but only attended classes on an irregular basis.

1 Emmy E. Scheyer (Renée), Flower Field, 1911, oil on canvas (Private collection).

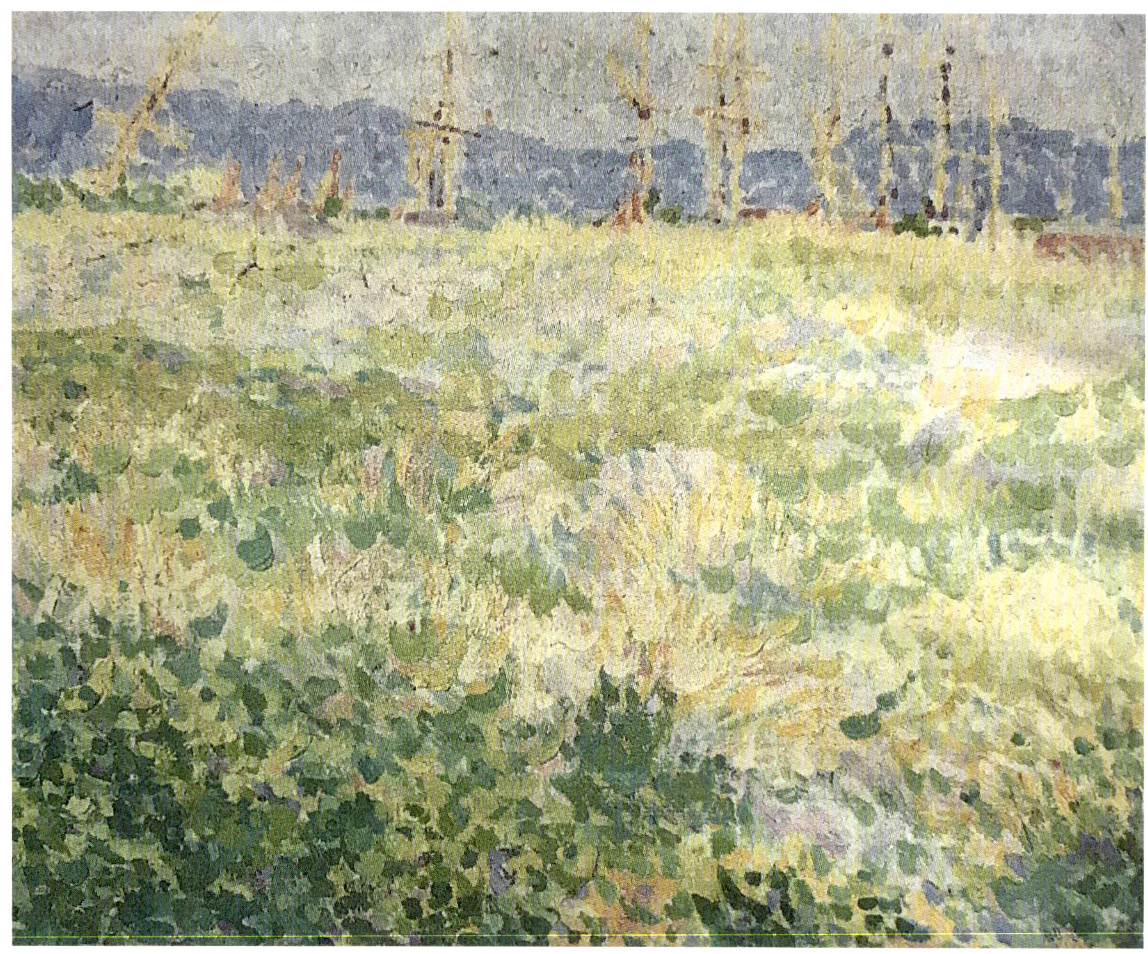

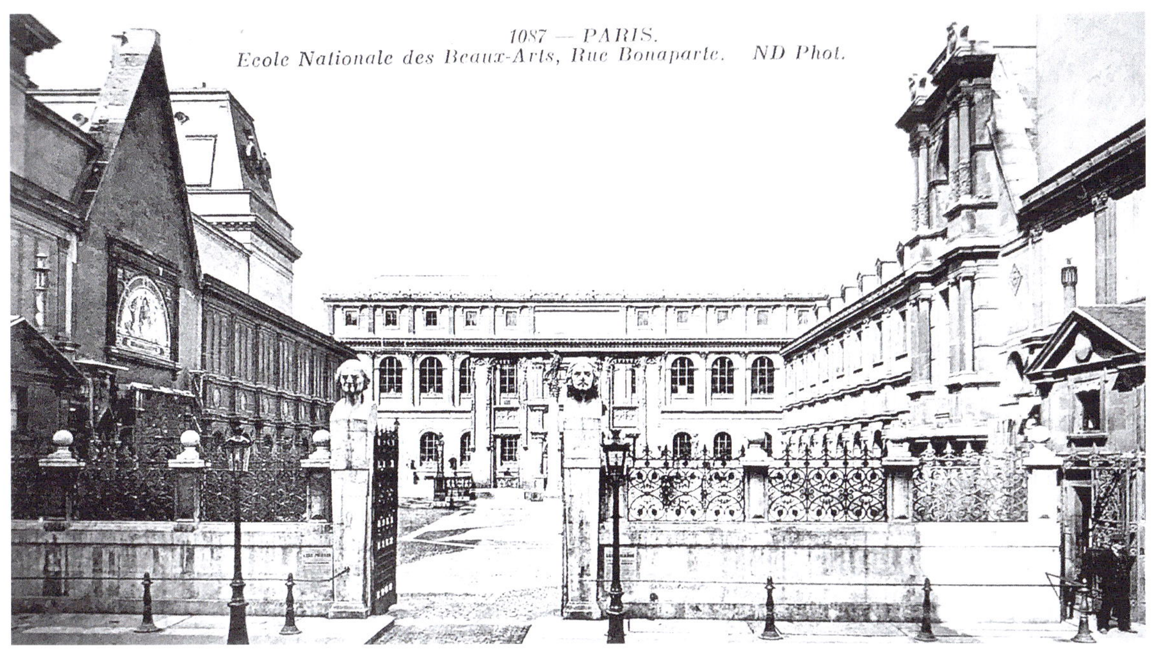

2 Historical postcard showing the École des Beaux-Arts, Paris, ca. 1900 (Photo: private).

3 (below) Annual table of students of the Conservatoire de Paris, Archives nationales, Pierrefitte-sur-Seine, AJ/37/181 (Photo: private).

Another qualification that Scheyer stated in her fellowship application was her language study at the Alliance française. Although enrollment lists of the renowned language school have not survived for the period of her stay in France, two diplomas Scheyer obtained still exist.[6] One diploma attests Scheyer's basic knowledge of French and the other her advanced language skills including the approval to teach French (Fig. 4). A closer look reveals that the diplomas were not issued at the language school's main location at Boulevard Raspail in Paris, as might have been expected. Instead, Saint-Valery-en-Caux – a small coastal town in Normandy, about 180 km northwest of Paris – is mentioned as site of the language courses. The possibility that Scheyer continuously studied French at the Alliance française in Saint-Valery-en-Caux during her two-year stay in Paris cannot only be excluded because of the long distance between the two places, but also because the diplomas clearly indicate that they were issued for

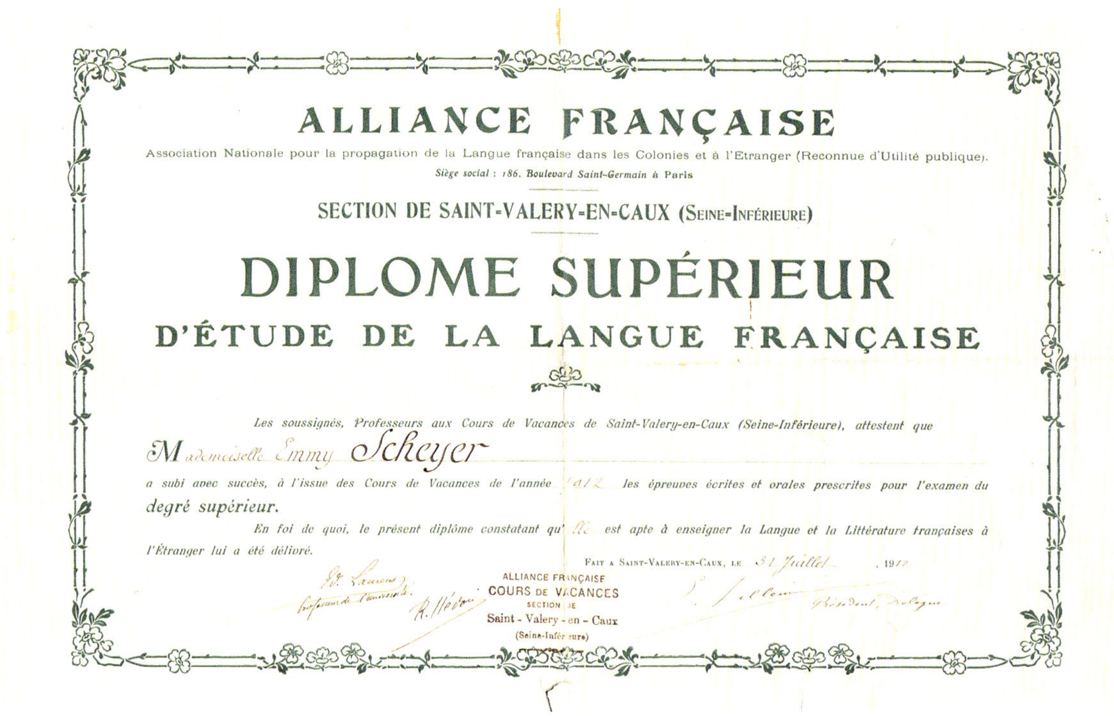

4 Galka Scheyer's "diplôme supérieur" for her language studies at the Alliance Française à Saint-Valery-en-Caux, July 31, 1912, (Courtesy of the Norton Simon Museum, Pasadena, CA).

the successful participation in summer language courses attended in Saint-Valery-en-Caux in July 1912.

Parisians are Selling in America[7]

It remains unclear to what extent Galka Scheyer attempted to establish contacts with artistic circles during her first stay in Paris, or whether she spent her time in the French capital by visiting museums or by familiarizing herself with current art movements while visiting gallery exhibitions. When she moved to New York in 1924 to promote the art of The Blue Four, she knew that in the US French art was preferred over German art.[8] Even though German art clearly was in the focus of her interest, Scheyer – as exhibition organizer and collector – was also open to French art. In the exhibition European Modernists, organized by Scheyer in Los Angeles in 1927, more than one third of the 27 artists presented were French, among them Derain, Léger, Maillol, and Matisse. The decision to show French artists seems not only to have been a concession to the American public, but also reflected Scheyer's taste in art: all works in the exhibition belonged to her private collection.

At about the same time as the exhibition, Scheyer was in contact with Christian Zervos, editor of the influential French art magazine Cahiers d'Art, who asked her for help. The Cahiers d'Art had run into financial difficulties and Zervos wanted her to support him in the US. Scheyer distanced herself from Zervos' request that she should directly ask people she knew in America to provide financial support for his magazine, with great clarity:

Je dois vous expliquer ma position … je ne m'approche jamais quelqu'un avec une demande d'acheter quelquechose [sic]. Ca [sic] se fait chez moi qu'on aime des œuvres d'art d'une telle façon qu'on se rapproche de moi de les acheter. Je ne peu [sic] pas changer cette politique pour demander des collecteurs pour supporter votre magazine.[9]

Later on, Scheyer, tried to reconcile and promised to support publication projects that Zervos at that time had planned together with Kandinsky. A possible reason for her change of mind could have been a longer trip to Europe she planned for the following year as European representative of the Oakland Art Gallery. In August 1932, she wrote to Kandinsky that she had "the intention

5 Letter by Marcel Duchamp to Galka Scheyer, n. d. (Courtesy of the Norton Simon Museum, Pasadena, CA, The Blue Four Galka Scheyer Collection Archives).

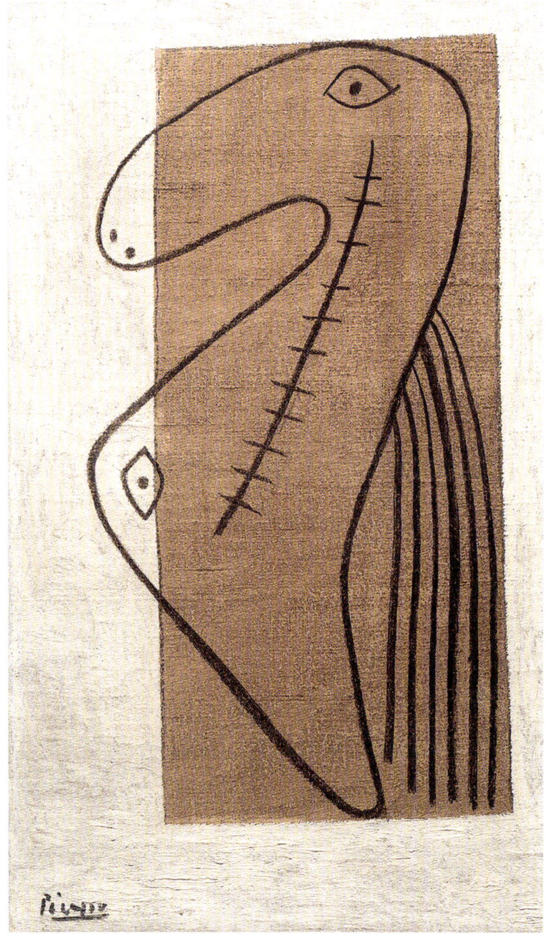

6 Pablo Picasso, Head of a Woman, ca. 1927, oil on canvas, (© Succession Picasso 2021).

to stay much longer in Europe this time, especially in Paris."[10] Her interest in the city and its art seems to have increased. In November 1932, she finally arrived in the French capital where she stayed at the Hotel de Castiglione in the Rue du Faubourg Saint-Honoré, not far away from the Louvre. She soon began to meet numerous artists. In her calendar, she noted meetings with the sculptor Constantin Brancusi and the painter Piet Mondrian. At these meetings, Scheyer seemed to have been primarily concerned with obtaining works of the artists, which she could later on

bring to the US. She missed the Italian painter Giorgio de Chirico, whom she had asked for a meeting by letter, because he was in Italy. In contrast, she was able to meet with the architect Le Corbusier, which shows that she pursued her interest in modern architecture during her trip to France.[11]

In Paris, Galka Scheyer also met with Marcel Duchamp, who even introduced her to various members of his family (Fig. 5).[12] She was not only interested in his works, but also in those of his brother, the painter and printmaker Jacques Villon, for which Duchamp willingly quoted his prices to her. He invited her to come to his brother's home in Puteaux, a small town about 15 km away from Paris, where Duchamp used to meet with artist friends such as Albert Gleizes, Jean Metzinger or Henri Le Fauconnier and which, at that time, involved a one-hour ride on the streetcar from Paris city center. Duchamp also recommended Scheyer see works by Salvador Dalí at the Galerie Pierre Colle, where just a few months later, in June 1933, such artists as André Breton, Max Ernst, and René Magritte presented their works at the *Exposition surréaliste*, the first major exhibition of surrealist art. Before Scheyer came to Paris in 1932, Duchamp had even been warned about her. Her reputation of being a temperamental person who tended to dominate others, preceded her all the way to France. Duchamp does not seem to have been particularly impressed by this as he met with Scheyer several times.[13]

In addition to works she could buy directly from artists, Galka Scheyer was also interested in the regular art market. Among the galleries she visited in Paris was the renowned art gallery of Paul Rosenberg in the Rue de la Boétie, which specialized in contemporary French art and represented Braque, Picasso, and Léger, among others.[14] During some of her gallery visits, Scheyer was advised by the artist and writer Henri-Pierre Roché, who was a friend of Duchamp. Along with Roché, she

7 Letter by Fernand Léger to Galka Scheyer, January 1935 (Courtesy of Norton Simon Museum, Pasadena, California).

visited the Galerie Percier near the Parc Monceau in the north of the city, where she bought a painting by Picasso. The artwork – the portrait *Head of a Woman* (Fig. 6) – remained in her private collection until her death.

A Missed Meeting

Among the artists Galka Scheyer missed during her stay in Paris in November 1932 was Fernand Léger. The French painter, whose artworks belonged to Scheyer's private collection, invited her to show her some of this works, but no date could be fixed because Scheyer left Europe earlier than planned. After her stay in France, a correspondence between her and Léger developed (Fig. 7).[15] Aware of her role as "European representativ" of the Oakland Art Gallery in California, the artist asked her in a letter dated October 1933: "Il y aurait-il un intérêt à organiser une exposition à Oakland Gallery? Petites toiles dessins et aquarelle[s]?"[16]

Galka Scheyer was immediately enthusiastic about the idea of a Léger exhibition in California. Even before the Oakland Gallery had agreed to the exhibition, she had the artist send her several art works, which she also wanted to show in her newly built home at 1880 Blue Heights Drive in Hollywood. After lengthy discussions about who would cover the transportation and exhibition costs, the gallery finally decided against exhibiting Léger's works. During the negotiations, Scheyer got in touch with the Renaissance Society of the University of Chicago, where a large monographic exhibition of Léger's work was shown in 1936.[17]

As an alternative to the cancelled exhibition at the Oakland Gallery, Léger offered Scheyer to come to California to give a series of conferences. In one of his letters, he described the planned lectures, some of which included film screenings:

Voici un programme possible:
1   Conference [sic] de F. Leger [sic] sur le Nouveau Realisme [sic] …
2   Projection du film "le Ballet Mecanique [sic]" de Fernand Léger. Epoque cubiste Mécanique [sic]
3   Projection du Film [sic] Entr'acte de René Clair – Picabia. Epoque Dadaïste
4   Projection du film le chien Andalou de Bunuel. Epoque Surealiste [sic][18]

The ambitious program was designed to give the American public an insight into recent French avant-garde developments. Scheyer reached out to the filmmaker Josef von Sternberg as well as to Charlie Chaplin for support, but was not able to convince them. Travel costs threatened to be high, so Léger's lectures were eventually cancelled. They would have been the last major event to result from Galka Scheyer's stay in Paris in 1932.

Conclusion

Galka Scheyer's stay in Paris from about 1912 to 1913, presented in the first part of the article, proved to be difficult to reconstruct. In her early years, Paris was just one of many places in Europe where the art, language, and music student stayed for a longer period of time. Much remains in the dark as evidence of enrollment in institutions such as the Conservatoire de Paris and the École des Beaux-Arts, which Scheyer stated to have attended, cannot be found. The fact that some details, such as the language lessons taken not in Paris but in Normandy, were probably not completely unintentionally disguised by Scheyer, does not make the situation clearer. It is doubtful whether the stay in Paris was really primarily devoted to education, as the curriculum vitae submitted to the Guggenheim Foundation in 1939 would make us believe.[19] The possibility that Scheyer, as her friend Lette Valeska wrote in a letter to Clemens Weiler in 1957, in Paris "in

Stellung ging,"[20] that means worked as a house-keeper just as she had done before in England and only took music and art lessons on the side seems more and more probable considering the lack of evidence for regular studies.

The second stay in Paris twenty years later, in 1932, to which Scheyer travelled from the US, took place under completely different circum-stances. The trip was closely linked to her work in international art business, not to her artistic train-ing. Her focus rested on contacting local artists and organizing works she could bring to the US. The role of Paris as a European metropolis for the arts and the art trade became much more impor-tant than during her earlier stay. The fact that her journey to Paris in 1932 was not as long as had previously been planned was due to the political situation. As early as late November, after not more than four weeks, Galka Scheyer left France for Germany. In May 1933, three months after Hitler's seizure of power, the Jewish art dealer and collector left for the USA and was never to return to France, nor to the rest of Europe.

1   For a selection on literature on Galka Scheyer, see Isabel Wün-sche, ed., *Galka E. Scheyer & the Blue Four: correspondence, 1924–1945* (Wabern and Bern, 2006); Sara Campbell, ed., *Feininger, Jawlensky, Kandinsky, Paul Klee: The Blue Four Galka Scheyer Collection, Norton Simon Museum of Art at Pasadena* (Pasadena, CA, 1976); Vivian Endicott Barnett, *The Blue Four Collection at the Norton Simon Museum* (New Haven, 2002); Vivian Endicott Barnett and Josef Helfenstein, ed., *Die Blaue Vier. Feininger, Jawlensky, Kandinsky, Klee in der Neuen Welt*, exhibition catalog Kunstmuseum Bern and Kunstsammlung Nordrhein-Westfalen, Düsseldorf (Cologne, 1997). For the ap-plication, see Norton Simon Museum, Pasadena, CA, The Blue Four Galka Scheyer Collection Archives, 1939 GES (Guggen-heim Fellowship 1940 Application); I thank Gloria Williams Sander, Britta Traub, and Stéphanie Baumewerd for their help in providing archival material and literature sources.
2   The Archives de la Préfecture de la Police de Paris do not hold any records that verify the duration of the stay.
3   Norton Simon Museum, Pasadena, CA, The Blue Four Galka Scheyer Collection Archives, 1939 GES (Guggenheim Fellow-ship 1940 Application).
4   The archives of the École des Beaux-Arts are held at the Ar-chives nationales, Pierrefitte-sur-Seine, see Archives nationales, AJ/52/470 (Élèves étrangers 1. 1879–1928); AN, AJ/52/573 (Répertoire alphabétique des élèves femmes, françaises et étrangères, autorisées à travailler dans les galeries 1. 1911–1949); AN, AJ/52/248 (Table du registre d'inscription); AN, AJ/52/553 (Répertoire alphabétique des élèves dans les ateliers. XIXe s.-1940).

5   As the archives of the École des Beaux-Arts, the archives of the Conservatoire de Paris are held at the Archives nationales, Pier-refitte-sur-Seine, see Archives nationales, AJ/37/135 (Enseigne-ment. Tableau annuel des classes, première série (1). Musique et déclamation : professeurs et élèves, 1911, 1912); AN, AJ/37/136 (ibid., 1912, 1913); AN, AJ/37/137 (ibid., 1913, 1914); AN, AJ/37/138 (ibid., 1914, 1915); AN, AJ/37/180 (Enseignement. Tableau annuel des classes, deuxième série (1). Musique et décla-mation : professeurs et élèves, 1er octobre 1911–30 septembre 1912); AN, AJ/37/181 (ibid., 1912, 1913); AN, AJ/37/182 (ibid., 1913, 1914); AN AJ/37/183 (ibid., 1914, 1915). I thank Marie Duchêne-Thegarid who prepares the publication of a da-tabase with all students of the Conservatoire. She is particularly interested in foreign students of the school, but could not find any trace of Scheyer, either.
6   Norton Simon Museum, Pasadena, CA, The Blue Four Galka Scheyer Collection Archives (1912 07 31_GES Alliance Fran-çaise Certificat Français Elémentaire; 1912 07 31_GES Alliance Française Diplôme Supérieur).
7   Letter by Kandinsky to Scheyer, November 17, 1934, in Wün-sche, *Galka E. Scheyer & the Blue Four* (see note 1), p. 250.
8   Wünsche, *Galka E. Scheyer & the Blue Four* (see note 1), p. 10.
9   "I have to explain my position to you … I never approach any-one with a request to buy something. It is at my place that peo-ple love artworks in such a way that they approach me to buy them. I cannot change this policy to ask collectors to support your magazine." Paris, Bibliothèque Kandinsky, Fonds Cahiers d'Art, CAPROV 3 (letter by Scheyer to Zervos, September 8, 1931).

10　Paris, Bibliothèque Kandinsky, Fonds Kandinsky, VK 304 (letter by Scheyer to Kandinsky, August 16, 1932): "Außerdem habe ich die Absicht, viel länger dieses Mal in Europa zu bleiben, besonders in Paris."

11　Norton Simon Museum, Pasadena, CA, The Blue Four Galka Scheyer Collection Archives, G dC 1932–1 (letter by de Chirico to Scheyer, November 25[?], 1932); ibid, LC 1932-2 (letter by Le Corbusier to Scheyer, November 10, 1932).

12　Ibid., M D 1932–3 (letter by Duchamp to Scheyer, not dated).

13　See Darcy Tell, "The Art Lover: Galka Scheyer's Higher Calling," *East of Borneo*, December 2, 2010, fn 18 [https://eastofborneo.org/articles/the-art-lover-galka-scheyers-higher-calling/] (accessed April 30, 2021): "The Arensbergs warned Marcel Duchamp not to let Scheyer "impose" on him during a visit to Paris. (As mentioned in Beatrice Wood's diary entry, dated December 13, 1945, Beatrice Wood papers, Smithsonian Archives of American Art);" the diary has been consulted, but Tell might have mixed up dates as the entry of December 13, 1945 does not refer to Duchamp [https://edan.si.edu/slideshow/viewer/?eadrefid=AAA.woodbeat_ref892] (accessed April 30, 2021).

14　Norton Simon Museum, Pasadena, CA, The Blue Four Galka Scheyer Collection Archives, F L 1933-1 (letter by Scheyer to Léger, August 15, 1933).

15　Ibid., F L 1933–1935 (correspondence Scheyer/Léger).

16　"Would there be interest to organize an exhibition at Oakland Gallery? Small paintings, drawings, and watercolors?" Ibid., FL 1933–2 (letter by Léger to Scheyer, October 26, 1933).

17　"Fernand Léger, Paintings, Watercolors, and Gouaches," March 6 to April 6, 1936, The Renaissance Society of the University of Chicago.

18　"Here is a possible program:
1　　Conference of F. Léger on New Realism…
2　　Screening of the film "Le ballet mécanique" by Fernand Léger. Mechanical cubist period
3　　Screening of the film Entr'acte by René Clair – Picabia. Dadaist period
4　　Screening of the film Le chien andalou by Bunuel. Surrealist period"
Ibid., FL 1935–6 (letter by Léger to Scheyer, n. d.).

19　Scheyer did not get the Guggenheim fellowship.

20　Wiesbaden, private archives for Impressionist painting (letter by Lette Valeska to Clemens Weiler, November 12, 1957).

Galka Scheyer
in the International Art Business

William M. Katin

A comparison of Galka Scheyer's representation of the Blue Four artists Paul Klee, Alexej von Jawlensky, Lyonel Feininger and Wassily Kandinsky with Alfred Flechtheim's galleries in Dusseldorf and Berlin offers insight into her success in business. The juxtaposition places Scheyer into the global economy of the Weimar Republic's 1923 hyperinflation and New York's 1929 stock market crash, while not neglecting the sales of art in uncertain times, causing consumers to exercise greater caution. This essay will trace the resemblances via five factors: the amount of invested capital, entrepreneurial skills, personality, location, and marketing ability.

The analogy is warranted since Scheyer (1889–1945) was a contemporary German-Jew of Flechtheim (1878–1937) and both represented several of the same artists, although Flechtheim primarily espoused French modernists.

Admittedly there is a major operational difference, since Scheyer departed Germany for the US in May 1924[1] whereas Flechtheim remained in the fatherland through September 1933. A third caveat is that Flechtheim needed large sums of capital to cover the fixed costs of owning stores. His wife's dowry was responsible for the opening of the Dusseldorf gallery in 1913, but the Berlin flagship required a bank loan in 1927–28.[2]

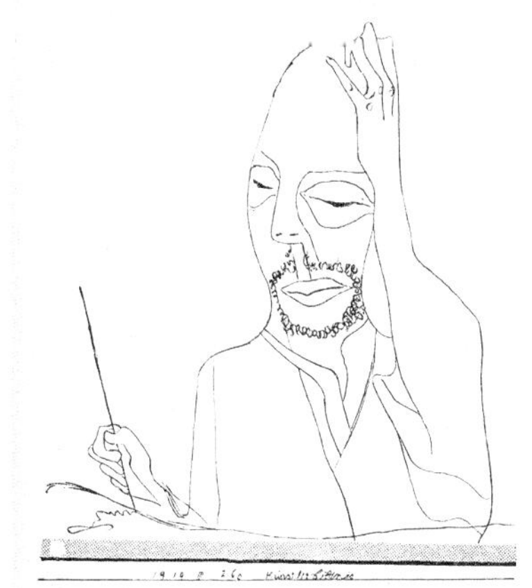

1 Exhibition catalogue "Paul Klee. Watercolors, drawings and prints from 25 years. Exhibition February 15 to March 10, 1930, Alfred Flechtheim Gallery, Düsseldorf (Courtesy of Verlag NIMBUS. Kunst und Bücher, Wädenswill/Switzerland).

The Amount of Invested Capital

Both received financial support from family-owned firms. Galka's stemmed from the W. Maseberg Cannery whereas Alfred's originated with father Emil's grain distributorship, the M. Flechtheim Company. It was typical for Jewish-owned businesses to employ family members and to receive capital from them. From late fall through early 1925 Scheyer negotiated for monthly financial assistance of $50 from her brothers.[3] Flechtheim's capital derived from his wife's dowry, which he spent on French art during the honeymoon.[4]

2 Flechtheim Gallery auction catalogue 1931 (Courtesy of Verlag NIMBUS. Kunst und Bücher, Wädenswill/Switzerland).

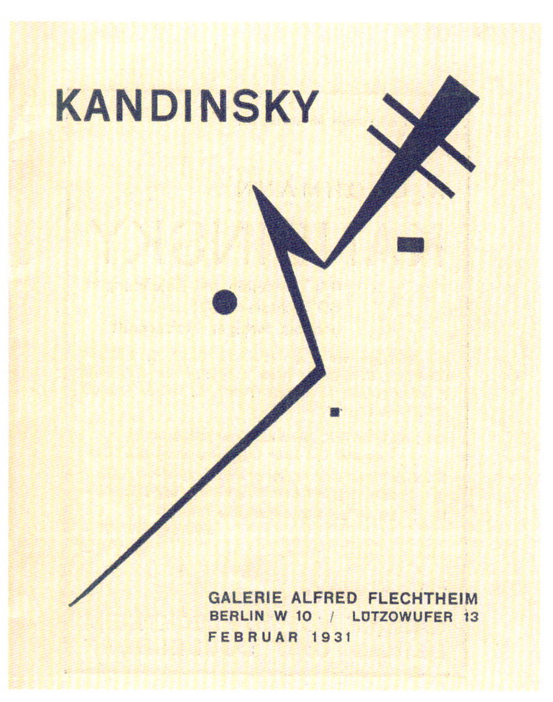

Entrepreneurial Skills

Three letters from January through April 1924 indicate Galka's entrepreneurial skill in paying the Blue Four artists with cans of food. The first mention derives from Lily Klee's acceptance of this creative financing and the two following pieces of correspondence indicate Feininger's and Jawlensky's acceptance of bartering.[5] A second example of Galka's non-traditional thinking was exemplified in her cooperation with Prentis Cobb Hale's department stores in California. Cobb utilized Galka's art to decorate displays of contemporary furniture in his San Francisco, Oakland, Sacramento and San Jose stores in order to stimulate sales. The experience taught Galka that business was more sales oriented than museums.[6] In addition, Galka would on occasion sell gifts given by the artist. Alfred incorporated a similar practice of placing works on commission in his apartment, which makes it difficult to discern which pieces were owned by him and which were on consignment. The extent of Flechtheim's assets thus become unclear.

Alfred displayed innovation in the 1927–28 grand opening in Berlin by having guests pay for the banquet and Josef Hauth supplied the wine from his wholesale company. As the economic crisis was worsened by anti-Semitism, Alfred received occasional aid from his cousin, the I. G. Farben attorney, Julius Flechtheim. Although Alfred was originally unwilling to sell Max Beckmann's self-portrait to Berlin's National Gallery Director Ludwig Justi in 1928, the depression forced Alfred to sell three of his favorite art pieces to the German banker Eduard von der Heydt in 1930. Since Justi had advised Heydt to purchase the Beckmann, it was loaned to the National Gallery.[7]

Another creative step implemented by both dealers was the symbiosis with literature and bookstores. In 1925, Galka received a monthly stipend from Hanover publisher Alfred Rose. Another example developed after Scheyer's move from New York to California. In 1926, she arranged for art to be displayed in Paul Elder's San Francisco bookstore. A third example was her appointment as a correspondent for the *San Francisco Examiner*. The association with the newspaper resulted in a marketing coup in which her artists were provided with a full-page story. As an advertisement it would have cost $1,500.[8]

Similarly, Flechtheim published *Der Querschnitt* from 1921 to 1936 and began the two-year publication of *Omnibus* in 1930. His stylized, elongated "AF" logo gained name recognition from art connoisseurs for the Dusseldorf and Berlin galleries. Although Scheyer could be congratulated by modern business consultants on obtaining free advertisement for the Blue Four artists, historians have criticized Flechtheim for hubris in attempting to use luminaries such as Alfred Barr of New York's MOMA and Ernest Hemingway in a distribution network far smaller than the Ullstein publishing house, which he had employed for his prior publication *Querschnitt*. Bookstores may have played a negative role in Flechtheim's business. After the Berlin gallery was closed, former Flechtheim employee Curt Valentin sold the inventory in Karl Buchholz's book shop.[9]

DIE BLAUE VIER

FEININGER
JAWLENSKY
KANDINSKY
PAUL KLEE

Allgemeiner Brief—

3.

Sacramento, California.
July 28 th 1925.
105 Grad Hitze im Schatten.
Fahrenheit.

Lieber König Feininger !

Die weiteren direkten Ausgaben, ausserhalb des Rosen- schen Geldes von 1925 , habe ich der Interesse halber vermerkt . Dieselben habe ich von meinen Privatgel- dern bezahlt. (z. B. Übersetzungen einiger Bücher u. Schriften vom französischen ins deutsche über den Radierer Bresdin. Dann 25 $ 14 % Verdienst vom verkauf ten Bildwerken.

Im Moment sehe ich keine weiteren extra Verdienstmög- lichkeiten,. Meine neue "Blaue Vier " Saison , die ich ständig jetzt schon vorbereite, fängt ca. am ersten October an. Ich erhalte aus Deutschland $ 75 monatlic Auskommen kann man unmöglich unter $ 150 .00 im Monat. Wie ich es machen werde wissen die Götter. Aber ich weiss, dass ich durchhalten werde, denn es ist sicher, dass meine Arbeit in Amerika schon seine Früchte brin- gen wird.

Eine grosse Idee hat noch nie , 1,2,3, Erfolg gehabt. Mein Vorschlag ist daher, nur event. Erleichterung der Lage, dass Rose, wenn es ihm möglich ist, und die Künstler damit einverstanden sind, mir vom ersten October bis 30 . März, also für 6 Monate, pro Monat 50 $ sendet,. Dann wären mir wenigstens im Ganzen 125 $ monatlich für die Saison in California gesichert, was ein freies Gefühl gibt u, den nötigen Schwung. Sollte ich gleich zu Anfang durch Vorträge endlich 50 $ per Stück verdienen so würde ich es Rose wissen lassen und das Geld wäre dann nicht nötig (weiter) Ich habe jetzt glänzende Empfehlungen und ich werde keine Gratisvorträge mehr annehmen, ausser für Universitäten , der Reklame wegen. Der Bürgermeister und Frau interessieren sich hier sehr für mich,. Das kann mein Glück in California sein. Frau Bürgermeister will mit mir nächste Woche nach San Francisco fahren und mich persönlich dort einführen. Aber alles ist Schicksal....... und warum , wenn mich keiner lieb hat, soll mich nicht mal das Schicksal liebhaben? (Natürlich nur um der "Blauen Vier" willen. Diesen Brief erhalten die 4 blauen Könige und Rose. Wenn beide Seiten einverstanden sind , bitte ich Sie sich/gegenseitig in Verbindung zu setzen und mich das Resultat wissen zu lassen.

Herzliche Grüsse dem König
u. der Königin Ihr erg. Minister Emmy.
bitte wenden.

3 Letter from Scheyer to the Blue Four mentioning Rose's funding, July 28, 1925 (Courtesy of the Norton Simon Museum, Pasadena, California).

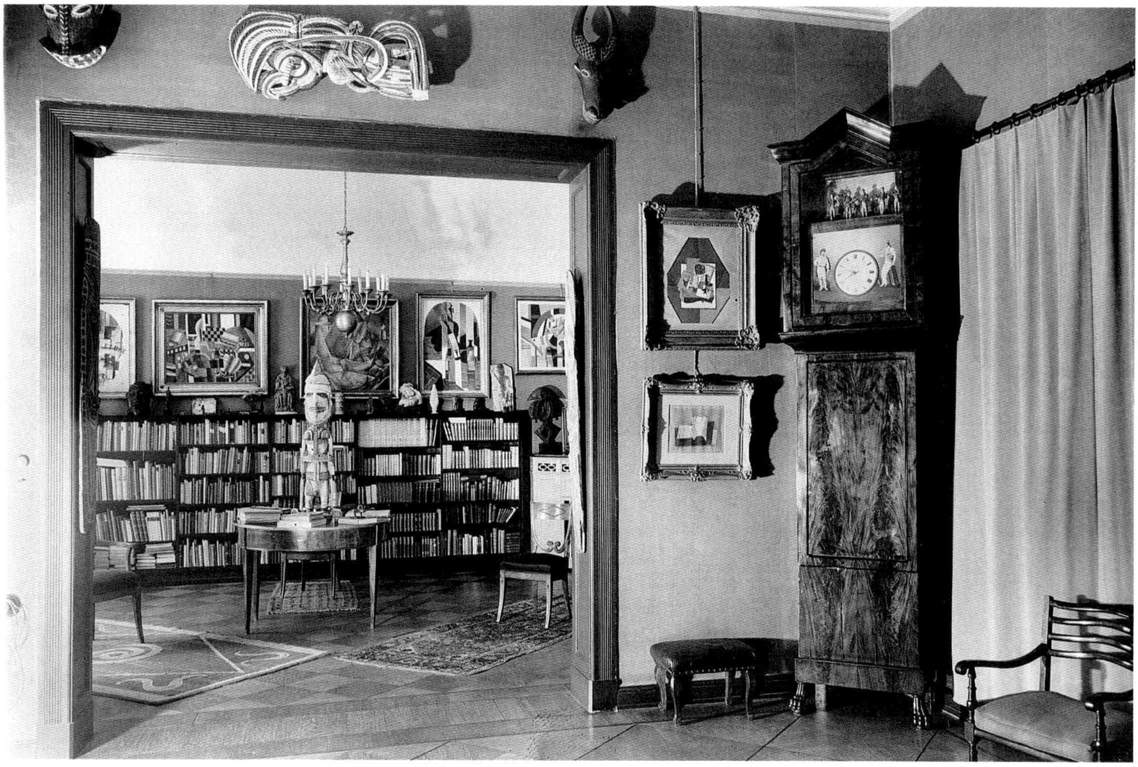

4 Marta Huth's photograph of Flechtheim's Picasso-filled apartment (Courtesy of Landesarchiv Berlin, F Rep. 290-05-01 Nr. 45, photographer: Marta Huth).

Personality

Galka's and Alfred's personalities were different. In the beginning of her business venture, Galka gave lectures to adults and provided creative art lessons to children. She viewed her activities more as a spiritual endeavor than as an opportunity to make a financial profit. She expressed her life mission in an October 19, 1925 open letter to the Blue Four: "I would rather speak free of charge to young, impressionable people, than for the money of the dead bodies in clubs."[10] Although Alfred did not give lectures, George Grosz depicted him as a relic from a prior age, more similar to a patron of the arts rather than a dealer. But at the same time Alfred also acted as a speculator, receiving two to three times the amount for cubist art purchased during his 1905 honeymoon to Paris.[11]

Location

Alfred's apartment was "an intimate extension" of his gallery on the Lützowufer with the walls covered from floor to ceiling with French and German pictures. Famous people, such as Josef von Sternberg and Max Schmeling, attended the dinners in his Bleibtreustraße home near the Kurfürstendamm, in which he offered great hospitality. The home provided an additional location from which to buy art. George Grosz learned about all von Sternberg's movies in the hope that Josef would buy some of his work during a Flechtheim party.[12]

As Galka returned to California from Europe in the summer of 1933, she rented a room in a Frank Lloyd Wright house for $60. Although she had received 250 new pictures on commission, the tiny room allowed her to display only three pieces at a time to potential customers. This difficulty was resolved by the availability of a lot overlooking Hollywood on which to build a house. The price of the land was only $150 and the renowned architect Richard Neutra agreed to design a custom house.[13] Both Alfred and Galka bought homes in expensive neighborhood in order to extend to wealthy guests a casual atmosphere in which to buy art, although Galka's real estate investment was made at a time in which Alfred's business was about to be "aryanized."

Marketing Ability

The film industry had a worldwide impact and thus some major participants in Hollywood were clients of both Flechtheim and Scheyer.

During a Flechtheim dinner party, von Sternberg exploited a lull in the conversation to ostensibly address the sculptor Rudolf Belling. In a raised voice audible to all, Sternberg announced "No, I don't earn so much money. At most, perhaps three times as much as the President of the US."[14] Large salaries in Hollywood drew those

5 Marta Huth's photograph of Flechtheim's Picasso-filled apartment Courtesy of Landesarchiv Berlin, F Rep. 290-05-01 Nr. 46, photographer: Marta Huth).

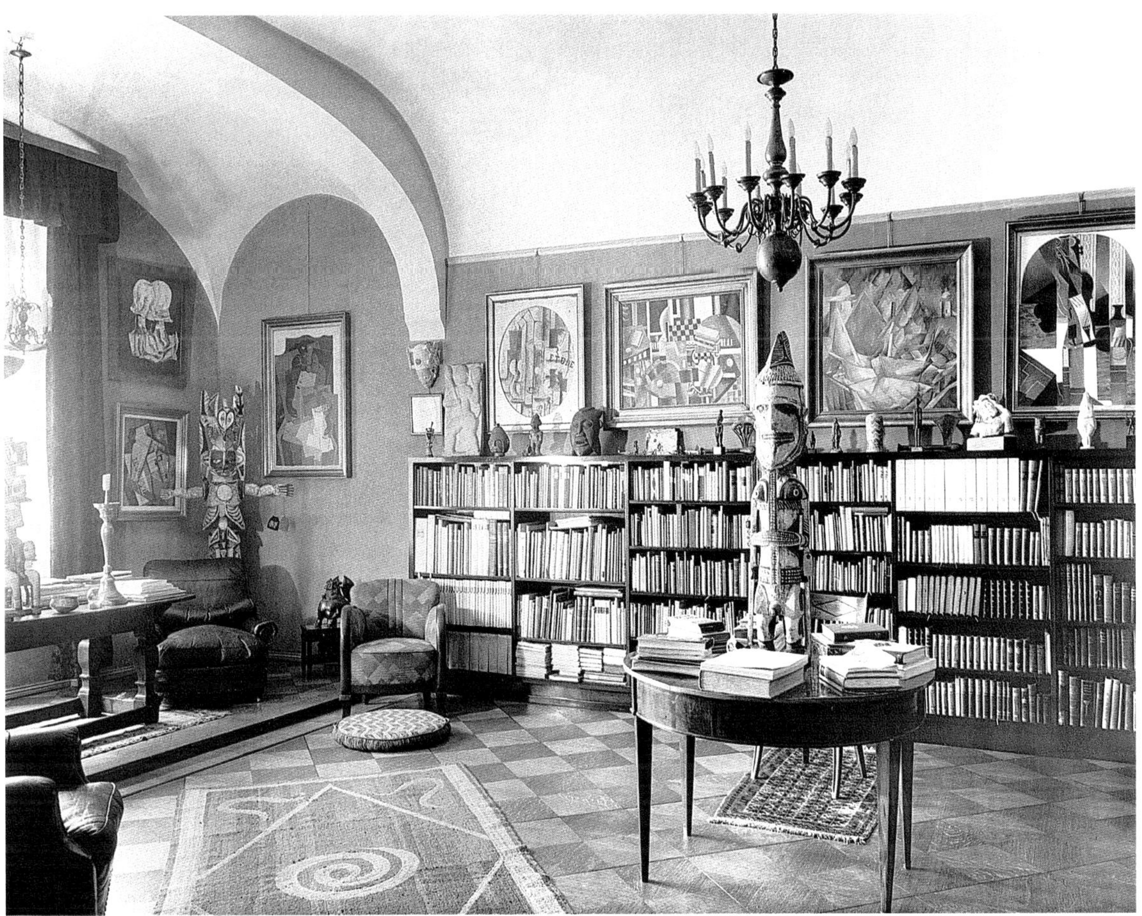

in the film industry away from Babelsberg, Germany. Sternberg had acquired a taste for Wassily Kandinsky as early as the 1913 International Exhibition of Modern Art. His tastes were also evident in the Packard in which he drove actress Georgia Hale in 1919. When the movie *Underworld* hit the box office in June 1929, Paramount doubled his salary from $10,000 to $20,000 per week, in addition to a $10,000 bonus. In contrast, UFA paid Germany's most successful screenwriter Robert Liebmann $500 per week in 1929. Scheyer warned the Blue Four not to succumb to Sternberg's bargaining, since he could well afford to pay. Sternberg spent the bare minimum on housekeeping in order to afford art and a house in which to showcase it. His house in Northridge CA, was designed by Neutra in 1933. The scale of Sternberg's collection can be seen by the exhibition of 133 of his works of art displayed by the LA County Museum of Art in June 1935.[15]

Scheyer attracted wealthy customers outside the film industry, including Walter and Louise Arensberg as well as Ruth Maitland. The Arensbergs assembled a large assemblage of Klee paintings of which the first was *Carnival Village* acquired through Scheyer in 1930.[16] Both Scheyer and Flechtheim catered to wealthy celebrities in Hollywood and Berlin, realizing they could well afford original art pieces.

The Fateful End of German-Jewish
Art Representation

Flechtheim's economic demise is often attributed to the slow recovery of the international market from the world crisis or the ascendency of National Socialism. Such an interpretation may misidentify the actual causes as well as may confuse a temporary problem in liquid assets with a need to enlist the services of Alfred E. Schulte, the outside auditor. Historians have justified the auditor's ef-

forts to avoid bankruptcy by liquidating the business. The scant evidence for this interpretation appears to originate with the lack of Flechtheim's sales at two sales opportunities during the fall of 1932 through the spring of 1933. The first failure was the September 11–November 13, 1932 exhibition of Picassos at the Kunsthaus Zurich. Prior studies have emphasized that Flechtheim's shipment of 17 paintings to Wilhelm Wartmann in Zurich did not strengthen his available cash. But the insurance value of Flechtheim's Picassos could just as well be underscored in evaluating the ability of his company to survive a temporary setback. For example, the insurance value of *The Head* was 10,000 Swiss Francs; *The Poet* was 25,000; *The Head of a Young Girl* was 5,500; *The Fireplace* was 12,500; and *The Welcome* was 4,000 Swiss Francs.

A number of issues regarding Flechtheim's sales require resolution. Why did customers with hard currency in Zurich need discounts? How deep were the discounts, which resulted in Flechtheim netting a mere 1,000 Swiss Francs? The import of these questions can be comprehended when it is observed that Wilhelm Wartmann acquired the Picasso painting *Guitar on a Pedestal Table* for 15,217 Swiss Francs in a purchase for the Kunsthaus. The discrepancy between 15,000 for one painting in contrast with 1,000 for all of Flechtheim's art is enormous, especially when it is considered that his selling price for the one Picasso painting *The Maternity* was 55,000 Swiss Francs.[17]

The significance of the above queries is underscored when one contrasts the Zurich buying practices with the purchasing mores of Scheyer's customers in Hollywood. Bargaining was not an acceptable practice among high-end American customers, such as the Arensbergs and the Maitlands.

The second setback concerned Hugo Helbing's Saturday March 11, 1933 auction of Old and New Masters at the Parkhotel Breidenbacher Hof. Police did not intervene as the SA disrupted the sales event. Worse than Flechtheim not receiving any revenue for his artwork was the fact that Dusseldorf branch manager Alex Vömel "aryanized" the gallery the following Thursday. On March 16, Vömel maintained in the city's commercial registry that the building and its inventory belonged to him, not Flechtheim.

Vömel could not have suddenly become the owner of the Dusseldorf gallery without assistance from a local bank, such as the B. Simon & Company Bank or the Bankhaus von der Heydt. Vömel informed the city's business registry that he was starting with operating capital of RM 10,000. Undoubtedly, he gave one painting to a financial institution as collateral for a RM 10,000 loan. The details of this transaction are unknown, but Vömel's pattern is clear from other financial undertakings. Flechtheim had owed the city of Dusseldorf the sum of RM 3,000. By claiming that

```
                          1380 Blue Heights Drive
                          Hollywood, California
                          May 14, 1939.
```

Mein langes Stillschweigen erklaert sich durch ein ziemlich bewegtes Leben, das ich fuhre. Das Haus auf der blauen Hoehe den herrlichen Kunstwerken der Blauen Koenige hat sogar die scheue Greta Garbo angelockt. Sie war bezaubert und bezaubernd und lief wie ein Kind von Bildern zu Blumen und freute sich an allem und seufzte:"Ach wenn ich doch auch einmal so leben koennte". Sie kochte Kaffee in meiner kleinen Kueche, bewunderte die Farben der Bilder, sagte sie verstehe davon nichts, moechte es aber gerne lernen. Sie faengt jetzt gerade an, an einem neuen Film zu arbeiten, was sie ueberaus beschaeftigt. Sowie sie damit fertig ist will sie wiederkommen und mehr sehen und hoeren. Sie ist sehr schoen, sah aus wie ein Stroemer und spazierte hier in meinen Bergen herum. Ihre Stimme ist das faszinierenste an ihr.

Der andere Stern, Marlene Dietrich, ist das Gegenteil von Greta Garbo. Kultiviert, raffiniert, ebenfalls schoen und lebhaft. Wir haben uns sehr angefreundet. Sie war oefter bei mir und ich noch oefter bei ihr. Ich half ihr ein Teil des neu gemieteten Hauses umzugestalten und hing das Haus mit Bildern von meinen Blauen Meistern, mit meinem Freunde den Schauspieler und Maler Koslock. Mit unserer Begeisterung steckten wir die Marlene an, die sich gerade in Paris Cezanne durch den Rat Remarques gekauft hatte. Sie erwartete ihn und zeigte uns alle Fotos von Bildern aus der Remarque Sammlung, der sit bis jetzt bis Van Gogh gegangen. Er kam morgens um 9 Uhr an und um 11 Uhr lautete mich Marlene schon an um mir freudestrahlend mitzuteilen, dass Remarque begeistert ist uber die Bilder. Wir hatten auch von Mrs. Maitland Toulouse Lautrec und Degas geliehen, da Marlene Angst hatte, dass Remarque die Bilder zu modern fand. Aber er war nur interessiert in die "Blauen" und erwahnte Degas und Toulouse Lautrec gar nicht. Marlene war sehr gluecklich daruber. Dann wurde sie sehr krank, dann e
Jetzt hoffe ich dass sie beide zu mir kommen und ich da wieder anknupfen kann, wo wir aufgehort haben.
Ich hatte Ihr angeboten ihr einige Bilder aus meiner Sammlung zu leihen, ebenso wie Mrs. Maitland. Diese Gelegenheit mit den Bildern zu leben, (sie hat sie sich selbst ausgesucht) wird entweder ein Verstandniss und Liebe dafur bringen, dass als Folge ein Besitzenwollen und Ankauf hat, oder, wenn das nicht geschieht, dann mutzt Kon..... (Auftragen) zum Verkauf. Diese Kunst ist keine Ware das es so schwer ist Bilder zu verkaufen
liegt vor allem daran
das die Menschen diese Kunst noch nicht verstehen und wenn man sie dazu ueberreden wuerde sich etwas in ihnen dagegen auflehnt. Daher halte ich es manchmal, wie in diesem Falle fuer angebracht ruhig Bilder zu leihen damit sie sich selbst verkaufen. Marlene giebt grosse Gesellschaften und die Werke werden von vielen Stars gesehen.
Ich hoffe das ich Ihnen bald Nachrichten geben kann das Marlene oder Remarque das Eine oder das andere Bild besitzen will

6 Letter from Scheyer to the Blue Four mentioning Greta Garbo's and Marlene Dietrich's visits to her house, May 14, 1939 (Courtesy of the Norton Simon Museum, Pasadena, California).

the inventory belonged to the Vömel-Suermondt collection, Vömel relinquished Barlach's bronze *Singing Man* and Georg Kolbe's *Bust of General von Einem* to the Dusseldorf City Museum at below market value, thus satisfying the debt. Similarly, Vömel wrote an October 21, 1933 letter to Kurt Poensgen, the owner of the former Jewish B. Simon & Company Bank, since the gallery in Dusseldorf was in arrears with regard to its monthly mortgage. Vömel brought the mortgage payments up-to-date through the sale of Picasso's *Beatrice*. The practice of selling an artwork to alleviate a debt owed to the Poensgen family or giving the family a piece of art was not novel, having been previously practiced with regard to Aristide Maillol's bronze *Bust of Renoir*. Some National Socialists may have been angered that Vömel was continuing Flechtheim's art business, but Vömel's repayment certainly satisfied most people including Kurt and Ernst Poensgen, who later became a member of Albert Speer's armaments advisory council.

Judges in the District Court would have supported Vömel's claim to being the new proprietor of both the building and the art. Providing another illustration of how Jewish-owned companies were "Aryanized," the Flechtheim Gallery was accepted by the city of Dusseldorf as Vömel's private property on Monday March 20.[18]

The lapse of only five business days between the interrupted auction to the city's acceptance of Vömel as the new owner indicates that Vömel had been planning this hostile takeover for months prior to the unsuccessful auction. Rather than laying the blame for the "Aryanization" on the SA violence, it appears more likely that the responsibility lays with the opportunistic employee, Alex Vömel, who was aided and abetted by German banks and the conservative legal system. Vömel continued to offer modern art for sale, so heclearly was not a Nazi, who would have objected to modern works as being "degenerate." Nevertheless, ethics played no role in his aspirations to pro-

mote himself from an employee to the owner of a recognized firm.[19]

When a historian reflects on Vömel's "Aryanization," Alex's shrewdness comes to the fore. For example, Paul Klee was worried about controlling the price of his pieces of art as well as ensuring their safety. As the SA requested that Klee's "degenerate art" be destroyed, Klee insisted that all German galleries return those items received on commission. This was another setback for Flechtheim, who had been the chief international distributor for Klee from 1927 through 1933, having sold 26 paintings and 5 watercolors at a gross price of RM 63,800. An October 24, 1933 contract required Flechtheim to transfer all Klee works to Daniel-Henry Kahnweiler's gallery in Paris. But the recall of works commissioned by Klee also adversely affected the Ferdinand Möller Gallery in Berlin and Rudolf Probst's Neue Kunst Fides in Dresden. Astonishingly, Vömel wrote to Kurt Valentin on October 30, 1933 that he was the sole German exception to Klee's return policy.[20]

In assessing the strengths and weaknesses of the two businesses, it should be observed that Scheyer did not insure the works by the Blue Four, due to the lack of available funds, whereas Flechtheim did. In addition, Scheyer found funding for exhibition catalogs from other art enthusiasts, rather than absorbing these variable costs. Thus, Scheyer avoided both the fixed cost of owning galleries and some variable costs as frequently as possible. This makes her activities at times appear as a personal venture rather than a recognized company.

The Nazi rejection of modern art ethically complicated art transactions. Karl Buchholz, Ferdinand Möller, Hildebrand Gurlitt and Bernhard Böhmer were the only four individuals allowed by the Nazis to buy art confiscated from German museums.[21] Flechtheim sold Klee's *Junger Garten (Rhythmen)* to the Dresden Painting

Gallery in 1929. Buchholz acquired it from the Propaganda Ministry for $240 in 1939 and then delivered it along with 14 others to Curt Valentin for sale in the US. Scheyer arranged for its sale in 1940 to Ruth Maitland in LA for $650, which was not noticeably different from the average mid-range sales price of $300–$910 during the period 1937–40. Lily Klee's March 14, 1940 letter to Valentin expressed relief that her husband's art had found a new home. But when this 64 x 50 cm oil painting was sold again in 2008 for $7.2 million, would she have expressed the same feelings?[22]

It could be argued that Scheyer established a more lasting memory. One piece of evidence for this view is a book originally published in German, which translates into English as *Strolls through Immigrant Hollywood*. The book was later translated into English as six tours of the greater Los Angeles area, noting on maps where foreign luminaries lived. The third tour was entitled "Famous Mansions in the Hollywood Hills," which included Galka's home along with those owned by Franz Werfel, Fritz Lang, Bruno Walter, Bruno Frank, and Conrad Veidt. The map illustrated how Scheyer lived between novelist Friedrich Torberg and composer Igor Stravinsky. Although Neutra's concrete building lacks the appeal of Werfel's or Walter's home, the accompanying photo of the panoramic view of LA from her home is stunning.[23]

1 Scheyer came to the US very early. Although following Berlin gallery owner J. B. Neumann in 1923, she preceded his colleagues Kurt Nierendorf in 1936 and Curt Valentin in 1937. See Marion F. Deshmukh, "The Visual Arts and Cultural Migration," *Central European History* 41, no. 4 (2008), p. 598.

2 Ottfried Dascher, *"Es ist was Wahnsinniges mit der Kunst," Alfred Flechtheim. Sammler, Kunsthändler, Verleger; mit einer Bibliographie* (Wädenswil, 2011), pp. 243–59.

3 Isabel Wünsche, *Galka E. Scheyer & The Blue Four: Correspondence 1924–1945* (Wabern, 2006), pp. 59–62.

4 George Grosz, *Ein kleines Ja und ein großes Nein: Sein Leben von ihm selbst erzählt* (Hamburg, 1986), p. 189.

5 Wünsche, *Galka* (see note 3), pp. 38–47.

6 Ibid., pp. 115, 160.

7 Dascher, *Alfred Flechtheim* (see note 2), pp. 259–76.

8 Wünsche, *Galka* (see note 3), pp. 97–125.

9 Dascher, *Alfred Flechtheim* (see note 2), pp. 277–78; Gesa Jeuthe, *Kunstwerte im Wandel* (Berlin, 2011), p. 53.

10 Wünsche, *Galka* (see note 3), p. 121.

11 Grosz, *Ein kleines Ja* (see note 4), pp. 188–89.

12 Ibid., pp. 189–92.

13 Wünsche, *Galka* (see note 3), p. 220.

14 Grosz, *Ein kleines Ja* (see note 4), p. 192.

15 John Baxter, *Von Sternberg* (Lexington, 2010), pp. 28, 43, 70–75, 94–117, 156–72, 193.

16 Jeuthe, *Kunstwerte* (see note 9), p. 213.

17 Dascher, *Alfred Flechtheim* (see note 2), pp. 281–87.

18 Ibid., pp. 293–300, 315–16.

19 Historians need to reassess their interpretation of Aryanization. It was often not a top-down procedure driven by the NSDAP occurring as late as 1938. Instead, it was a bottom-up operation by opportunistic non-Nazi German businessmen, who had the financial support of the banks and the legal protection of the courts. For examples from other business sectors see William M. Katin, *Hostile Takeovers of Large Jewish Companies, 1933–1935* (Lanham, 2021).

20 Dascher, *Alfred Flechtheim* (see note 2), pp. 317–18.

21 Uwe Fleckner, "Zweifelhafte Geschäfte," in *Markt und Macht* (Berlin, 2017), p. 6.

22 Jeuthe, *Kunstwerte* (see note 9), pp. 220–21.

23 Cornelius Schnauber, *Hollywood Haven: Homes and Haunts of the European Émigrés* (Riverside, 1997), pp. 13–14, 61–88.

German-Jewish Artists, Dealers and Collectors between 1910 and 1938

Marian Stein-Steinfeld

Undeterred, true to myself, to my idea, I must walk my path. Homeless, like the eternal Jew, but with a flag. And I won't trade it for anything. No one can carry it like I can. And I know that without being proud.[1]

This quote from Galka Scheyer paraphrases the problematic nature of the subject of Jewish artists, art dealers and collectors in the context of Galka Scheyer.

Today, most museums research the provenances of their collections and document losses due to Nazi confiscation actions. In 2019, the Städel Museum in Frankfurt am Main presented an empty frame on a pedestal in the center of one of the first rooms in its "van Gogh Exhibition." On the wall behind it the *Portrait of Dr. Gachet*,[2] was reproduced oversized and in black and white. This portrait was confiscated in 1937, the empty frame was left in the museum.[3]

It is important for heirs to reconstruct stations of the works of art from family property. It seems equally important to me to remember the individuals who were associated with these works – their creators, their mediators as well as their former owners.

Much of what will follow is based on research into the biography of Hanna Bekker vom Rath,[4] who was well connected in the German art scene of the interwar period as a painter and above all as a patron and collector. Using selected examples, some Jewish artists, art dealers, and art collectors will be introduced of whom little more than a frame – their vital records – remains. With Galka Scheyer, these contemporaries shared love, joy and commitment to art and carried the same flag as she did.

Ludwig and Else Meidner

While the painter and poet Ludwig Meidner (1884–1965) had been rediscovered in Germany since the 1960s – he had returned from his English exile to Germany – his wife Else (1901–87) is nearly forgotten, today.

Hanna Bekker vom Rath had regularly invited Meidner and his family, whom she had known since the mid-1920s, to Hofheim am Taunus. Her "Blue House" became a refuge for artists, which the Meidner family last visited in 1937 before they fled to England.

Else Meidner refused to return to the country of the perpetrators, who had killed her entire family of origin. But the hard and lonely life in exile made the once eccentrically cheerful woman bitter and impoverished:

> All lost, nothing gained! … When I came here as
> a beggar, I could not draw for a long time, not to
> mention painting … Long story short, I have not
> proved myself, I am as unsuitable for emigration
> as possible … I have not stained myself with glory,
> nor have I settled in, nor do I fit here![5]

she wrote to Hanna Bekker vom Rath in the spring of 1949 to Hofheim am Taunus. At this time, Else Meidner, her husband, and their son David were still living in exile in London. Then, David made Aliyah and lived in the religious Kibbutz Shluhot to which he later bequeathed the inheritance of his parents.[6]

Ludwig Meidner could no longer cope in London. He returned to Germany, lived for a few years in a district of Hofheim before spending his last years in Darmstadt. During the Hofheim period he again produced numerous paintings and drawings.[7]

Ludwig Schames (1852–1922)

Hanna Bekker had acquired first works of her later collection from the art dealer Ludwig Schames (1852–1922). The Kunstsalon Schames had been located at Börsenstraße 2–4 in Frankfurt since 1906, near the Frankfurt stock-exchange. Exhibitions of expressionist artists had been on show here since 1914. Ernst Ludwig Kirchner, who was presented many times at Schames', created an impressive wood cut-portrait of the art dealer in 1918, to which he later added this obituary:

> That was the art dealer Ludwig Schames, the
> fine altruistic friend of art and the artist … In the
> noblest way he enabled me and many others to
> create and live. We lose in him the man who was
> unique like a good father, a friend, a subtle and
> understanding patron of the art of our time.[8]

Ludwig's nephew Manfred Schames continued to run the Kunstsalon, but had to move the gallery's

location several times. After being banned from his profession in 1934, he emigrated to Palestine. In 1954, he turned to Hanna Bekker vom Rath, asking her as a witness to confirm his claims for compensation. Manfred Schames died in Israel that year.

Samson Schames (1898–1967), another nephew of Ludwig Schames, studied painting at the Offenbach School and later at the Frankfurt School of Arts and Crafts. He fled to London in 1939 and emigrated to New York in 1948. The Jewish Museum in Frankfurt dedicated an extensive retrospective to him in 1989.[9]

In November 1920, Ludwig Schames presented the Jawlensky exhibition, a tour-show organized by Galka Scheyer, which continued in January 1921 to Wiesbaden, Jawlensky's new residence. Jawlensky and Hanna Bekker vom Rath met around 1926 in Wiesbaden – he advised her artistically and she bought works from him. In 1928, she sent a letter calling for the foundation of the "Jawlensky Society":

> In order to preserve the creative power and joy
> of the artist, whose further work is currently
> in danger, and thus serve not only the artist
> himself, but above all also art and our culture.
> In order to achieve this goal, these friends need
> the help of personalities close to art, and they
> therefore turn to you with the request to help
> make the plan a reality through a monthly
> contribution.[10]

In doing so she followed the example of the Braunschweig collector Otto Ralfs, who had similarly supported Klee. Ralf's commitment to "Friends of Young Art" (Freunde Junger Kunst) was honored at the Schlossmuseum Braunschweig in 2019.

Robert von Hirsch (1883–1977)

Among the twelve founding members of the Jawlensky Society were at least five Jewish art collectors: the factory owner's daughter Clara Gans, the two lawyers Dr. Moritz Mannheimer from Wiesbaden and Dr. Paul Simon from Mainz, psychoanalyst and collector Dr. Margarete (Marga) Stegmann from Dresden as well as leather manufacturer Robert von Hirsch.

For Robert von Hirsch, descending from a culturally open-minded, assimilated family of the Frankfurt Jewish upper middle class, the friendship with Georg Swarzenski (1876–1957) was formative. The director of the Städel-Museum in Frankfurt had acquired French impressionists and German expressionists for the museum since 1906. He was dismissed as director of the municipal museum in 1933, but remained director of the private Städelsches Kunstinstitut until 1937, then emigrated to the USA in 1938.

Swarzenski succeeded in building up the collection of modern art for the Städel with the support of the Frankfurt bourgeoisie, including Jewish collectors such as: Heinrich Simon, Harry Fuld, Hugo Nathan, Ludwig Schames, Carl Sternheim, Dr. Kohnstamm, Fritz Gurlitt, Martin and Ernst Flersheim, Paul Hirsch and Robert von Hirsch.[11]

At Swarzenski's request, Hirsch donated the painting *Fleurs et céramique* by Henri Matisse to the Städel in 1917, painted between 1911 and 1913. It was confiscated in 1937 and auctioned at the Fischer Auction in Lucerne in 1939. This painting was bought back by the museum in 1967.[12] As a paying member of the Jawlensky Society, Hirsch received the painting *Abstract Head, Symphony in Pink*,[13] which he donated to the Städel in 1932. He revoked this donation in 1932, but renewed it in 1964.[14]

In September 1932, Hirsch registered a second residence in Basel and became the owner of Lederhandels AG there. In September 1933, he finally emigrated. His brother Paul managed to

escape to England, his brother Karl Siegmund was deported to Buchenwald. Robert von Hirsch paid a large ransom for his brother, but Karl Siegmund died before his release as a result of the camp conditions.

Robert von Hirsch never stepped on German soil again. Apart from a few legacies, he decided that his collection should be put up for auction after his death: Just as he had fought for every piece, so new collectors should conquer the works, and so they would remain alive. The auction took place in London in 1978, Frankfurt museums were able to bid for a number of objects.

Ludwig und Rosy Fischer

Since 1906, Ludwig Fischer (1860–1922) and his wife Rosy (1869–1926) built up their collection of modern art and since 1913 they devoted themselves mainly to the expressionists. When Ludwig Fischer died, inflation prevailed, so it was not possible for his widow to continue collecting. On the contrary, she was forced to sell works against a lifetime pension. Director Max Sauerlandt acquired many of them for the Städtisches Museum für Kunst und Gewerbe in Halle. Nevertheless, Rosy Fischer still tried to promote artists of the second generation of expressionists, including the Jewish painter Lasar Segall (1891–1957). For a short time she even opened the gallery for "Neuzeitliche Kunst"[15] in her Frankfurt apartment. The Fischer parents died before the question of emigration arose. However, their sons Max and Ernst Fischer were forced to leave Germany. Ernst Fischer (1896–1981), who had lost his position as a private lecturer, emigrated to the USA in 1934 and was able to take his inheritance with him. Max Fischer (1893–1954) worked as a journalist until his last-minute escape in 1938. He had already had to sell some of the artworks and was only allowed to take a limited part of his inheritance with him.

Rosa Schapire (1874–1954)

The art historian received her doctorate in Heidelberg in 1904. She made her living through publications and lectures. Rosa Schapire was a well-connected scientist, women's rights activist, mediator, patron and collector. As a passive member of the Brücke she was actively involved in the promotion of the artists' works in Hamburg. However, she ceased her initial support for Emil Nolde because of his anti-Semitic attitude. As co-founder of the supra-regional "Frauenbund zur Förderung deutscher bildender Kunst" (1916), she mediated between artists and collectors supported purchases by German museums as well. In 1897, she published "Ein Wort zur Frauenemanzipation" in *Sozialistische Monatshefte* rejecting the bourgeois women's movement. In 1931, she was a founding member of the first German Zonta Club in Hamburg.

Schapire had a lifelong friendship especially with Karl Schmidt-Rottluff. His numerous portraits of her bear witness to this, as does the catalog raisonné of his graphic works that she published in 1923.[16]

After 1933 she was banished from her most important places of work, the Hamburger Kunsthalle and the library of the Kupferstichkabinett in Hamburg. From then on, she could only give lectures in her apartment and in the "Jüdischer Kulturbund," the only place where Jews could still attend cultural events. In her travelogue on the ghetto in Prague, she described the history of the Jews in detail – a subject she had never dealt with before.

Ever since her visit to the Munich exhibition *Degenerate Art*, she had sought to emigrate to the US: She tried in vain to sell her collection; in consultation with Schmidt-Rottluff, she burned his letters and stored a container with his handcrafted furniture at a shipping company in the port of Hamburg. In August 1939, – the American visa had not arrived – she took the chance to flee to London on a transit visa. She managed to take along some of Schmidt-Rottluff's works, part of her graphic collection, and artists' postcards she had received. Her stored container was confiscated by the Nazis, its contents probably destroyed.

In London, she put all her energy into promoting the expressionists, who were yet little appreciated there. After the end of the war, she sent care packages to her German artist friends. In gratitude for having been accepted as a refugee, she donated works from her collection to the Tate Modern and the Victoria & Albert Museum in London. Schapire died in 1954 on her way to the Tate Modern.[17]

I. B. Neumann (1887–1961)

Israel Ber Neumann founded his first Graphisches Kabinett in Berlin in 1911. It was a combination of antiquarian bookshop, publishing house, bookstore and art gallery. After the end of WWI, he opened branches, under the management of Peter Zingler in Frankfurt (until 1926) and of Günther Franke in Munich. Like Galka Scheyer, Neumann decided to introduce Expressionist artists to the American art market as early as the mid-1920s and founded his own gallery in New York. Neumann handed over the management of the Berlin cabinet to Karl Nierendorf (1889–1947). Despite all the economic difficulties and some personal conflicts, they stayed in contact. Through Neumann's mediation, Nierendorf was able to show the first exhibition of Alexander Calder in Germany in 1929. Since 1933, the former Berlin cabinet was operated under the name Galerie Nierendorf.

Karl Nierendorf arrived in New York in 1936. Initially planned as a journey, it turned into a stay of more than a decade. After reconnecting with

I. B. Neumann, he traveled to California and met Galka Scheyer, who had previously worked for I. B. Neumann at his New York gallery.

Alfred Flechtheim (1878–1937)

Initially a collector of French Modern art during stays in Paris from 1906, Flechtheim was one of the organizers – and also lender – of the famous *International Art Exhibition of the Sonderbund Westdeutscher Kunstfreunde und Künstler 1912* in Cologne. A year later, he opened his first gallery in Düsseldorf. After 1921, branches followed in Berlin, Frankfurt, Cologne and Vienna. He represented German modern art and, in collaboration with Daniel Henry Kahnweiler (1884–1979) in Paris, French contemporary artists as well.

The Flechtheim branches had to close in 1933, only the Düsseldorf gallery under the management of Alex Vömel continued to exist as Galerie Vömel. Alfred Flechtheim fled to London via Paris. His wife Berta was with him when he died, but returned to Berlin. After she received the deportation order, she took her own life in 1941.

Curt Valentin (1902–54)

After working in several renowned galleries, Valentin was hired as an assistant to Alfred Flechtheim in Berlin in 1927. After Flechtheim's escape, Karl Buchholz hired him to set up the Galerie Buchholz in Berlin. It was only when Valentin had to provide proof of his "Aryan status" that he learned that he had four Jewish grandparents. After his escape he founded the New York branch Buchholz-Gallery. Karl Buchholz was one of four art dealers officially authorized to sell "degenerate" art from confiscations for foreign currency. Through Va-

lentin, many of these works paved the way for European modernism to enter museums and the art market in the US. Neumann, Nierendorf and Valentin were able to reestablish their art-network in the US and even reconnected with the German market from the late 1940s on.

Conclusion

In summary, emigration was life-saving, but the experience of exile left extreme caesurae in each biography. Exile studies in the 1970s focused primarily on authors. Meanwhile, there is also a growing number of publications on persecuted artists, collectors, and art dealers.

I would like to conclude this overview with three open questions:

First, are these biographical studies overshadowed by provenance research, a topic that seems easier to deal with on the "factual" level – the issue that is highly promoted by public research funds?

Second question: are individual relations of the persecuted to Judaism – religious, political, secular or solely attributed by the Nazis – ignored or even excluded as a historical research subject – and if so, why?

The empty frame in the Frankfurt van Gogh exhibition mentioned at the beginning was very popular: visitors photographed their partners standing behind the frame. This observation leads to my third question:

In what ways and by what means can future mediators stimulate visitors' empathy for the human side of all these losses due to inhumane policies?

1 "Unbeirrt, treu mir selber, meiner Idee, muss ich meinen Weg wandern. Wohl heimatlos, wie der ewige Jude, aber mit einer Fahne. Und die tausche ich für nichts ein. Die kann keiner so tragen wie ich. Und das weiß ich, ohne stolz zu sein." Clemens Weiler, "Galka Scheyer. Bildnis einer Braunschweigerin," in *Brunsvicensia Judaica. Gedenkbuch für die jüdischen Mitbürger der Stadt Braunschweig 1933–1945* (Braunschweig, 1966), pp. 94–96.

2 In 1912, the art lover Victor Mössinger had donated the portrait to the Städel Museum at the request of the then director Georg Swarzenski. It was confiscated as "degenerate art" in 1937 and last appeared at a New York auction some 30 years ago. At 82.5 million dollars, it reached its highest price and has not been seen in public since.

3 For the history of this painting cf. https://www.staedelmuseum.de/en/podcast-finding-van-gogh (accessed September 23, 2019).

4 Marian Stein-Steinfeld, *Hanna Bekker vom Rath, Handelnde für Kunst und Künstler* (Frankfurt a. Main, 2018). For more details cf. https://hanna-bekker-vom-rath.org/en/hanna-bekker-vom-rath/.

5 Archive Hanna Bekker vom Rath Frankfurt, Else Meidner, Letter to Hanna Bekker vom Rath, London April 16, 1949.

6 Interview with former kibbutz secretary Shlomo Samson about the Meidner family: http://ludwig-meidner.de/de/ludwig-meidners-erbe/#more-1421 (accessed November 8, 2019).

7 Cf. Stadtmuseum Hofheim, ed., *Jugend und Alter. Ludwig Meidners Porträts aus den 1950er und 1960er Jahren*, catalog (Hofheim am Taunus, 2016).

8 Ernst Ludwig Kirchner, "Ludwig Schames, woodcut in memoriam Ludwig Schames," *Der Querschnitt* 2, no. 3: Weihnachtsheft (1922), pp. 156–57.

9 Jüdisches Museum Frankfurt am Main, ed., *Samson Schames (1898–1967) Bilder und Mosaiken*, catalog (Frankfurt, 1989).

10 *Aufruf der Vereinigung der Freunde der Kunst von Alexej von Jawlensky*, Ende 1928, Museum Wiesbaden, Freunde der Kunst (Museum Wiesbaden – Jawlensky/Bekker vom Rath).

11 Cf. Vereinigung für Neue Kunst im Frankfurter Kunstverein, ed., *Die Neue Kunst in Frankfurter Privatsammlungen,* catalog (Frankfurt, 1917).

12 Cf. https://sammlung.staedelmuseum.de/en/work/flowers-and-china-the-capuchin-cress (accessed May 7, 2021).

13 Cf. Ingrid Koszinowksi, "Wiesbaden 1921–1941: Collectors and Friends," in Volker Rattemeyer, Renate Petzinger, eds., *Jawlensky: Meine liebe Galka!*, catalog Museum Wiesbaden (Wiesbaden, 2004), p. 226, fig. p. 203.

14 Cf. https://sammlung.staedelmuseum.de/en/work/abstract-head-symphony-in-pink, accessed November 11, 2019.

15 Biographies of Ludwig und Rosy Fischer, cf. Georg Heuberger, ed., *Expressionismus und Exil. Die Sammlung Ludwig und Rosy Fischer*, catalog Jüdisches Museum Frankfurt (Frankfurt, 1990), p. 170.

16 Rosa Schapire, *Karl Schmidt-Rottluffs graphisches Werk bis 1923* (Berlin, 1923).

17 Cf. Museum für Kunst und Gewerbe Hamburg, ed., *Rosa. Eigenartig Grün. Roda Schapire und die Expressionisten* (Ostfildern, 2009).

GALKA E. SCHEYER
AND THE MODERNIST ART SCENE IN CALIFORNIA

Isabel Wünsche

After a ten-day sea voyage, Galka E. Scheyer arrived in New York on May 18, 1924, carrying a suitcase full of paintings by her "Blue Four" artists. She was greeted by Rajah von Rubio, with whom she stayed in Ossining, in upstate New York, in May and June.[1] Scheyer moved to New York City in the summer and started a "massive mailing campaign" with the intention of organizing a lecture tour throughout the United States.[2] She sent out several hundred letters to universities and colleges, offering a series of 6–8 slide lectures on art history topics from Rembrandt and Delacroix to the Blue Four, and nearly four hundred letters, offering exhibitions to museums and other cultural institutions (Fig. 2). The response was meager; disillusioned she began to look for alternatives.

Angelica Archipenko's planned journey across the United States and on to Western Canada gave Scheyer a welcome opportunity to leave New York and pursue her luck on the West Coast. On May 30, 1925, Scheyer and Archipenko set off on the first leg of their long journey, which led them from New York via Niagara Falls to Chicago. They continued on to Ames, Iowa, where Scheyer gave a lecture at the State University of

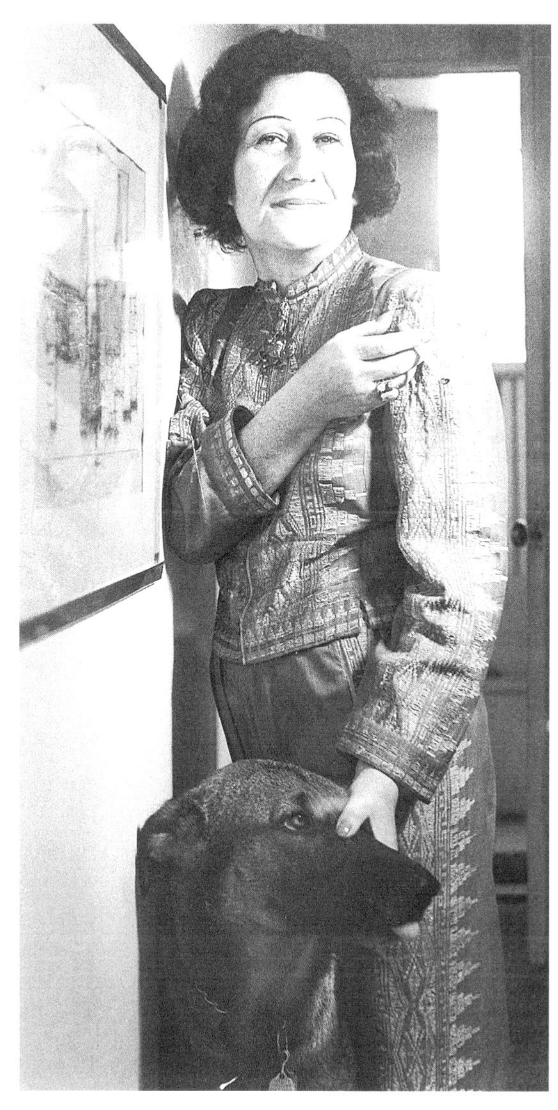

1 Galka E. Scheyer, ca. 1940 (Photo by Alexander Hammid).

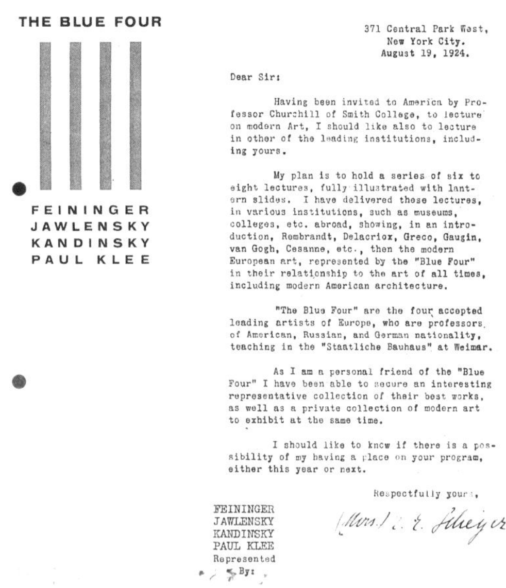

2 Pamphlet from Scheyer's mailing campaign, New York, August 1924.

Iowa, then via Denver and Colorado Springs to Santa Fe, New Mexico. This was followed by a visit to the Grand Canyon and an almost two-week stay in Los Angeles (Fig. 3). Continuing their trip up the Pacific Coast, Scheyer arranged for future lecture engagements in Santa Barbara and San Francisco. In Sacramento the two women parted ways, Archipenko continuing her voyage north to Canada, Scheyer spending the rest of the summer with her "aunt," Sophie Hymann, in Sacramento.[3]

In August 1925, Scheyer settled in San Francisco. She took a room at the Hotel Normandie and immediately began to give lectures and show the works of the Blue Four to invited guests and art patrons. One of her first acquaintances in San Francisco was Ernest Bloch, then director of the San Francisco Conservatory of Music, where she gave one of her first lectures on the Blue Four.[4] In September 1925, Scheyer met the painter Maynard Dixon and his wife, photographer Dorothea Lange. Dixon introduced Scheyer to art dealer

Beatrice Judd Ryan and to Roi Partridge, director of the Art Gallery of Mills College in Oakland, and his wife, photographer Imogen Cunningham, and also sculptor Ralph Stackpole and painter Frank van Sloun. Furthermore, Dixon wrote to Aurelia Reinhardt, president of Mills College, about the importance of Scheyer's arrival in the Bay Area and her suitcase full of paintings for the local art scene:

> There is now in town a very interesting little woman from Germany with a collection of modern paintings and some 600 lantern slides. She is seeking lecture dates with the purpose of furthering the ideas of modern art in this country. She knows her subject well, -- + I have brought Bender and Partridge in contact with her in the hope that they also will be interested. Her name is Mrs. E. E. Scheyer, at Hotel Normandie. I am doing what I can do to secure attention for her, as we artists believe her kind of work is badly needed here.[5]

Unlike New York, California had neither an advanced art scene nor a well-developed network of galleries, collectors, and art institutions. During the 1920s, the San Francisco art scene was quite small and rather traditional. The Panama-Pacific International Exposition of 1915 had introduced West Coast artists to European modernism, particularly cubism, futurism, and abstract art. However, the majority of the painters on the West Coast worked in an impressionist or post-impressionist style.[6] The established art institutions in the Bay Area, among them the California School of Fine Arts, the East Bay California School of Arts and Crafts, and the Art Department of the University of California, Berkeley, under Eugen Neuhaus, were also quite conservative.[7]

Radically modern artists and intellectuals in San Francisco of the mid-1920s often congregated at the studio of Ralph Stackpole and at the Beaux Arts Gallery, founded by Ryan in 1925. Other Bay Area venues for modern and avant-garde art included the art gallery of Mills College, established by Partridge in 1925, and, between 1918 and 1935, the Oakland Art Gallery, under the leadership of William H. Clapp.[8] Not until the establishment of the San Francisco Museum of Modern Art in 1935 did the city gain a civic institution focused specifically on the promotion of contemporary art.

During a lecture in San Francisco in September 1925, Scheyer met Arthur B. Clark, professor in the Art Department at Stanford University, who invited her to show a Blue Four exhibition there in October. Shortly thereafter, on November 1, 1925, the article "Prophetess of 'The Blue Four': Mme Scheyer, the The Blue Four and Their Art" was published in *The San Francisco Examiner*. (Fig. 4). Roi Partridge asked Scheyer to organize a the Blue Four exhibition at Mills College in February 1926, and through him she got lecture appointments at the California School of Fine Arts, the San Francisco State Teachers College, and the State Teachers University, San Jose.

Another important connection Scheyer made was the acquaintance of William Henry Clapp, director of the Oakland Art Gallery and one of the most engaged promoters of modern art in the Bay Area. Like Dixon, Clapp realized the importance of Scheyer's presence in the San Francisco art scene. He not only gave her the opportunity to organize a major exhibition with works by the Blue Four at the Oakland Art Gallery in May 1926, but also appointed Scheyer European representative of the Oakland Art Gallery. This unpaid but prestigious position was of great importance for Scheyer as it gave her the needed institutional credentials. As director of the Western Association of Art Museum Directors, Clapp also made it possible for exhibitions organized by Scheyer to travel up and down the West Coast, from San Diego to Seattle.

From 1926 to 1929, Scheyer showed the works of the Blue Four in exhibitions accompanied by

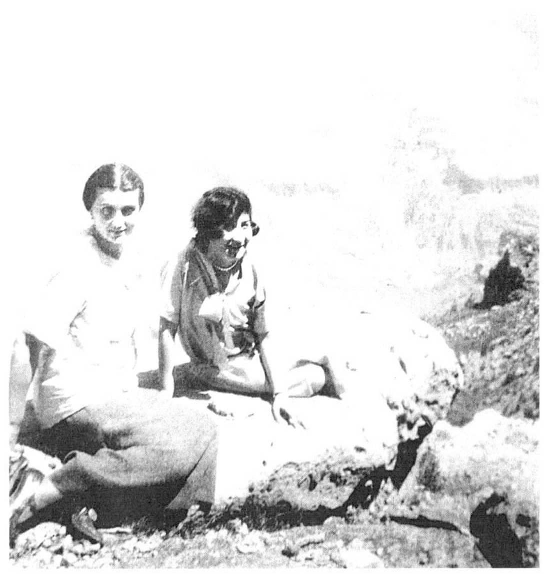

3 *Galka E. Scheyer and Angelica Archipenko at the Grand Canyon, summer 1925.*

lectures in Oakland, San Francisco, Los Angeles, San Diego, Portland, Spokane, and Seattle. She also organized shows with works of other artists, among them a Franz Marc exhibition in San Francisco and San Diego in 1927, the exhibitions Constructivists with works by Willi Baumeister, El Lissitzky, László Moholy-Nagy, Oskar Schlemmer, and Kurt Schwitters at the University of California, Los Angeles, and European Modernists, with works by Alexander Archipenko, Otto Dix, Ernst Ludwig Kirchner, Oskar Kokoschka, Wilhelm Lehmbruck, Emil Nolde, Karl Schmidt-Rottluff, Arthur Segal, and others, in the Los Angeles Museum in 1927 and at the Oakland Art Gallery in 1928.

Scheyer not only prepared numerous exhibitions and supported William H. Clapp and Florence Wieben Lehre in their efforts to introduce the general public to modern art, she also worked with them on the designs for a new museum in which the latest methods of integrated exhibition design and progressive art education for all ages would be realized.[9] The resulting plans for a new Oakland Art Gallery building were well ahead of their time and not realized until much later. Scheyer's ideas for the new museum as well as her participation in the presentations of the Hales department stores in 1928 confirm her status as an early promoter of cooperative relationships between art and commerce and new forms of arts underwriting.

When Scheyer returned to Germany in 1928, she traveled as the European representative of the Oakland Art Gallery and correspondent for the *San Francisco Examiner*.[10] In her function as art director of the Anna Head School in Berkeley, she attended the VI. International Congress for Drawing, Art Education, and the Applied Arts in Prague, where she delivered the paper "Free, Imaginative and Creative Work," in which she outlined her pedagogical approach to children's art.[11]

Although Scheyer worked tirelessly for the acceptance of the art of the Blue Four and other German artists, she was also receptive to the work of American artists and was often able to support the enterprising modernists among them by including their works in the annual exhibitions of the Oakland Art Gallery and elsewhere.[12] She exhibited works by Dixon and Stackpole during the Week of the San Francisco Artists in 1926 and forcefully defended the work of Forest Brissey and Hagedorn in the morality dispute that arose in the Fifth Annual Exhibition of 1927. Through her personal acquaintance with Imogen Cunningham and Edward Weston, she also influenced the development of photography in the Bay Area. The lively debates she had with Weston during her stays in Carmel in 1929 and 1930 suggest the influence of Scheyer's activities on the transition from pictorialism to straight photography and the emergence of Group f/64.[13] Her interest in the development of modern photography by Cun-

4 Newspaper article "Prophetess of 'The Blue Four': Mme. Scheyer, The Blue Four and Their Art," The San Francisco Examiner, November 1, 1925.

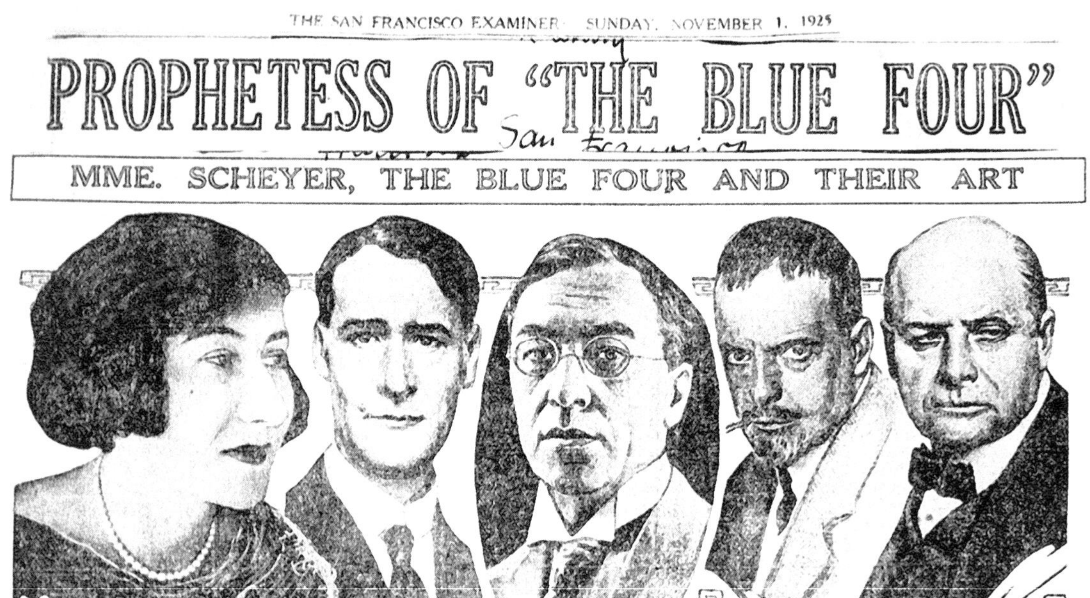

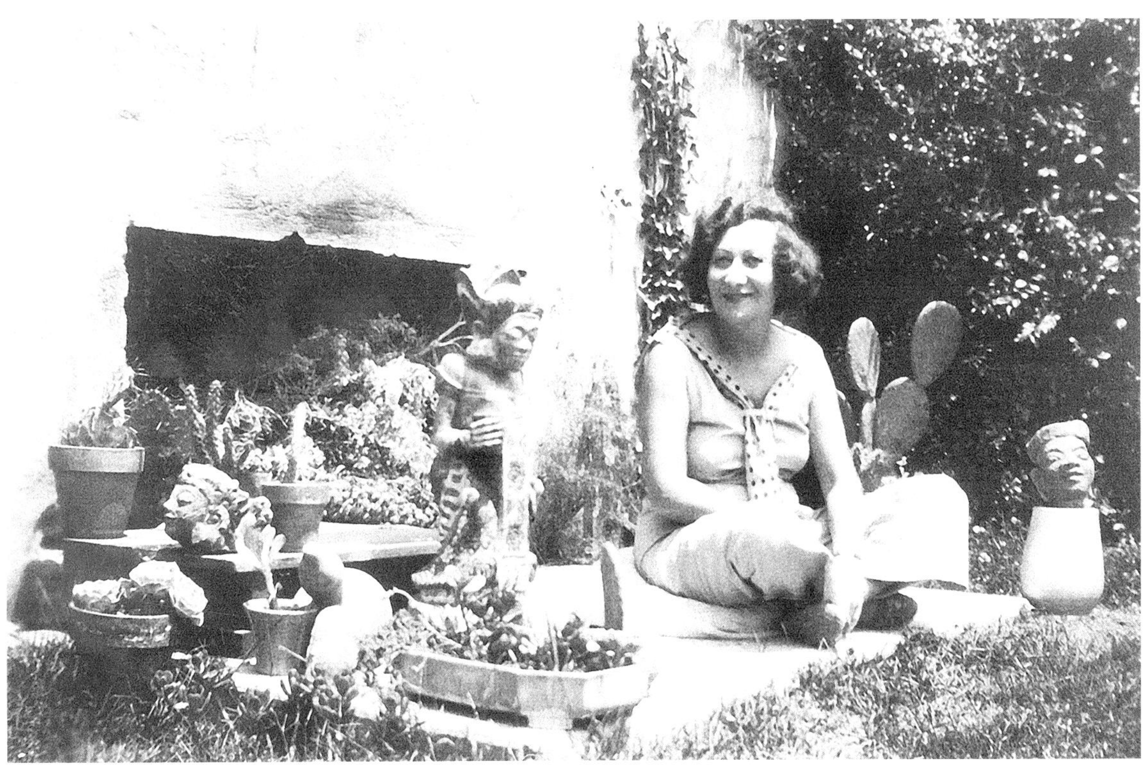

5 Scheyer with her Balinese sculptures in the garden of the Schindler House, Hollywood, ca. 1931–32.

ningham, Brett and Edward Weston is reflected in her collection.

Furthermore, Scheyer was open to the cultural influences and local traditions of the West Coast, which were shaped as much by Indian and Hispanic art and the Asian cultures of the Pacific Rim as they were by the East Coast and European modernism. Her lively interest in Chinese theater in San Francisco, the works of the Pueblo Indians in New Mexico, and in Mexican mural painting as well as in Hawaiian folk art and Balinese art stemmed from her expressionist grounding and her belief in the creative power of non-Western art. She saw in these art forms an important source of inspiration for contemporary Western art (Fig. 5).

Scheyer was not only active in the Bay Area, but also in Los Angeles. In fall 1926, she opened a

Blue Four exhibition at the Los Angeles Museum that was later also shown at the University of California, Los Angeles. As in San Francisco, she quickly established contacts with museum workers, art teachers, and artists such as Ben Berlin, Boris Deutsch, and Peter Krasnow. In February 1927, she participated in a wild party at Krasnow's studio,[14] and the summer months of 1927 she spent at the house of the architect Rudolph Schindler on Kings Road in Hollywood. The intensity of her appearance and her performances is captured in the drawings *Mme Moderne Kunst* (1925) by Maynard Dixon and *Recalling Happy Memories* (1927–29) by Peter Krasnow[15] (Fig. 6).

From fall 1929 to early summer 1930, Scheyer constantly traveled back and forth between the Bay Area and Los Angeles, and in December

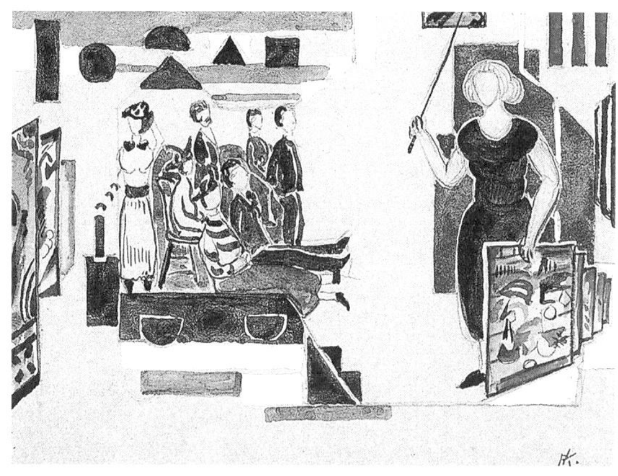

6 *Peter Krasnow, Recalling Happy Memories, ca. 1927, watercolor with silver pigment and pencil (Courtesy of Norton Simon Museum, Pasadena, California).*

1929 and spring 1930, she also stayed for some time at the artists' colony Carmel, south of San Francisco, where Edward Weston was living during that period. In early 1930, she prepared four individual exhibitions of the Blue Four artists which were shown at Harry Braxton's new gallery in Hollywood. At about the same time, Scheyer met the East Coast art collectors Louise and Walter Arensberg, who had settled in Los Angeles in 1927 and owned a remarkable collection of modern art with works by Constantin Brancusi, Paul Cézanne, Henri Matisse, Georges Braque, and Pablo Picasso. The main focus of their collection, however, was the work of Marcel Duchamp.[16] Between 1930 and 1934, the Arensbergs were her most promising clients.[17]

From July 1930 to February 1931, Scheyer traveled with Angelica Archipenko through Asia. After her return to San Francisco, she met Mexican painter Diego Rivera and his wife Frida Kahlo who was staying in town while Rivera was executing the murals *Allegory of California* at the Luncheon Club of the San Francisco Stock Exchange and *The Making of a Fresco* at the California School of Fine Arts. Scheyer befriended Kahlo and Rivera, who shared her love of the art of the

Blue Four.[18] At their invitation, she exhibited works by the Blue Four in Mexico City in 1931 and bought paintings by Angel Bracho and Rivera for her own collection. In 1932, she showed works by Carlos Merida at the Oakland Art Gallery (Fig. 7).

In October 1932, after having presented Blue Four exhibitions at the Faulkner Memorial Gallery in Santa Barbara, the Arts Club of Chicago, and the Renaissance Society of the University of Chicago, Scheyer returned to Europe, staying first in Paris, where she met with Giorgio de Chirico, Marcel Duchamp, Le Corbusier, Fernand Leger, and others in their studios,[19] and then travelling on to Germany, where she spent the holidays with her family in Braunschweig.

Scheyer was unprepared for the rise of the National Socialists to power and the political changes taking place in Germany, and in January 1933 hastily returned to the United States. Her first concern then became the construction and furnishing of her new home in the Hollywood Hills. Her life on 1880 Blue Heights Drive, surrounded by nature and modern art, provided her with an ideal setting and became increasingly her trademark in the 1930s (Fig. 8). The energetic woman with the unusual home at the top of the mountain was an attraction in Hollywood circles. A visit to Scheyer's place promised a real adventure, beginning with Scheyer's driving on the unpaved winding access road. Her visitors included actors Billie Burke, Marlene Dietrich, Greta Garbo, and Edward G. Robinson; film directors Dorothy Arzner, Fritz Lang, and Josef von Sternberg; writer Erich-Maria Remarque and composer Leopold Stokowski. Wolo von Trutzschler's 1935 *Carricature of Galka E. Scheyer and Angelo Ravagli's* 1936 *Depiction of Scheyer* reveal the extent to which Scheyer's personality, lifestyle, and house on Blue Heights Drive had merged into one in the eyes of her contemporaries[20] (Fig. 9).

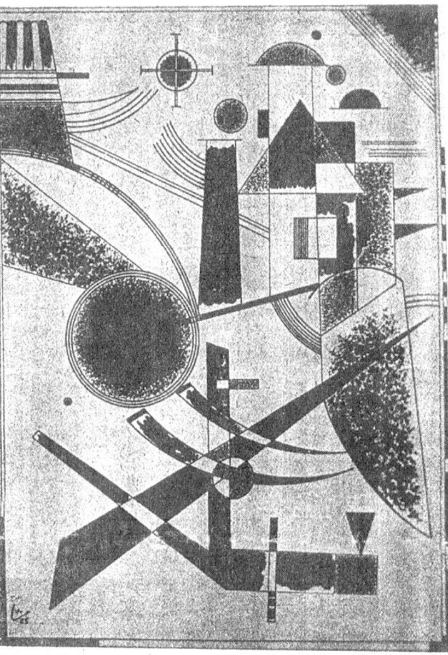
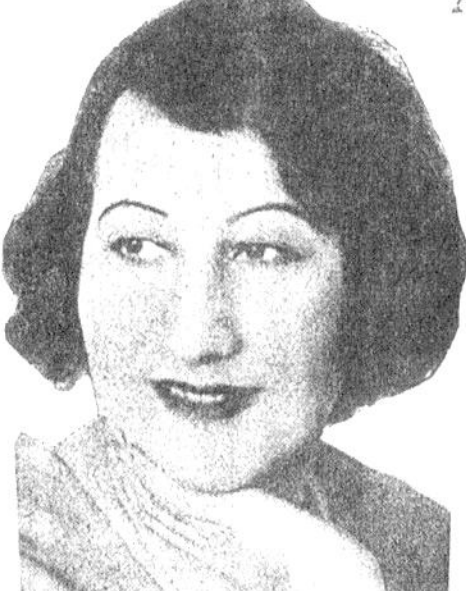
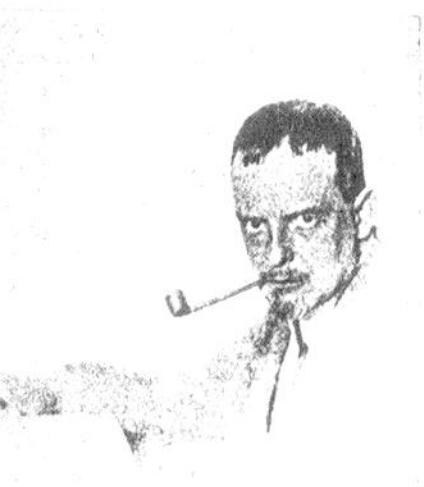
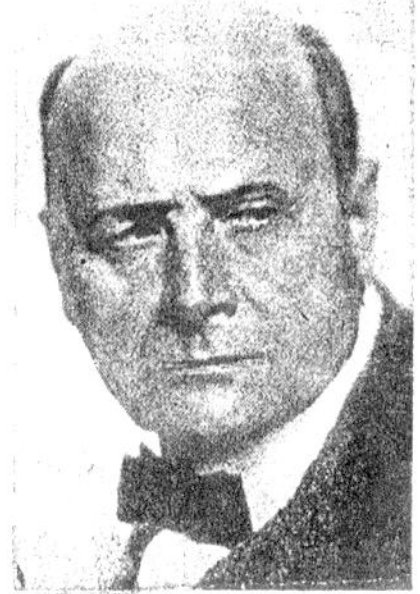
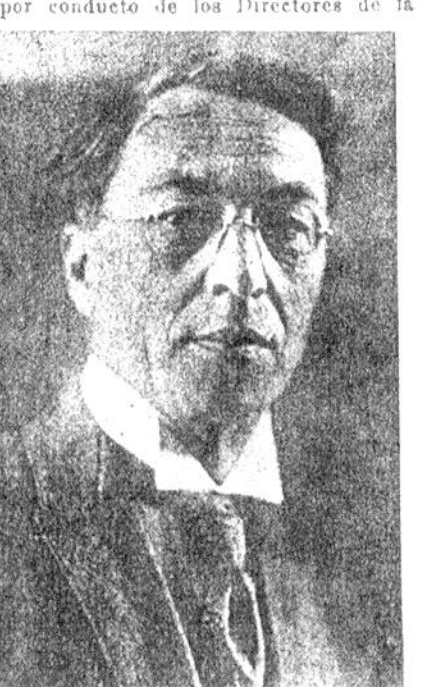
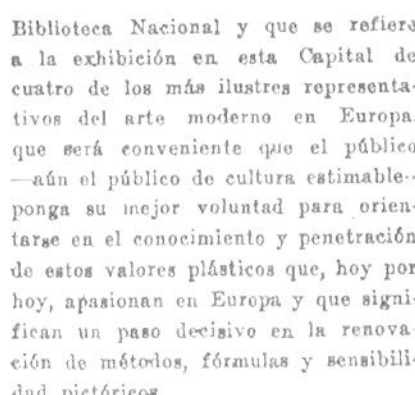
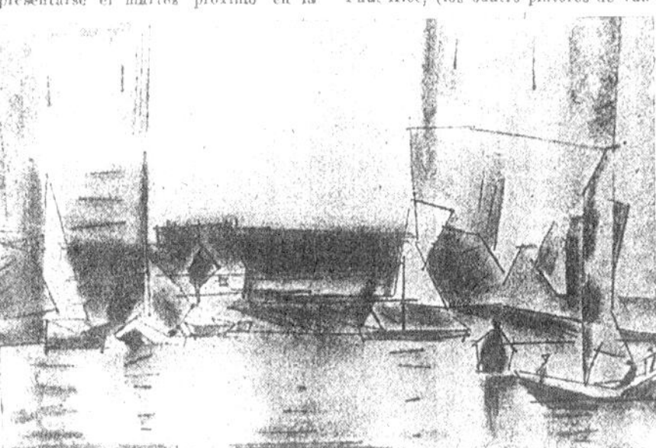
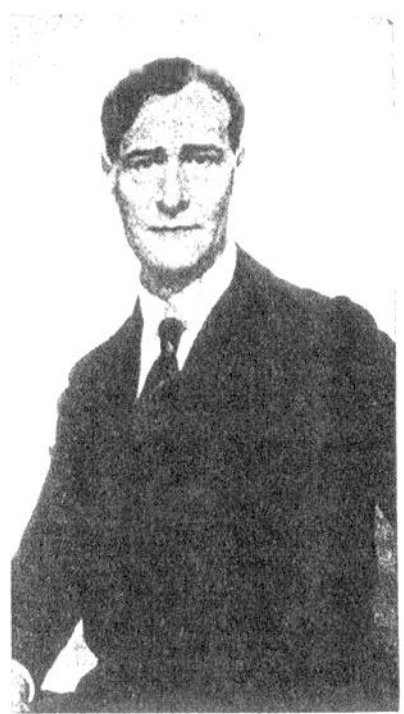

"CUATRO AZULES"
LOS PINTORES VANGUARDISTAS

Abrirán su Exposición el próximo día 24, en la Biblioteca Nacional

Litografía, por Kandinsky

El martes próximo—24 de noviembre—será la solemne apertura de la exposición de los "Blue Four" en la Biblioteca Nacional de México. Esta presentará, en su hermoso vestíbulo, la extraordinaria exhibición de "LOS CUATRO AZULES", nombre que designa el grupo que forman cuatro de los más eminentes pintores vanguardistas de la actualidad: Feininger, Kandinsky, Jawlensky y Paul Klee, consagrados por los más ilustres críticos universales.

En los anales de las Exposiciones celebradas en México, indudablemente la que hoy anunciamos ocupará un lugar y significación culminantes. La crítica europea ha hecho objeto a estos célebres pintores de las más encendidas alabanzas. Su prestigio descansa sobre bases de estricta probidad artística, y en su producción se refleja uno de los avances más considerables para determinar los lineamientos definitivos del arte nuevo, que en lo que va corrido del siglo se ha desperdigado por los caminos más disímiles, en anhelosa busca por una expresión formal.

El contingente que va a exhibirse lo forma una bellísima colección de óleos, litografías y acuarelas, que indudablemente, como en todas partes, apasionará a nuestros críticos de arte y al público conocedor. "LOS CUATRO AZULES", repetimos, es la más insigne entidad creadora de obras pictóricas.

El Departamento de Bellas Artes de la Secretaría de Educación Pública, por conducto de los Directores de la Sala de Arte de la propia Secretaría, los pintores Francisco Díaz de León y Gabriel Fernández Ledesma, coopera con la Biblioteca Nacional para presentar esta magnífica exposición.

La apertura de la "EXPOSICION DE "LOS CUATRO AZULES", será el martes 24 del actual, a las 19 y media horas, en el vestíbulo de la Biblioteca Nacional de México, esquina Uruguay e Isabel la Católica.

Los Sres. Francisco Díaz de León y Gabriel Fernández Ledesma, nos dicen, con relación al notable acontecimiento de orden artístico que va a presentarse el martes próximo en la Biblioteca Nacional y que se refiere a la exhibición en esta Capital de cuatro de los más ilustres representativos del arte moderno en Europa, que será conveniente que el público —aún el público de cultura estimable— ponga su mejor voluntad para orientarse en el conocimiento y penetración de estos valores plásticos que, hoy por hoy, apasionan en Europa y que significan un paso decisivo en la renovación de métodos, fórmulas y sensibilidad pictóricos.

Y añaden: Posiblemente el arte de Kandinsky, Jawlensky, Feininger y Paul Klee, (los cuatro pintores de vanguardia a que nos referimos) pueda aparecer abstruso a una buena mayoría del público que visite esta notable exposición. En tal caso, sería oportuno que los interesados en dilucidar estas difíciles manifestaciones de arte, se orientaran a tal respecto conversando con artistas nuestros que constantemente habrán de estar en el vestíbulo de la Biblioteca Nacional o se acercaran al sitio en que se exhibirán notables monografías editadas en Europa, de estos cuatro ilustres representativos.

ACUARELA POR FEINNINGER

ALISAY TAWLENSKY

PAUL KLEE

WARRILG KANDIUSKY

BEJNEL FEINNGER.

Mme GALKA E. SHEYER

7 Newspaper review, "'Cuatro Azules' Los Pintores Vanguardistas" (Reprinted from El Popular, *1931. p. 2).*

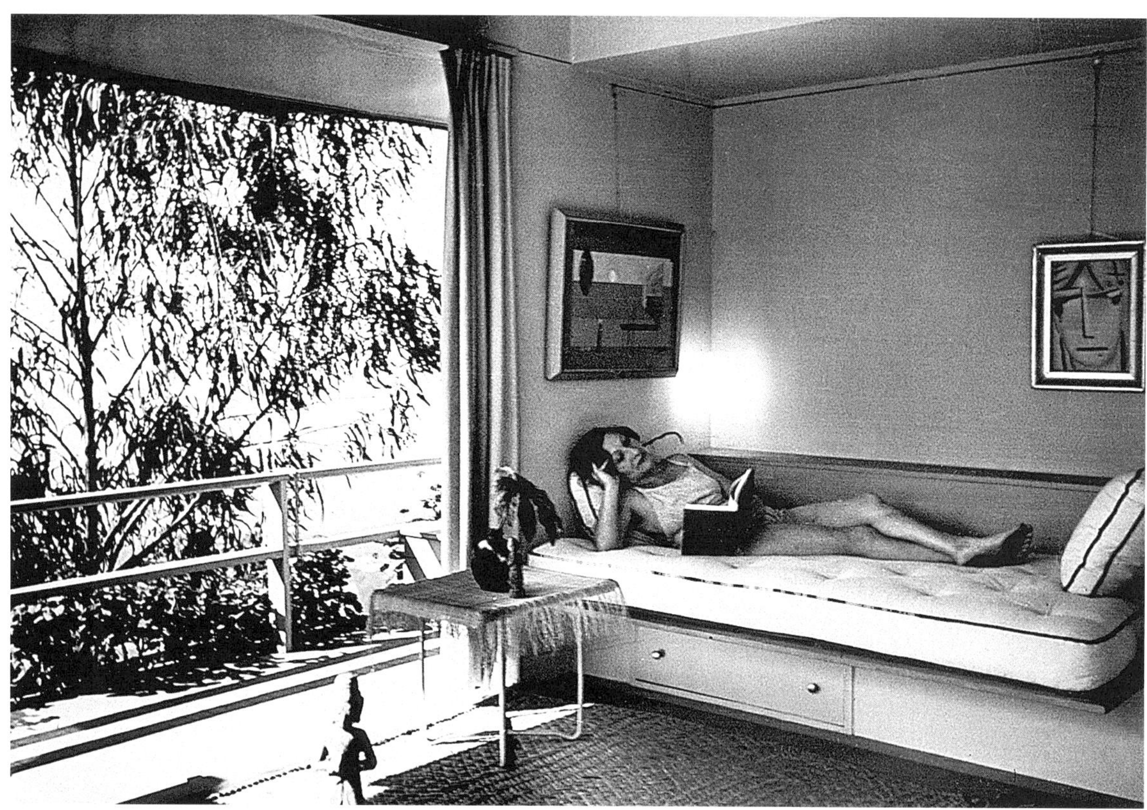

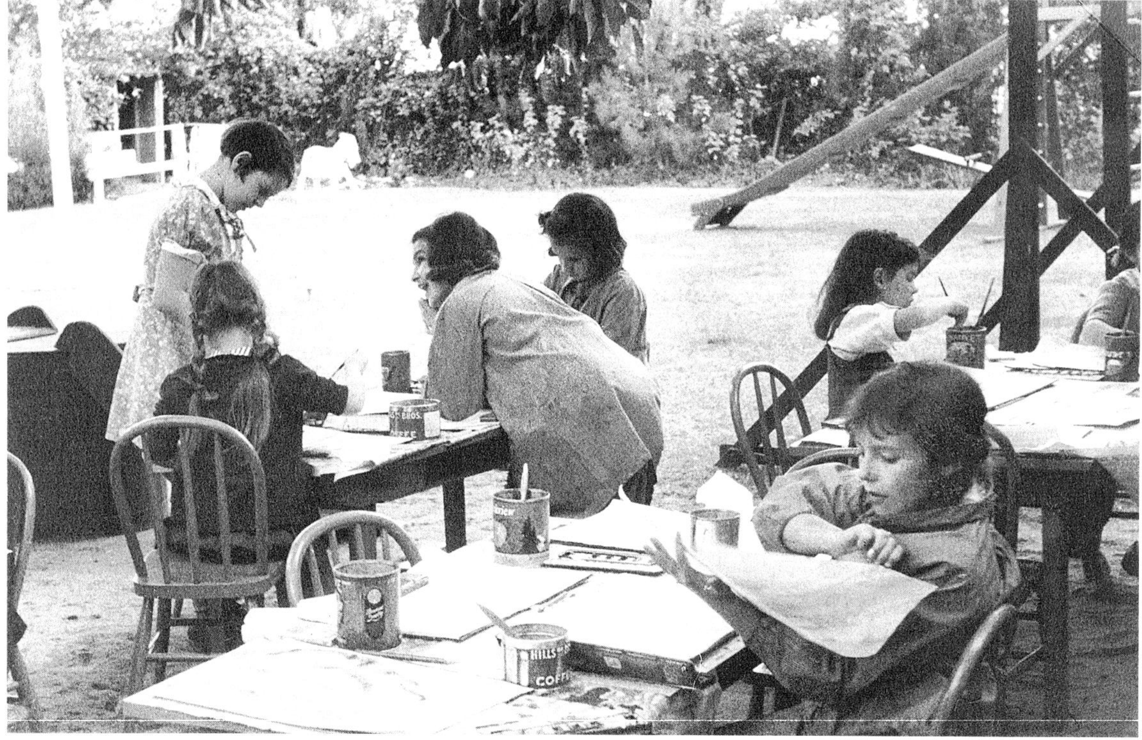

After 1933, as the exodus of artists and intellectuals from Germany gradually turned Los Angeles into one of the world's largest cultural diasporas, Scheyer's house on Blue Heights Drive in Hollywood became an important landing spot for many emigrants.[21] Her presence in Los Angeles and her work of the previous years had paved the way for them and offered emigrants such as Arnold Schönberg, Alois Schardt, Elfriede and Oskar Fischinger, Karl Nierendorf, and Lette Valeska a point of contact for cultural-intellectual exchanges, new occupations, and supportive networks.

The considered presentation of an artist's works in an suitable environment, created and controlled by her, served as a desirable alternative to the discouraging situation at the Los Angeles art market in the 1930s (at the same time that the situation in Germany was flooding the American art market with art and causing prices to drop, the American public's interest in international modernism was waning in favor of realism and regionalism). Scheyer had been almost alone in showing modern European art in the Bay Area and in Los Angeles between 1925 and 1933, but thereafter her competition increased significantly.[22] Since Scheyer was not running a commercial art gallery, she collaborated in the 1930s with the art dealers Howard Putzel and Earl Stendahl, book dealers Stanley Rose and Jake Zeitlin, and impressario Merle Armitage.[23]

After Louise and Walter Arensberg, Scheyer owned one of the most important collections of modern art in Los Angeles; one that became a

o. p.:
8 Scheyer in her house on Blue Hights Drive in Hollywood, 1930s.
9 Scheyer's art class, 1940s.

source of inspiration for many artists as well as the art interested public. Her presence in Los Angeles meant encouragement and support for sculptor Peter Krasnow as well as for the expressionist painter Boris Deutsch and painter and actor Martin Kosleck. The works of Kandinsky and Klee in her collection and exhibitions served to inspire the organic abstractions of Henrietta Shore, the mystic paintings of Agnes Pelton, and the cosmic abstractions of Oskar Fischinger.[24] Danish artist Knud Merrild, influenced by Kurt Schwitters' Merz pictures and constructions in Scheyer's collection, began to develop relief constructions of metal and wood in the 1930s and then, in the early 1940s, inspired by the works of Hans Arp, Max Ernst, Kandinsky, and Klee, his organic abstractions.[25]

Scheyer even influenced the emergence of post-surrealism, as formulated by Lorser Feitelson and Helen Luneberg in 1934. This movement by West Coast artists was the first American response to French surrealism. However, in contrast to the European surrealists, the California artists emphasized the constructive elements of surrealism.[26] In 1935, in collaboration with Feitelson, Scheyer organized a Klee as well as an expressionist exhibition at Feitelson's newly founded Hollywood Gallery of Modern Art.

Scheyer's personal and financial situation and health began to worsen in the mid-1930s. In July 1936, she had to undergo a throat operation and several dental surgeries and in April 1938 she was involved in a serious car accident. In 1936, after increasing difficulties with the German authorities, the monthly support payments from her brothers stopped entirely. In the summer of 1938, her family's property was forcibly appropriated; now it was they who were dependent upon her help and support.

Given the changing situation in the Los Angeles art market in Los Angeles in the 1930s, Scheyer

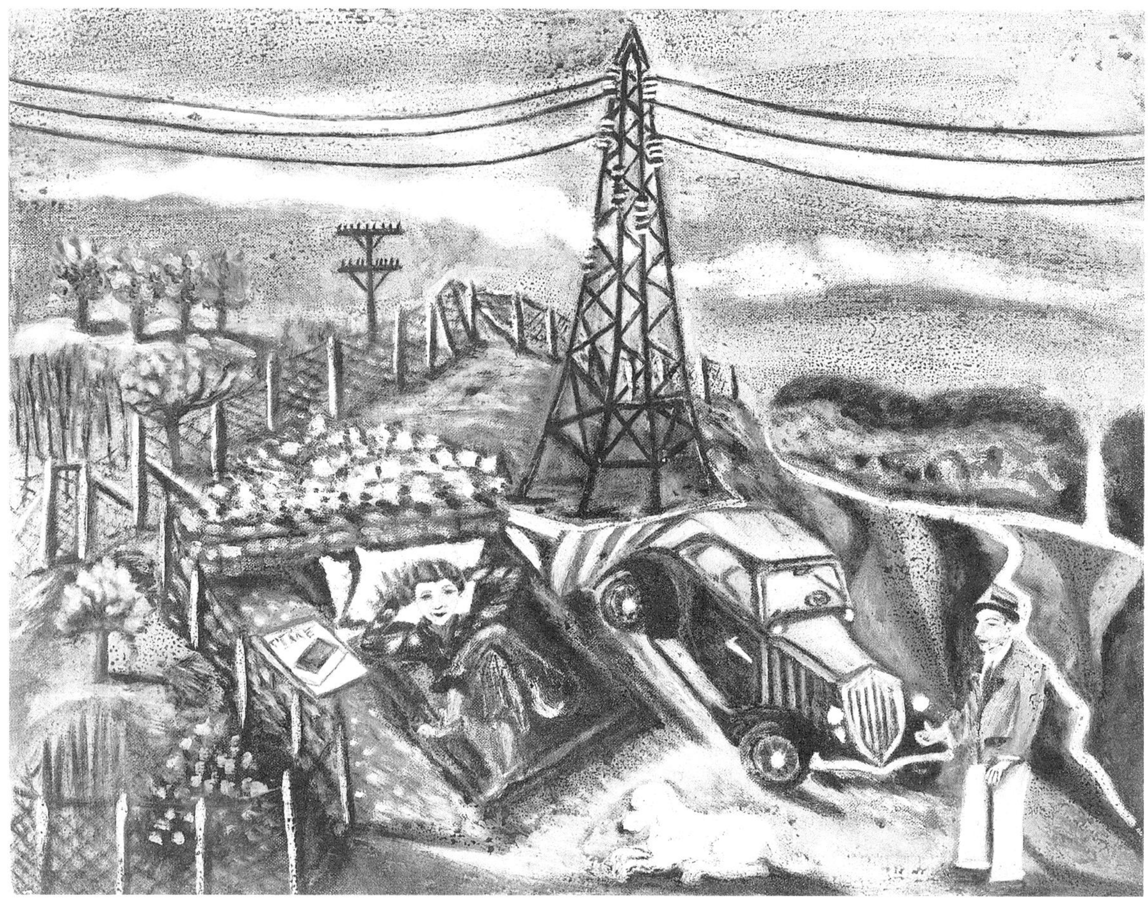

10 Angelo Ravagli, Galka Scheyer, April 1936, oil on canvas (Courtesy of the Norton Simon Museum, Pasadena, California).

increasingly focused on art education for children, which not only brought her joy and recognition, but also increasingly served to provide a means of support. Between 1933 and 1939, Scheyer taught at the Broadoaks School of Education and at the Grant School in Pasadena and she gave private lessons in Beverly Hills and at the School of Childhood in Los Angeles; from 1936 to 1939 she served as art director of the Brentwood Town and Country School in Los Angeles (Fig. 10).

During the war, Scheyer's opportunities to organize exhibitions were limited and sales of art works difficult. In spring 1940, she showed once more four individual the Blue Four exhibitions at Earl Stendahl's gallery in Los Angeles. Of the Blue Four exhibitions planned for 1942 and 1943 at the Raymond & Raymond Galleries in San Francisco only two were realized.[27] Instead, between 1936 and 1944, Scheyer supported other institutions with loans of works by the Blue Four. In 1936 and 1937, she sent works from her own collection to the Feininger exhibitions in Oakland and San Francisco, which were held on the occasion of Feininger's summer courses at Mills College. She also lent works by the Blue Four to the exhibitions *Contemporary German Watercolor Painting* at the California Palace of the Legion of Honor in summer 1936, *Modern Art: Eighty-Fifth Anniversary Exhibition* at Mills College in spring 1937,

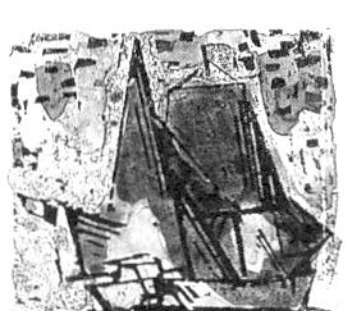

11 Lyonel Feininger, letter to Galka E. Scheyer, December 13, 1945.

and *Abstract Art*, also at Mills College in fall 1939, as well as the *Nineteenth International Exhibition of Watercolors* at the Art Institute of Chicago in spring 1940. She also contributed to the exhibi-

tion *Paintings by Wassily Kandinsky: A Summary 1923 to Present* at the San Francisco Museum of Art in summer 1939, the *Jawlensky Retrospective* exhibition at the Nierendorf Gallery in New York in November 1939, and the *Paul Klee Memorial Exhibition*, organized by the Museum of Modern Art and also shown at the San Francisco Museum of Art and at the Stendahl Art Gallery in Los Angeles in the spring.

Emily "Galka" Scheyer died of cancer on December 13, 1945 (Fig. 11). In her untiring efforts on behalf of the Blue Four as well as other progressive artists and art educators, she moved the hearts of her contemporaries, gave inspiration and support to like-minded souls, and paved the way for artists to come. She remained, however, often misunderstood, and by traditional measures of success hers were small, but in her exhibitions and lectures, her art education for children and adults, and with her collection, she was an important catalyst for modern art in California. After her death, Earl Stendahl publically acknowledged what many might have felt:

> I did not pay enough attention to Galka, … She had vision and understood the importance of modern art … I learned so much from her … when she died I cried, because I realized how much she had done for all of us.[28]

1   Galka E. Scheyer, collective letter to the Blue Four, May 28, 1924, The Blue Four Galka Scheyer Collection Archives, Norton Simon Museum, Pasadena (thereafter Pasadena), BF 1924-3, in Isabel Wünsche, *Galka E. Scheyer and the Blue Four: Correspondence, 1924–1945* (Bern, 2006), p. 68.

2   Galka E. Scheyer, letter to Lyonel Feininger, August 30, 1924, copy only, Pasadena, LF 1924-16.

3   Galka E. Scheyer, collective letter to the Blue Four, July 21, 1925, Pasadena, BF 1925–2, in Wünsche, *Galka E. Scheyer and the Blue Four* (see note 1), pp. 91–96.

4   Galka E. Scheyer, collective letter to the Blue Four, September 24, 1925, Pasadena, BF 1925–4, in Wünsche, *Galka E. Scheyer and the Blue Four* (see note 1), p. 117.

5   Maynard Dixon, letter to Aurelia Reinhardt, September 16, 1925, original at Mills College, Oakland. See also Vivian Endicott Barnett, *The Blue Four Collection at the Norton Simon Museum* (New Haven, 2002), p. 452.

6   Peter Joyner Flagg, "The Well-Painted Painting: Northern California's Academic Tradition and the Panama-Pacific International Exhibition," in *From Exposition to Exposition: Progressive and Conservative Northern California Painting, 1915–1939,* ed. by Joseph Armstrong Baird, Jr. (Sacramento, 1981), pp. 8–13.

7   Cynthia Charters Foley, "Modernism in the Bay Area: The Role of the Art Schools," in Baird, *From Exposition to Exposition* (see note 6), pp. 29–36.

8   Lynne Baer Smith, "The Relationship between Paris, New York and San Francisco," in Baird, *From Exposition to Exposition* (see note 6), pp. 13–19.

9   Nancy Boas, *The Society of Six: California Colorists* (Berkeley, 1998), p. 158.

10 William H. Clapp, letter to Galka E. Scheyer, May 15, 1928, original, Pasadena, Oakland Art Gallery 1928–2.

11 Galka E. Scheyer, "Free Imaginative and Creative Work," in *VI. International Congress for Art Education, Drawing and Art Applied to Industry in Prague, 1928: General Report of the Congress* (Prague, 1931), pp. 193–97.

12 Paul J. Karlstrom, ed., *On the Edge of America: California Modernist Art, 1900–1950* (Berkeley, 1996), pp. 5–6.

13 Therese Thau Heyman, "Modernist Photography and the Group f.64," in Karlstrom, ed., *On the Edge of America* (see note 12), p. 249.

14 See Nancy Newhall, *The Daybooks of Edward Weston* (New York, 1961), 2:3.

15 Maynard Dixon, *Portrait Galka Scheyer,* 1925, ink drawing, with the dedication "to Mme Moderne Kunst" and Peter Krasnow, *Recalling Happy Memories,* ca. 1927, watercolor with silver pigment, both The Blue Four Collection, Norton Simon Museum, Pasadena.

16 Winifred Haines Higgins, "The Louise and Walter Arensberg Collection," in *Art Collecting in the Los Angeles Area, 1910–1960* (PhD diss, University of California, Los Angeles 1963; Ann Arbor, 1986), pp. 162–81. See also: Naomi Sawelson-Gorse, "Narrow Circles and Uneasy Alliances: Galka Scheyer and American Collectors of the Blue Four," in *The Blue Four: Feininger, Jawlensky, Kandinsky, Klee in the New World*, ed. by Vivian Endicott Barnett, and Josef Helfenstein (Cologne, 1997), pp. 51–61.

17 Ibid.

18 See Scheyer's correspondence with Frida Kahlo and Diego Rivera in Pasadena.

19 See Scheyer's correspondence with Giorgio de Chirio, Marcel Duchamp, Le Corbusier, and Fernand Leger in Pasadena.

20 Wolo von Trutzschler, *Carricature Galka E. Scheyer,* 1935, crayon drawing and Angelo Ravagli, *Galka Scheyer,* April 1936, oil on canvas, both The Blue Four Collection, Norton Simon Museum, Pasadena.

21 Cornelius Schnauber, *Spaziergänge durch das Hollywood der Emigranten* (Zürich, 1992).

22 Vivian Endicott Barnett, "The Last Years of the Blue Four, 1933–1945," in *The Blue Four* (see note 16), pp. 263–71.

23 Victoria Dailey, Natalie Shivers, and Michael Dawson, *LA's Early Moderns: Art, Architecture, Photography* (Los Angeles, 2003).

24 Paul J. Karlstrom, and Susan Ehrlich, *Turning the Tide: Early Los Angeles Modernists 1920–1956* (Santa Barbara, 1990).

25 Susan M. Anderson, "Journey into the Sun: California Artists and Surrealism," in Karlstrom, *On the Edge of America,* (see note 12), p. 188.

26 Jules Langsner, "Post-Surrealists and Other Moderns, Hollywood: Stanley Rose Gallery, 1935," in *Pacific Dreams: Currents of Surrealism and Fantasy in California Art, 1934–1957*, ed. by Susan Ehrlich (Los Angeles, 1995), p. 20.

27 See correspondence between Scheyer and den Raymond & Raymond Galleries in Pasadena.

28 Earl Stendahl, interview with Winifred Haines Higgins, February 2, 1961, in Higgins, *Art Collecting in the Los Angeles Area, 1910–1960* (see note 16), p. 195.

Galka Scheyer – Catalyst for Modern Architecture in California

José Parra-Martínez & John Crosse

Upon Galka Scheyer's relocation to the West Coast in 1925, her relationship with Frank Lloyd Wright's disciple Barry Byrne via Lyonel Feininger facilitated her introduction to Rudolph and Pauline Schindler in Los Angeles, with whom, on her way to San Francisco, she spent two hectic weeks in July. The alternative architecture and the vibrant cultural atmosphere of the house that they had created in Kings Road in 1922 were a real find and a stroke of luck for her. The Schindlers took Scheyer into their West Hollywood circle, where she met Austrian-born architect Richard Neutra, art scholar Annita Delano, kindred spirit, interior designer Herman Sachs and numerous other members of a community of friends and lovers who, sharing "the excitement of making important breaks with tradition,"[1] were shaping the modernity of the unique cultural geography of Southern California.

The Schindlers' network led her to the most radical artists of the region. Among others, in the Bay Area she befriended photographers Edward Weston, Dorothea Lange and Imogen Cunnigham, sculptor Ralph Stackpole, Lange's husband, graphic artist Maynard Dixon and Cunnigham's husband, printmaker Roi Partridge, who was in charge of the Art Gallery at Mills College.

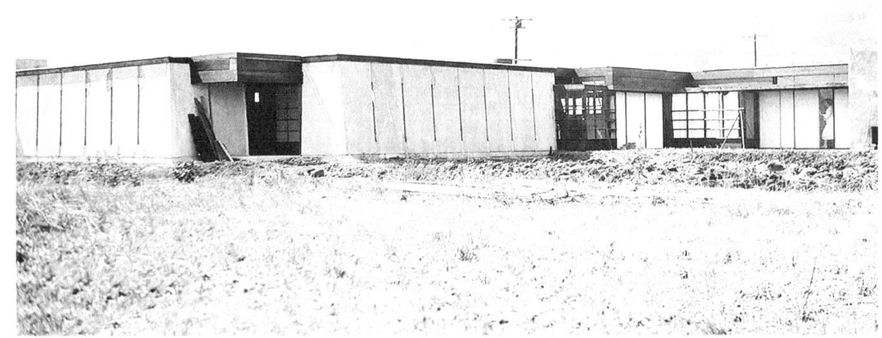

1 Rudoph M. Schindler, Kings Road's house and studio soon after its completion in 1922 (Courtesy of the Architecture and Design Collection, Art, Design & Architecture Museum, University of California, Santa Barbara, henceforth ADC/UCSB).

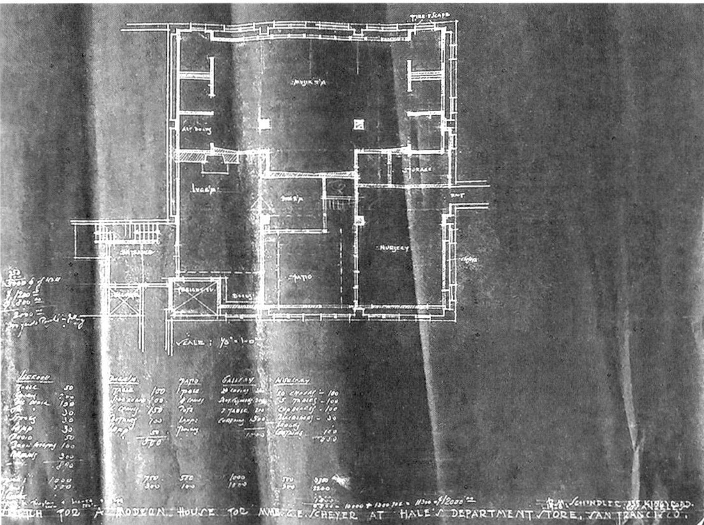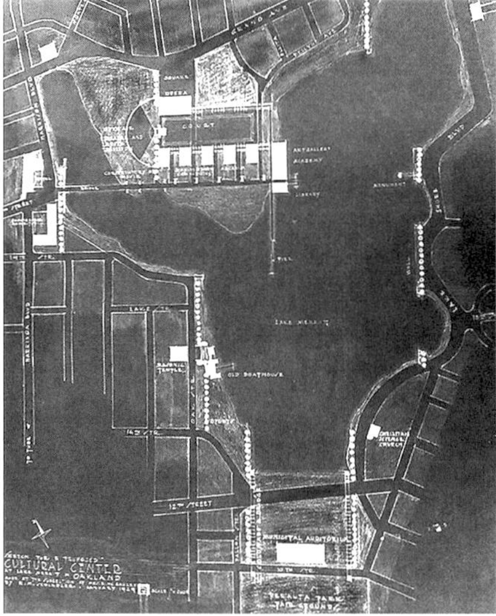

2 Left: Rudolph M. Schindler, "Sketch for a modern house for Mme. G. E. Scheyer at Hale's Department Store," San Francisco, 1928. Right: Rudolph M. Schindler, "Sketch for a Cultural Center at Lake Merrit, Oakland," January 1929 (Courtesy of the ADC/ UCSB).

Although in the mid-1920s, San Francisco Bay was still a small, conservative art center, Scheyer found unconditional support from these and other artists receptive to the European avant-gardes, such as the director of the Oakland Art Gallery, William Clapp, who was instrumental in providing Scheyer with both an exhibition space and contacts with various galleries on the West Coast.

This chapter delves into Galka Scheyer's manifold contributions to the local architectural avant-garde within and beyond these groups in both Northern and Southern California. Notwithstanding her role as maven and patron of modern architecture, her efforts to mobilize and expand architectural culture were linked to her resolution to use every resource, including architecture, to teach about the emancipatory nature of modern art.

In the summer of 1927, Scheyer spent three months at the Schindlers' guest apartment in Kings Road to study with Rudolph those aspects of modern architecture that she could apply to her art lectures and to better market the Bauhaus-oriented Blue Four's work with modernist clientele. During her stay, she witnessed the separation of her hosts. Still shrouded in mystery, the circumstances explaining Pauline's departure most likely affected the decision of the well-known naturopathic physician and *Los Angeles Times* health columnist Philip Lovell to remove Schindler from the project of his iconic house. Regardless of the speculation about the professional and personal reasons behind such a decision, there is historical consensus that Neutra was initially reluctant to replace his friend until Scheyer successfully interceded for him to take over the commission of the Lovell Health House. Therefore, "Scheyer's presence changed the course of modern architecture"[2] in California.

In February 1928, months before her European tour to lecture at the 6th International Congress for Art Education in Prague and to visit the Bauhaus's new site in Dessau, Scheyer met artist Marjorie Eaton, whom she would greatly influence. Scheyer passed on to Eaton her enthusiasm for modern architecture and for the architects she introduced to her. Indeed, Eaton and Schindler's correspondence reveals her and her stepmother Edith Cox Eaton's determination to land several commissions for the architect in San Francisco,[3] as well as to commercialize Schindler's pieces of furniture.[4]

Upon returning from Europe, in October 1928, Scheyer resumed her frantic pace of presentations in the Bay Area by lecturing at the Hale Brothers Department Store's *Exhibition of Modern Art* organized by her sponsor William Clapp.[5] In the wake of the 1925 Paris exhibition, the event was part of a burgeoning movement by big city department stores to educate the public on new industrial arts and decorative objects coming onto the market. Having been witness to the art deco craze sweeping New York department stores, like Macy's, Loeser & Co., and Lord and Taylor, Scheyer must have exchanged ideas with her travel companion and strong Los Angeles supporter Annita Delano, who was preparing a similar exhibition in Los Angeles to be held at Bullock's in December. Both friends were interested in the new techniques of retail design, such as the staging of furnished model rooms, to capture the public's attention. Cognizant of the importance of advertising as an essential component of modern art and architecture, Scheyer aimed to promote both of them simultaneously.

To do so, she tried to persuade Hale Brothers executives to create a Schindler-designed model home inside their Oakland store in order to display exclusive goods in an innovative, comprehensive fashion. The Schindler papers keep a blueprint of a temporary "modern house" to be installed around a patio. It would be accessible from the elevator and visited in a U-shaped tour of the living room, dining room and music room – conceived as a versatile space for social gatherings, recitals, art exhibitions and lectures – before leaving the exhibition through the nursery.

Although Scheyer was in the end unable to get Hale Brothers on board with this project, immediately afterwards, she persuaded the Oakland Public Library Board to consider commissioning Schindler with the extension and modernization of the Oakland Art Gallery, which was then located at the Municipal Auditorium, on the southern shore of Lake Merritt. In January 1929, the architect presented a master plan for an ambitious cultural forum around the lake. This would include an opera house, an open-air amphitheater, an aquarium, an academy of art, a music conservatory, a hotel and several commercial buildings, all of which were to be organized into a system of perpendicular axes which sought

3 Rudolph M. Schindler, Braxton Gallery at 1624 N. Vine Street, Hollywood, 1929, exterior view (Photo by Viroque Baker) and floor plan (Courtesy of the ADC/UCSB).

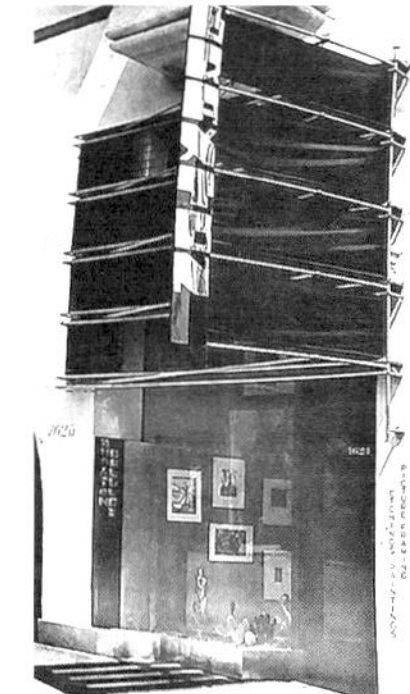

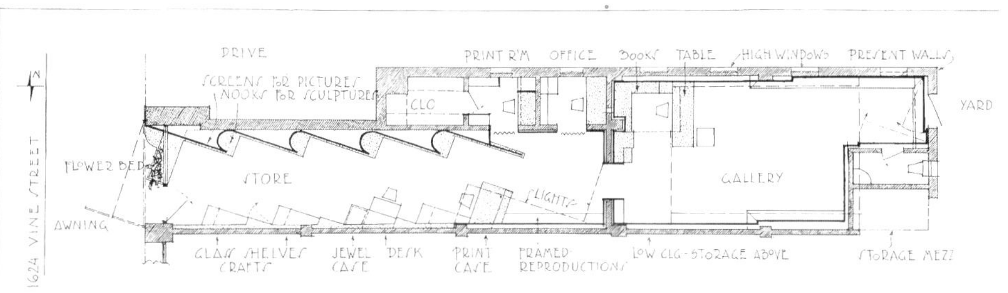

to harmonize the layout of the streets so as to produce a homogenous vision of the complex.

Despite Scheyer's tenacity, none of her efforts to achieve commissions for Schindler came to fruition until May 1929, when she discussed with Los Angeles gallerist Harry Braxton a long-term collaboration and, despite the fact that her new partner had Wright in mind,[6] she prevailed on him to sign a contract with Schindler for the design of an avant-garde gallery in Hollywood.

In order to make the most of the depth and narrowness of the premises, Schindler laid out an interior perimeter of leaning shelves, which, as well as regulating its geometry, allowed for the exhibition of works of varying formats such as sculptures, paintings, photographs, books, etc. The exterior image consisted of an effective and economical solution of black oilcloth canvasses stretched over a metal frame, which served as advertising, over the white background of the existing Spanish Revival façade. Art critic Arthur Millier praised the striking contrast between the neutral background of the dark interior and the metallic clarity of the display furniture, whose finished surfaces he compared to the elegance and modernity of a zeppelin.[7]

For Scheyer, the Braxton Gallery was a major turning point in her entrepreneurial career. Not only could she hold various Blue Four group or solo exhibitions there, but it also allowed her to establish solid contacts in the Los Angeles artistic world of movie studios which, during the Depression, would be one the few thriving businesses that could provide her with a wealthy clientele.

In 1930, after her several-year stay in Carmel, the peripatetic Pauline Schindler returned to Los Angeles. She had plans to act as agent for some architects,[8] including Richard Neutra, Kem Weber, Jock Peters, J. R. Davidson, Frank Lloyd Wright and son Lloyd, as well as her estranged husband

with whom she continued to collaborate professionally, often with Scheyer as an intermediary.[9] After her failure to edit a monograph issue of *The Carmelite* devoted to "Contemporary Architecture of the Pacific Coast," Pauline's first order of business was to curate a traveling exhibition for the group. Scheyer, who advised her on the catalogue, circulation and publicity for the show, quickly joined her. Entitled *Contemporary Creative Architecture in California*, it was premiered in April 1930 at UCLA. Most of the exhibitors in this seminal event would later figure prominently in the 1932 *Modern Architecture* exhibition at MoMA.

After her seven-month collecting expedition to Southeast Asia, in March 1931, Scheyer moved permanently to Los Angeles. She first installed herself in Chace's former apartment on Kings Road and seized its interior spaces and garden for a display of the Blue Four's paintings and other artists', such as Diego Rivera. Schindler's idiosyncratic architecture allowed her to arrange her collection in very personal, unconventional ways, placing such expressionist masterpieces in relation with design objects, modern furniture and classical works of non-Western art, like her treasured Balinese sculptures.

Initially, her symbiotic relationship with Schindler, whom she affectionately named the "honorary fifth" member of her group,[10] was very fruitful. Schindler, who undoubtedly benefited from her connections and experience as a modern art promoter and critic, enhanced Scheyer's love of modern architecture and, during various months, she savored the freedom of her new life in Kings Road.

However, living together gradually affected their personal relationship. Scheyer requested a great deal of modifications to her apartment that the architect did not always willingly accept, such as painting the existing concrete walls in colors or

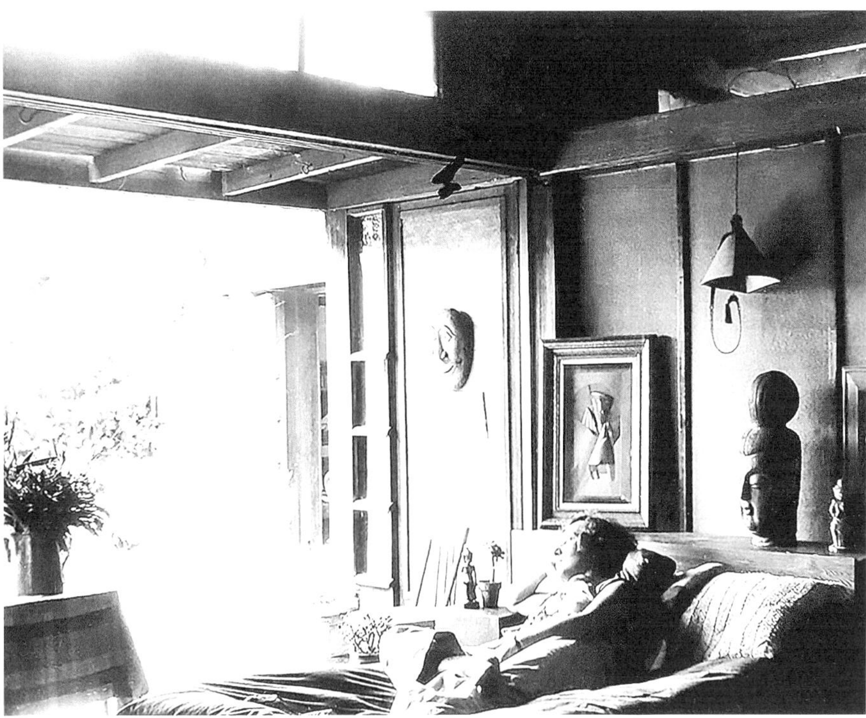

4 Galka Scheyer at Kings Road, circa 1931 (Courtesy of the Bibliothèque Kandinsky, MNAM/CCI, Centre Pompidou. Legacy of Nina Kandinsky).

the addition of curtains. The Schindler papers contain numerous requirements from his tenant, from the creation of painting frames and pieces of furniture, to never-ending lists of maintenance problems. The tone of her requests soon abandoned cordiality and the complaints began, for example, reprimanding him for the lack of comfort. The architect, who, like Scheyer, was short of money, scolded her for her late payment of rent or for the amenities used, to the point of telling her off for leaving the lights on or talking too much on the telephone. This back and forth of complaints and bills led to a spiral of disaffection, which would last for years, with strongly-worded letters in which Schindler called on her to settle her debts in exchange for a Jawlensky.[11]

Late in 1932, Scheyer visited her family and the Blue Four in Germany for the last time. The deterioration of the political situation led her to return to the United States ahead of schedule with 250 works in tow. In 1933, after the Nazis' rise to power, the North American market was literally flooded with modern art coming from Europe, which made its sale all the more difficult to a public largely interested in local movements.[12] After so many years in the country, Scheyer was still a dealer without a gallery. Feeling that the only option to her art business was to create a space of her own, where she could present herself in a different way from competitors, the idea of building a house-gallery-studio became a matter of utmost urgency.

After her falling out with Schindler and subsequent interest in working with J. R. Davidson, to whom Scheyer was very close because of her friendship with his wife, German designer Greta Wollstein,[13] the Davidsons' temporary move to Chicago, made her finally look for another architect. Frank Lloyd Wright was never an option for Scheyer; she had already stayed for some periods

2. HOUSE FOR GALKA SCHEYER, SANTA MONICA RANGE   RICHARD J. NEUTRA, ARCHITECT, GREGORY AIN, ASSOCIATE

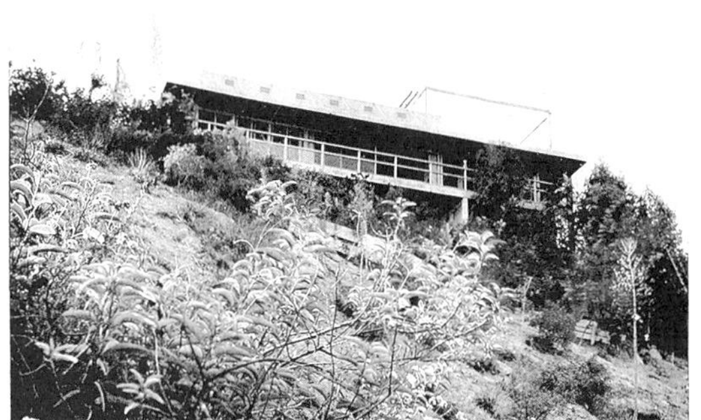

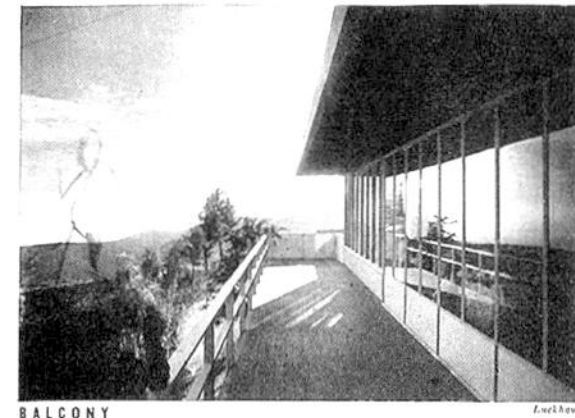

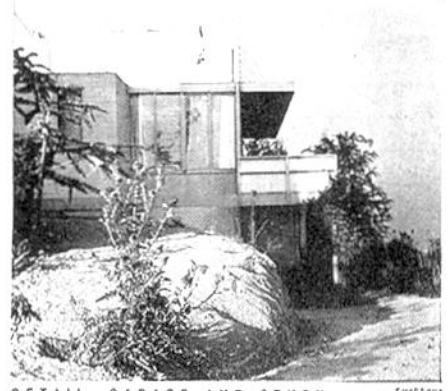

PROBLEM: The house stands on the peak of one of the highest mountains in the Santa Monica range. It has a view of the Pacific Ocean, frequently over fog banks and interesting cloud formations. As much glass as possible on the ocean side was indicated, as well as a balcony for use when weather permitted. The owner is a collector of modern art, and required a maximum of wall space for hanging pictures, as well as a fully fireproof workroom in which to store her pictures

The gallery, most important room in the house, serves as living room, dining room, and exhibition space for the owner's collection of pictures by Klee, Kandinsky, Picasso, etc. One large glazed opening extends the length of the room, and access to the terrace is provided by a sliding door 16 feet long. To permit an unobstructed view large sheets of plate glass were used, with no muntins, and metal frames as thin as possible. The conflicting requirements of maximum glass area and wall space were each satisfied by the adoption of panels which could be set over the glazed openings when it was necessary to increase the exhibition space. The other elements of the house are simple, consisting of a small kitchen, dressing room, and bath, but are quite adequate for the owner's needs. A roof garden is connected with the leveled-off top of the mountain, and the building's two lower stories open on three patios. Cost: under $3,000, or about $2.75 a square foot of net floor area.

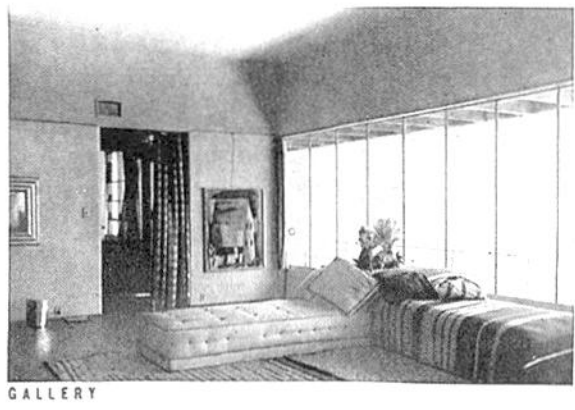

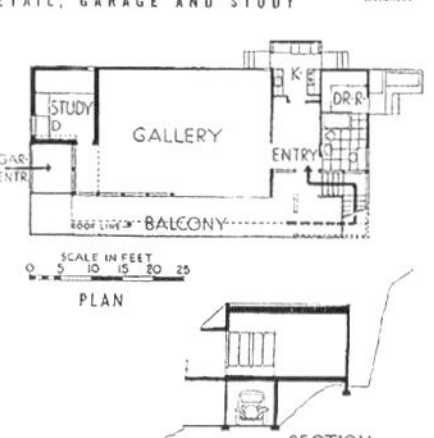

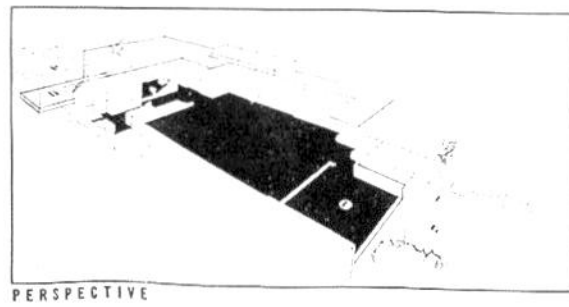
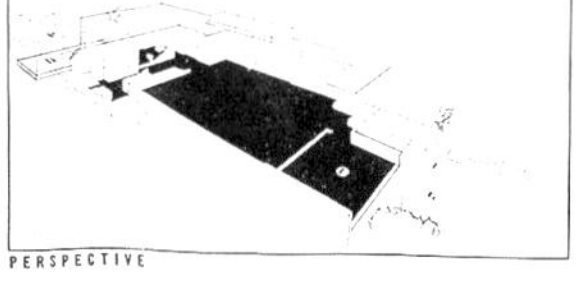

CONSTRUCTION OUTLINE

FOUNDATION
Walls—concrete 1:2½:3½. Riverside Portland Cement Co.
Cellar floor—3" cement paving No. 10 mesh reenforcing.
Waterproofing—"Pabco" by The Paraffine Companies, Inc.

FRAME CONSTRUCTION
Douglas Fir throughout with exception of redwood sills

MASONRY CONSTRUCTION
Cement block for fireproof study. Tiles by Gladding, McBean & Co.

EXTERIOR SURFACE
Stucco—Riverside cement plaster. Cemelith brushcoat.
Steel—suspension plate supporting porch overhang—U. S. Steel Co.

ROOF
Gutters / Flashing / Down spouts — Galvanized Iron—No. 1 "Armco" by American Rolling Mill Co.
Composition sheathing paper—"Pabco" composition roof by The Paraffine Companies.

DOOR AND WINDOW FRAMES
"Druwhit" casement type steel sash and sliding door, 16 feet long, by Druwhit Metal Products Co.

GLASS
Libbey-Owens-Ford double strength grade A.

EXTERIOR PAINT
Oil paint by National Lead Co. for exterior.
Sash—"Alcoa" aluminum paint.

LATH AND PLASTERING
Lath—U. S. Gypsum felt covered Rocklath and ½" Celotex lath.
Plastering—"Empire" hardwall plaster.

INTERIOR WOODWORK
Shelving and cabinets—vertical grain Douglas fir.

INSULATING
Outside walls—Celotex lath.
Roof—Celotex under composition roof.

INTERIOR FINISHES
Floors and trim—gray shingle stain by National Lead Co.

Doors—3 coats eggshell enamel by National Lead Co.
Sash—"Alcoa" aluminum paint.
Wallpaper—Sanitas.

WIRING
Cable—American Steel & Wire Co.
Switches—General Electric Co.

LIGHTING
Direct—"Light Control" lenses.
Indirect—Blue Ridge Manufacturing Co. diffusing glass.

PLUMBING
Kitchen.
Sink—Kohler Co.
Stove—"Magic"—American Stove Co.
Refrigerator—General Electric Co.

BATHROOM
Fixtures—Kohler.
Seats—Church Mfg. Co.
Tile—Gladding, McBean & Co.

PIPES
Puddled wrought iron pipe by Reading Iron Co.

HARDWARE
Locks for interior and exterior doors by Schlage Lock Co.

5 Richard Neutra, Galka Scheyer House, 1934 (Reprinted from Architectural Forum *62, October 1935, pp. 236–37).*

of time at the Wright-designed Storer and Freeman residences and her opinion of these textile block houses was not very high.[14] Given that her purpose was to create a truly innovative space, Richard Neutra, the most avant-garde architect in California, as he advertised himself, must have appeared as a natural choice to her.

No longer able to count on financial support from her family, Scheyer's ambitions were stifled by her budgetary limitations. Fortunately, in the summer of 1933, through Neutra's help, she was able to purchase a lot in the Hollywood hills for only $150. The total cost of the house was just $3,500,[15] of which a large part would go towards land development costs,[16] including the cutting of a road giving access to the house at 1880 Blue Heights Drive, which she managed to have named after her Blue Four friends.[17]

Focusing on what she considered essential, Scheyer prioritized the gallery as the very core of her house, which she would gradually finish. Used as an exhibition space and lecture room, as well as a place for various domestic activities, the gallery could be completely opened up by way of a large 16-foot sliding door to a long terrace from which Scheyer enjoyed impressive views of the mountains, the city and the ocean. Depending on the occasion, Scheyer made free use of all the rooms in the house, as is documented in the numerous photographs of her daily life, which she sent to the Blue Four. This extraordinary versatility, which challenged the normative bases of the usual domestic programs assumed by most of the modern homes intended for middle-class families, was, however, in tune with other houses that Neutra built for independent single women, such as that of art teacher Constance Perkins in the 1950s. Like Scheyer, Perkins preferred to sacrifice her own comfort in favor of a larger lounge-studio where she could work, receive visitors, give lessons to her students and even sleep, a mix of functions that was not easily accepted by the municipal authorities.

Although Scheyer wrote about the pleasure she gained from the night view of Los Angeles at her feet, or seeing her paintings filled with the morning light, she asked Neutra for less window glass in favor of a larger surface for exhibiting paintings. While the architect did not give in to this, it seems that they arrived at a compromise, consisting, according to architectural historian Thomas Hines,[18] of a system of removable panels for insertion over windows, allowing for an expandable exhibition surface without permanently closing off the breathtaking panorama. That said, this solution is not visible in any of the existing images of the house, and neither are the necessary profiles to receive such panels, which leads us to conclude that it was a basic and impractical system that, despite the publicity describing it as a highly sophisticated solution, was barely used.

While Scheyer envisioned her home gallery as a complex architectural device producing multiple art and life experiences, Neutra's drawings prioritized his own architectural formal values over those of art. His cut axonometric views seem more focused on explaining construction processes and technological innovations than in capturing the distinctive character of the house.

Tellingly, the only walls that are not drawn are those intended for paintings. Similarly, the rudimentary mechanism proposed to exhibit Scheyer's pictures, which simply consisted of pulling a

steel wire from wall to wall, speaks volumes about Neutra's disregard of the very issue of the hanging that was so important to his client.

Although still incomplete, in February 1934, Scheyer moved into her new home, where for some months she practically lived as if camping while providing a modicum of the construction labor herself in order to further keep costs down. Even if she told the Blue Four about the fatigue and discomfort of living in a half-finished house,[19] her inexhaustible energy and passion for the project is palpable in the photographs portraying her having fun while supervising the construction site, driving a bulldozer or joking with the workers.

After completion, Neutra made sure that both the local and international architectural press published Scheyer's house, which between 1934 and 1938 appeared in at least a dozen publications worldwide.[20] Correspondingly, Scheyer's "home-gallery-church of advanced art"[21] was open at all times for shows, lectures, viewings and parties. It soon became a gathering place for architects, artists, gallerists, such as Earl Stendahl and prominent members of the Hollywood film industry, like Josef von Sternberg – a contact that most likely facilitated Neutra's commission for the director's spectacular house in the San Fernando Valley.[22]

Surrounded by nature and plenty of avant-garde masterpieces, architecture provided Scheyer with an ideal setting to carry out her mission. As Isabel Wünsche elucidates,[23] it soon became her trademark in the 1930s, since her personality, lifestyle and modern house merged into one for her contemporaries.

Certainly, her house allowed the organization of the most varied of events, but the preparation of all these activities involved a great deal of work and the alleged flexibility of Neutra-designed

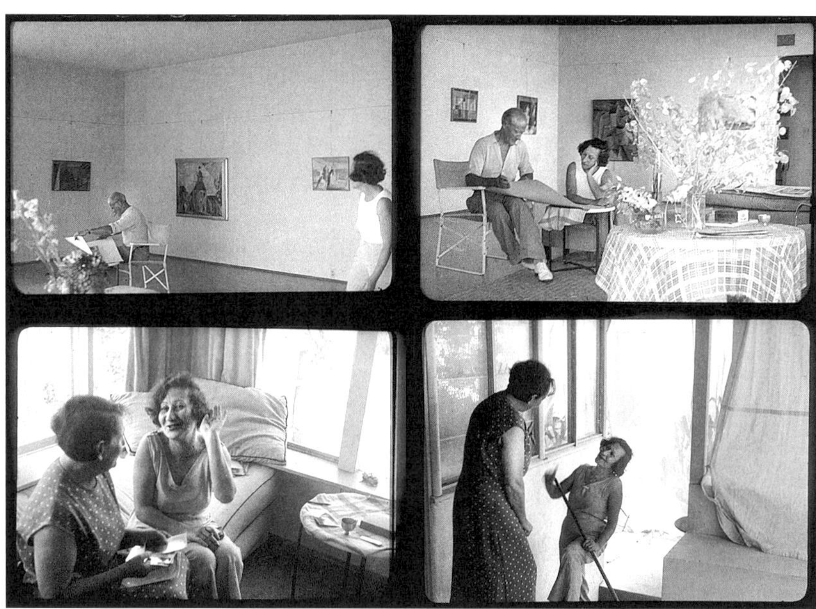

6 Galka Scheyer with Lyonel and Julia Feininger during their visitation to her Hollywood house in June 1936 (Courtesy of the Harvard Art Museums).

exhibition space required a lot of effort on her part. In 1936, in a collective letter to the Blue Four, Scheyer described such a struggle in detail:

> What does it mean to give lectures in my home? Hanging pictures, so splendidly, so lovingly, each related to the others. Picking them up myself and then returning them ... Hanging takes an entire day. Cleaning, filling the house with flowers, a second, the lecture a third, and cleaning up afterward, a fourth.[24]

The need for this continuous metamorphosis of the space explains why, from the first photographs taken by Arthur Luckhaus to her own snaps, the house transmits a sensation of disorder or temporariness. The gallery is always portrayed with few pieces of furniture, dispersed around an empty space, as was necessary in order to facilitate its transformation from domestic to exhibition space.

It is interesting to compare the architectural photographs released by Neutra with those showing the true experience of the house. Luckhaus's exterior pictures, like abstract models on a landscape still without vegetation, and icy interiors, which seem to emulate industrial photography, are the images on which Neutra sought to construct his prestige. In counterpoint, the photographs taken by Scheyer or her friends are not the usual images of a Neutra interior as they place all emphasis on showing the ordinary details of everyday life. For example, when in the summer of 1936, Lyonel Feininger and his wife Julia visited Scheyer at her home, their photos show a happy woman entertaining her friends, being photographed with them in the most carefree of situations, chatting on the balcony, happily working and even cleaning up.

The photographs which Julius Shulman took of Gregory Ain's addition are not among the best taken by the renowned architectural photographer, who at the time was learning his craft. Far from his brilliant compositions from the 1940s and '50s, Shulman's aseptic pictures of this house, with no people, contrast with the portraits taken by Lette Valeska of Galka Scheyer in the same spaces. In these, she appears sunbathing, doing the garden – two of her favorite pas-

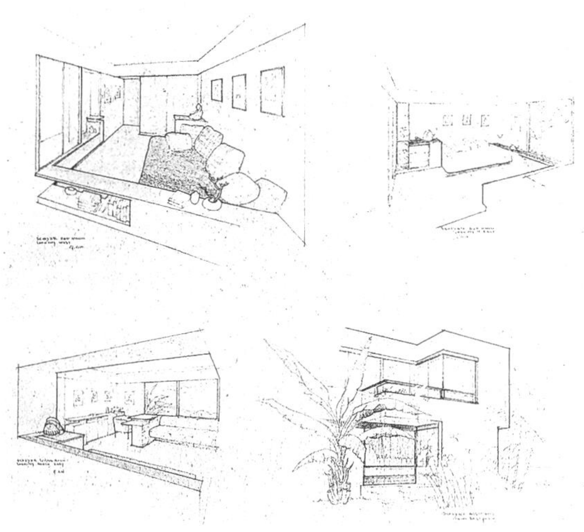

7 Gregory Ain, sketches for the second floor addition to Scheyer's house, 1936.

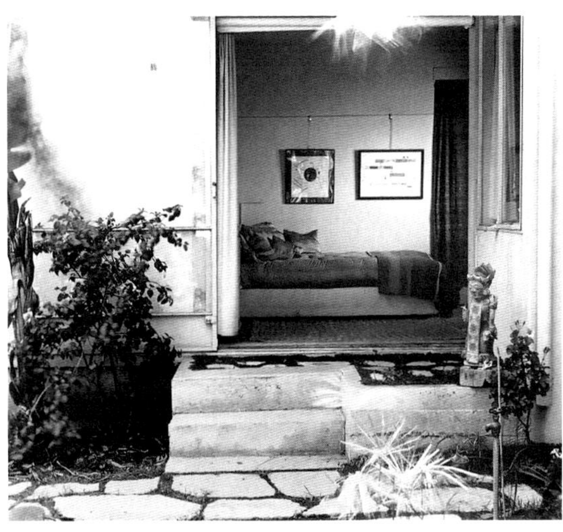

8 Julius Shulman's photo of the house after Ain's intervention (Courtesy of the ADC/UCSB).

times – and even dangerously posing in the window frames. Some of these photographs, which brought together the daily enjoyment of art and architecture, – like the one in which she is portrayed in a bathing suit atop the edge of the cantilever smiling at the camera – predate by more than a decade the famous photographs of Charles and Ray Eames celebrating their new house in Pacific Palisades perched on its metal structure.

The Feiningers' visit further strengthened Scheyer's resolve to extend her house in order to add a guest apartment. Yet, instead of Richard Neutra, she turned to his disciple and collaborator in the project, Gregory Ain, who took this commission as an opportunity to set up an independent practice. Thomas Hines intimates that Scheyer's "tense relationship with Neutra" was the explanation behind her decision; also that the architect was tired of their "numerous confrontations" and her telephoning "at all hours of the day and night."[25] Whatever their reasons, Scheyer was not the only one of Richard Neutra's clients who, after having worked and fought with him, did not call on him again for future alterations to their homes.

The second floor apartment, which included two rooms, a bathroom, a kitchen and an independent entrance, was finished in June 1937. Ain achieved a proposal which managed to take full advantage of the scarce existing surface space by way of the design of integrated furniture, a clear Schindler influence. In contrast to the modernity of its volume, the construction was a traditional wood-frame and stucco house. The plywood panels for the interior walls were arranged according to the four-foot module, also characteristic of Schindler. In their careful subdivision Ain integrated a discreet steel rail for curtains which, in this case, also served as a way of hanging Scheyer's paintings, solving this particular problem with a solution which was more refined than Neutra's in the lower floor gallery.

Hines has shown some reticence with respect to this intervention, declaring that

> Ain's competent, but boxy, addition sacrificed the building's horizontal serenity for a less compelling vertical orientation.[26]

Yet, this consideration of architecture from the only point of view of form ignores both its spatial condition and the needs of the user, which are downgraded in favor of image. Moreover, this criticism overlooks the interweaving of the building with its surroundings, which Ain's perspectives already showed – his drawings were indeed based on the idea that the rapid growth of vegetation made a complete vision of the house impossible, and only fragments of it could be glimpsed through the eucalyptuses.

During the construction work, Marjorie Eaton's frequent visits to Scheyer's house and meetings with Ain planted seeds for her 1939 commission to the fledgling architect to design a new home and art space for her in Palo Alto. Eaton's family owned the historic complex of Juana Briones de Miranda Ranch, to which she wanted to add her own place. Eaton discussed with Ain her desire to build in adobe brick, both as it was a relatively inexpensive material and also reminded her of much happier times living and painting in Taos. She must have heard directly from Ain as well of his boyhood experience building with adobe while living with his family at the ill-fated socialist colony of Llano del Rio in the Mojave Desert.

Eaton's one-floor house was organized on a gentle slope and its directions aligned with the pre-existing planting of almond trees. In the mid-1950s, Ain added a small outdoor amphitheater adjoining the rear patio, which served both as a rehearsal area for the artist – who was by then transitioning to an acting career – and a performance space for entertaining her guests. More than 5,000 adobe bricks were made on site for the house's walls. One of Ain's most significant contributions was his modern interpretation of an old building technique, of which Edith Cox Eaton's ranch provided interesting historical examples. In her Mesa Alta property, he found an unusual but effective case of traditional reinforced adobe construction consisting of a mixed system of mud bricks and redwood panels. Ain combined adobe walls with embedded wooden supports, which he secured with horizontal metal bars every 4 courses. This technique improved the already good natural insulation of adobe and solved its two most important drawbacks: the erosion of its surface and poor structural response to earthquake-induced forces.

The existing photos of Galka Scheyer's visits to Marjorie Eaton's construction site show her fasci-

9 Galka Scheyer in the second floor apartment added by Gregory Ain, photos by Lette Valeska, ca. 1938 (Courtesy of the Norton Simon Museum, Pasadena, CA).

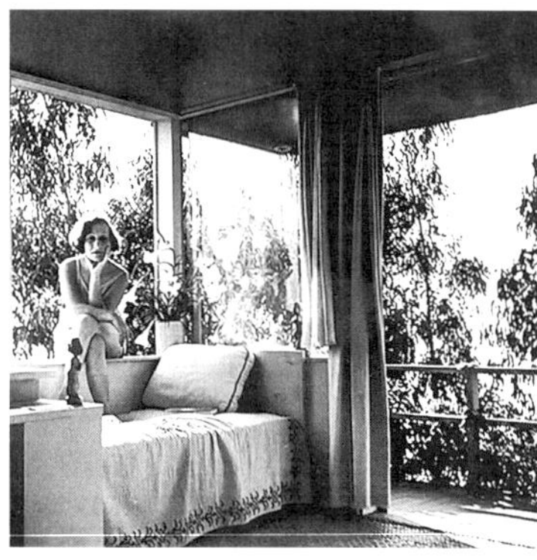
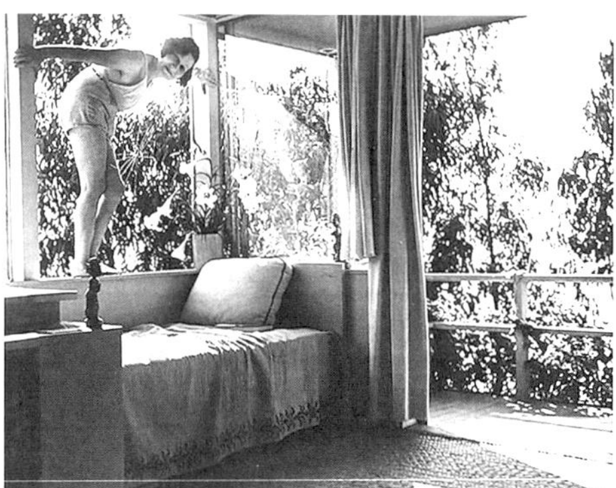
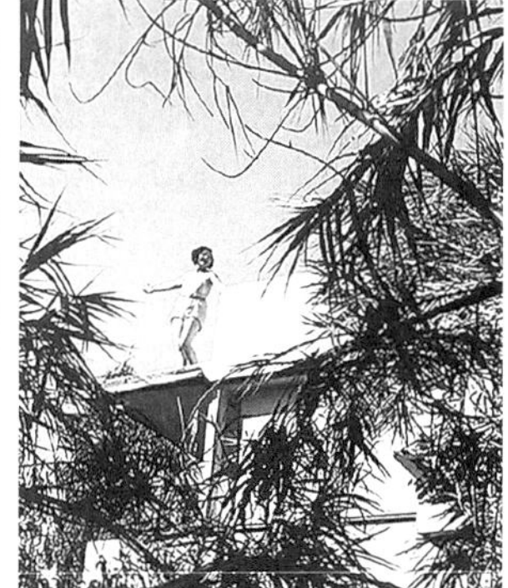

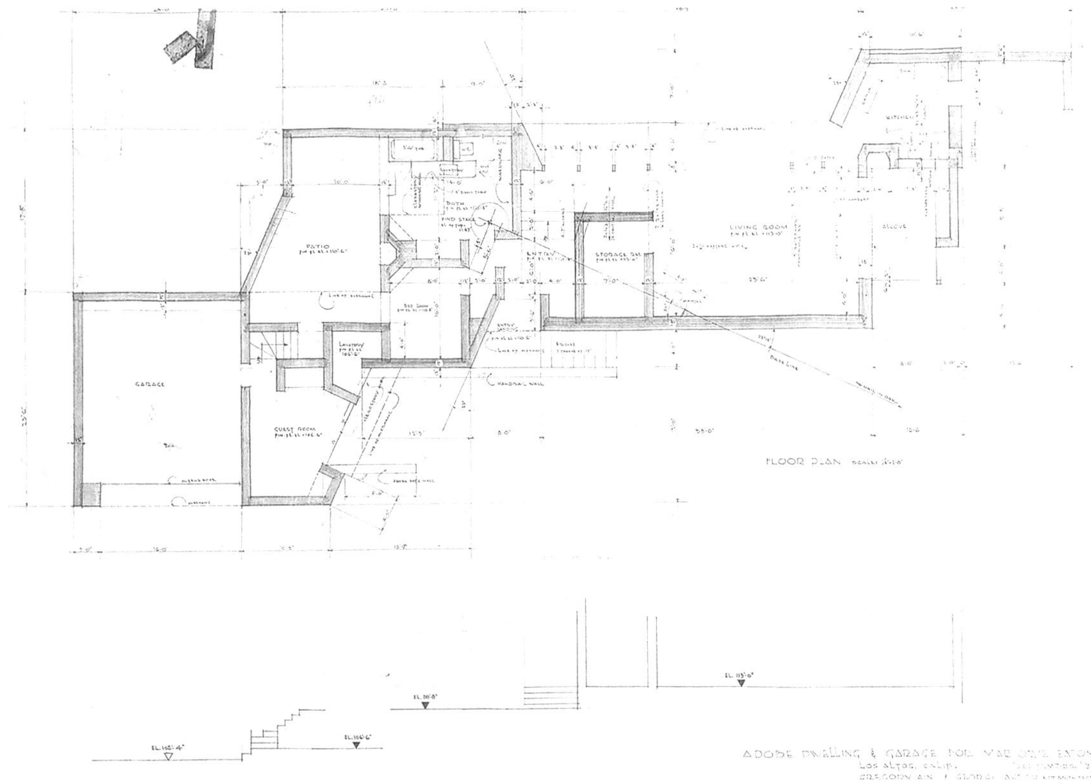

10 Gregory Ain, Marjorie Eaton House in Palo Alto, floor plan, September 1939 (Courtesy of the ADC/UCSB).

11 Galka Scheyer (in foreground) and Marjorie Eaton's visit to Eaton construction site, ca. 1940 (Courtesy of Susan Kirk).

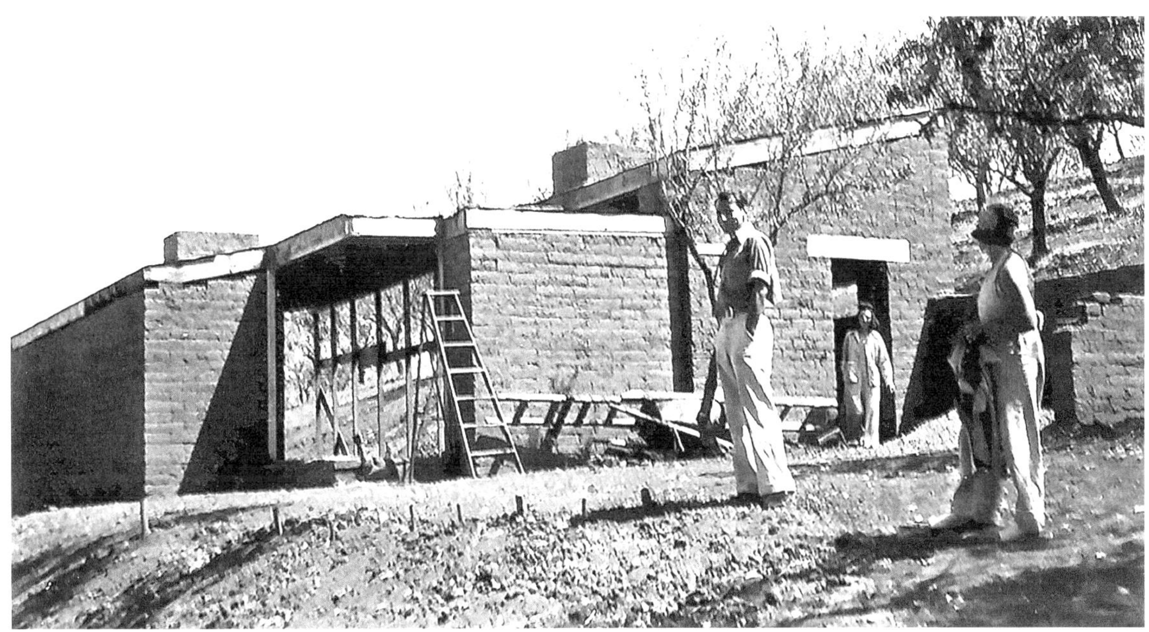

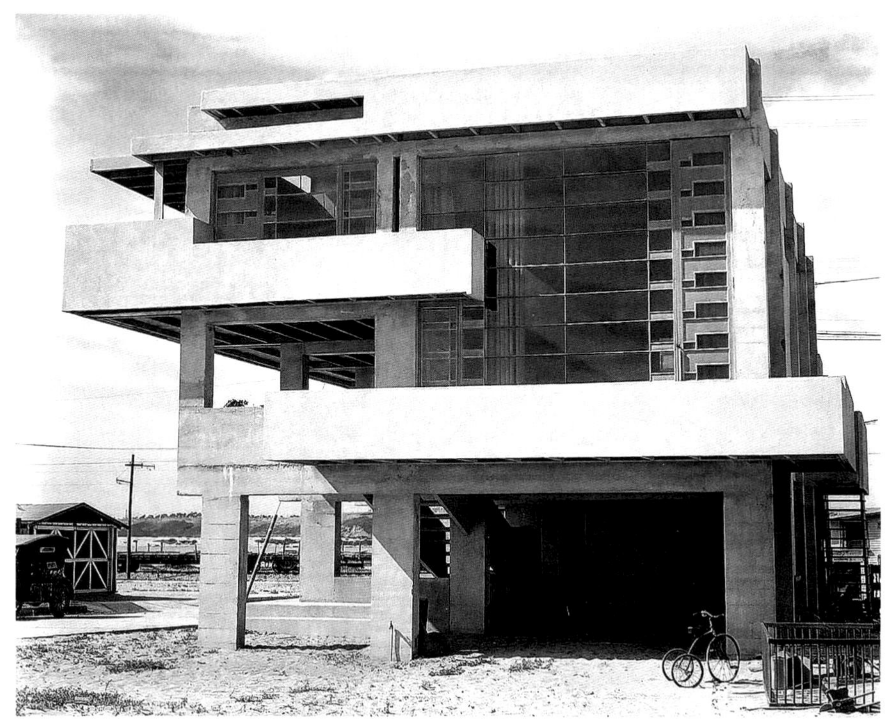

12 Rudolph. M. Schindler's Lovell Beach House used by Galka Scheyer to illustrate her lectures on art and architecture (Photo by Edward Weston, 1927; Courtesy of the ADC/UCSB).

nation and involvement with her friend's venture. It lasted throughout much of the 1940s as Eaton was strapped for funds. In this house, many of Scheyer and Eaton's mutual friends – among others, artists such as Lucrecia Van Horn and Louise Nevelson –, would spend long periods of time. Contrary to other conventional middle-class programs of modern architecture, Marjorie Eaton initiated a family-like arts colony around Briones's original home on the hill. Eaton's community flourished for most of the middle decades of the 20th century, encouraging women in the arts and challenging racial barriers amid the de facto segregation and increasing conservatism that accompanied Cold War fears in the South San Francisco Bay Area.[27]

Not only did Galka Scheyer everything she could to patronize architecture, but everything related to architectural culture and its relationships with other artistic disciplines. In her exhibitions and lectures, she tried to involve her audiences by way of expansive events. In these, Scheyer creatively linked artistic concepts to architectural proposals, especially those of her house, where content and container came together in perfect resonance. More than a medium, the architectural space was also a message given that, in her presentations, she herself created this framework by directly interacting with the exhibited works, alone or in combination with other media, such as modern photography. Among other images, Scheyer frequently turned to the pictures of Schindler's Lovell Beach House taken by their mutual friend Edward Weston, whose architectural photography, like that of his son Brett, she helped promote.

In her architectural circles, women like Pauline Schindler, Harriet Freeman, Leah Lovell or her inseparable friend Marjorie Eaton not only commissioned houses that were fundamental to California modernism, but also mobilized affections and wove the professional and personal networks that most contributed to the cultural environment which made these works possible. Unfortunately, records of the much-neglected contributions of these women as both patrons and facilitators are for the most part inaccurate and biased in the canonical accounts of modern architecture, in which Scheyer herself often appears as an inopportune and annoying woman exasperating her architects.

In the 1930s, having clear ideas and a strong character were valued as remarkable qualities in a man, but they used to be considered as socially unacceptable flaws in a woman. For this reason, contemporary studies cannot simply continue to accept these prejudices without criticism. In this sense, although both Neutra and Ain remembered Scheyer as an educated, intelligent woman, her architects' biographers have not hidden a pejorative discourse towards her figure, insisting on Scheyer's depiction as an "eccentric,"[28] "volatile,"[29] "very difficult to get along with," "highly neurotic woman and very demanding," "utterly impossible" client.[30]

In the history of 20th-century architecture, there are barely any cases of houses commissioned by women in which, when they requested innovative spaces for their equally unusual ways of life,[31] patrons and architects easily reached an agreement, mainly because gender biases have usually led male architects to show who was in control, both of the project and its narrative. Yet, without the

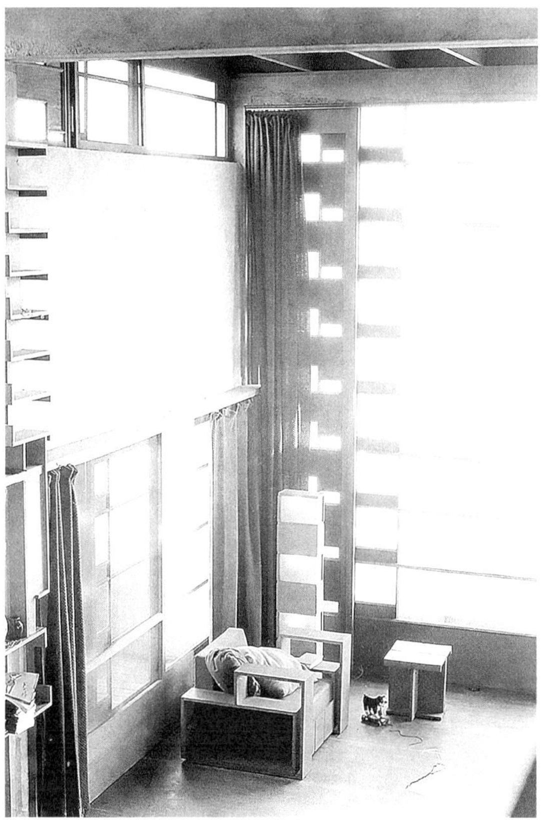

13 Rudolph. M. Schindler's Lovell Beach House used by Galka Scheyer to illustrate her lectures on art and architecture (Photo by Edward Weston, 1927; courtesy of the ADC/UCSB).

role of Galka Scheyer, as an essential catalyst for innovation, without this "dynamo of energy,"[32] as Edward Weston called her, the path taken by modern architecture in California would most likely have been a very different one.

1   William Deverell, "Introduction," in Victoria Dailey, Natalie Shivers, and Michael Dawson, *LA's Early Moderns. Art/Architecture/ Photography* (Los Angeles, CA, 2003), pp. 6–14, especially: p. 13.

2   Robert Sweeney, "Life in Kings Road: As It Was 1920–1940," in Michael Darling, and Elizabeth A. T. Smith, eds., *The Architecture of R. M. Schindler* (New York, NY, 2001), pp. 86–115, especially: p. 103.

3   Marjorie Eaton, letters to R. M. Schindler (RMS), spring-summer 1930; Edith Eaton Cox, letter to RMS, May 8 1929. Schindler papers, Architecture and Design Collection, Art, Design & Architecture Museum, University of California, Santa Barbara (henceforth ADC/UCSB).

4   Marjorie Eaton, letter to RMS, June 22, 1928 (ACD/UCSB).

5   "Exhibition on Modern Art Opens October 4 in Oakland," *The Argus* 4, no. 1 (San Francisco, CA, 1928), p. 17.

6   Harry Braxton and Viola Brothers Shore also commissioned Schindler to design their new home in Venice Beach, one of his most noticeable exercises of "space architecture." Yet, while it was on Schindler's drawing board, the couple divorced and gave up this project.

7   Arthur Millier, "'Ultra' Gallery Arrives," *Los Angeles Times*, September 15, 1929, p. B13.

8   Pauline Schindler, contract draft to represent and promote the work of local "contemporary creators," March 10, 1930 (ADC/UCSB).

9   Galka Scheyer to RMS, ca. winter 1929 (ADC/UCSB). Scheyer refers to Pauline's preparation of a monograph on modern architecture, in which she encourages Schindler to take part.

10 Galka Scheyer, letter to RMS, April 12, 1931 (ADC/UCSB).

11 RMS, letter to Galka Scheyer, September 12, 1934 (ADC/UCSB).

12 Isabel Wünsche, "In Pursuit of a Spiritual Calling: Katherine S. Dreier, Galka E. Scheyer, and Hilla von Rebay," in *Gender, Sexuality and Museums. A Routledge Reader*, ed. by Amy K. Levin (London, 2010), pp. 213–28, especially: p. 220.

13 As part of her busy networking activity, Scheyer introduced J. R. Davidson to her friend and client, Ruth McClymonds Maitland, one of the country's leading collectors, who commissioned the future Case Study House architect to take over the renovation work on her home.

14 Galka Scheyer, collective letter to the Blue Four, August 2, 1933. Compiled in Isabel Wünsche, *Galka E. Scheyer and the Blue Four: Correspondence 1924–1945* (Bern, 2006), p. 220.

15 F. W. Brown, ed., *California Homes Plan Book for 1938* (San Francisco, CA, 1938), p. 101.

16 The house was paid for through a loan from the Federal Housing Administration that allowed Scheyer to take on a mortgage of just $30 a month, insurance and taxes included, that is, less

17 Galka Scheyer, collective letter to the Blue Four, February 13, 1934. Compiled in Wünsche, *Galka E. Scheyer and the Blue Four* (see note 14), pp. 238–40.

18 Thomas S. Hines, *Richard Neutra and the Search for Modern Architecture* (New York, 2005), p. 138.

19 Galka Scheyer, collective letter to the Blue Four, February 13, 1934. Compiled in Wünsche, *Galka E. Scheyer and the Blue Four* (see note 14), pp. 238–40.

20 In December 1935, the San Francisco-based *Architect & Engineer* magazine, in an issue guest-edited by Pauline Schindler herself, covered the project. That very year, it was also included in the monograph exhibition that MoMA devoted to *Contemporary Architecture in California* and which, as its title reveals, could not have ignored the above-mentioned Schindler and Scheyer's almost homonymous show in 1930. Scheyer's house was also included, among other journals, in *Casabella* (January 1935), *Architects' Journal* (February 1935) and *Architecture* (August 1935); in October 1935, it was widely covered by Architectural Forum and, in March 1936, reviewed by the Japanese journal *Kokusai Kenchiku.*

21 Amy B. Sandback, Blue Heights Drive, *Artforum* 28, no. 7 (1990), pp. 123–27, especially: p. 123.

22 Neutra rubbed shoulders with Josef von Sternberg at Scheyer's exhibitions at the Braxton Gallery in the spring of 1930. Although Neutra never revealed how he had met the filmmaker, their simultaneous presence at Scheyer's events seems a reliable clue. Authors' conversation with Raymond Neutra, December 2020.

23 Wünsche, *Galka E. Scheyer and the Blue Four* (see note 14), p. 229.

24 Galka Scheyer, collective letter to the Blue Four, March 10, 1936. Compiled in Wünsche, *Galka E. Scheyer and the Blue Four* (see note 14), p. 256.

25 Thomas S. Hines, *Richard Neutra* (see note 18), pp. 138–39.

26 Ibid., p. 139.

27 Jan Rindfleisch, ed., *Roots and Offshoots: Silicon Valley's Arts Community* (Santa Clara, CA, 2017).

28 Thomas S. Hines, *Richard Neutra* (see note 18), p. 96.

29 Ibid., p. 138.

30 Anthony Denzer, *Gregory Ain. The Modern Home as Social Commentary* (New York, 2008), p. 48.

31 Alice T. Friedman, *Women and the Making of the Modern House: A Social and Architectural History* (New York, 1998).

32 Edward Weston and Nancy Newhall, ed., *The Daybooks of Edward Weston*, vol. 2: *California.* (New York, 1966), especially: p. 151.

Provenance Galka Scheyer – Works by Paul Klee in the Museum Berggruen

Sven Haase

There are different ways to approach Galka Scheyer: one is the story of a woman from Braunschweig in post-WWI-Germany, who went to the United States on a mission of modern art, others involved the art scene in California in the 1920s and '30s and then there is her engagement for the artist group the Blue Four. All of these are exciting topics. But I came to know Galka Scheyer through provenance research. Investigating the collection of the Museum Berggruen in Berlin, my focus was on the origin and history of the artworks and her name appeared in the provenance chain of several works by Paul Klee. Then there was the name of an art dealer with a Jewish background. Far from being an expert on her biography, I had to check her connection to the artworks along with a deeper study of time and circumstances of possession. So I started with a suspicious provenance and ended up with an impressive story.

The following essay presents four works from the Museum Berggruen with the provenance of Galka Scheyer and also some remarks on the significance of these examples. The goal is to show a spectrum of what provenance Galka Scheyer could mean and to contribute an interpretation of her efforts in dealing and collecting art and making the Blue Four – Lyonel Feininger, Wassily Kandinsky, Paul Klee, and Alexej Jawlensky – popular in the USA.

The Museum Berggruen is part of the Nationalgalerie Berlin and home to the former private collection of Heinz Berggruen (1914–2007). Within a three-year project, this research project covered 135 artworks, including paintings, works on paper and sculpture created before 1945 by artists Pablo Picasso, Paul Klee, Georges Braque, and Henri Matisse. My first goal was to check the provenance of the inventory between 1933 and 1945 in order to exclude having looted art in the collection.[1] During research, it became clear that there were many stories to tell. The names of those who came in contact with the works or those who owned them read like a dictionary of the modern art world during the first half of the 20th century: Alfred Flechtheim, Paul Rosenberg, Daniel-Henry Kahnweiler, Karl Buchholz, Alphonse Kann, Douglas Cooper, and Marie-Laure Comtesse de Noailles – just to name a few. The artworks not only remind us of their owners and proprietors whose biographies are embedded in historical events. Their provenances also express the variety of topics that shaped the history of 20th century art: the popularization of modernism, the development of an international art market, the art theft of the National Socialists and the emigration of art dealers and collectors. This is how we draw near to Galka Scheyer.

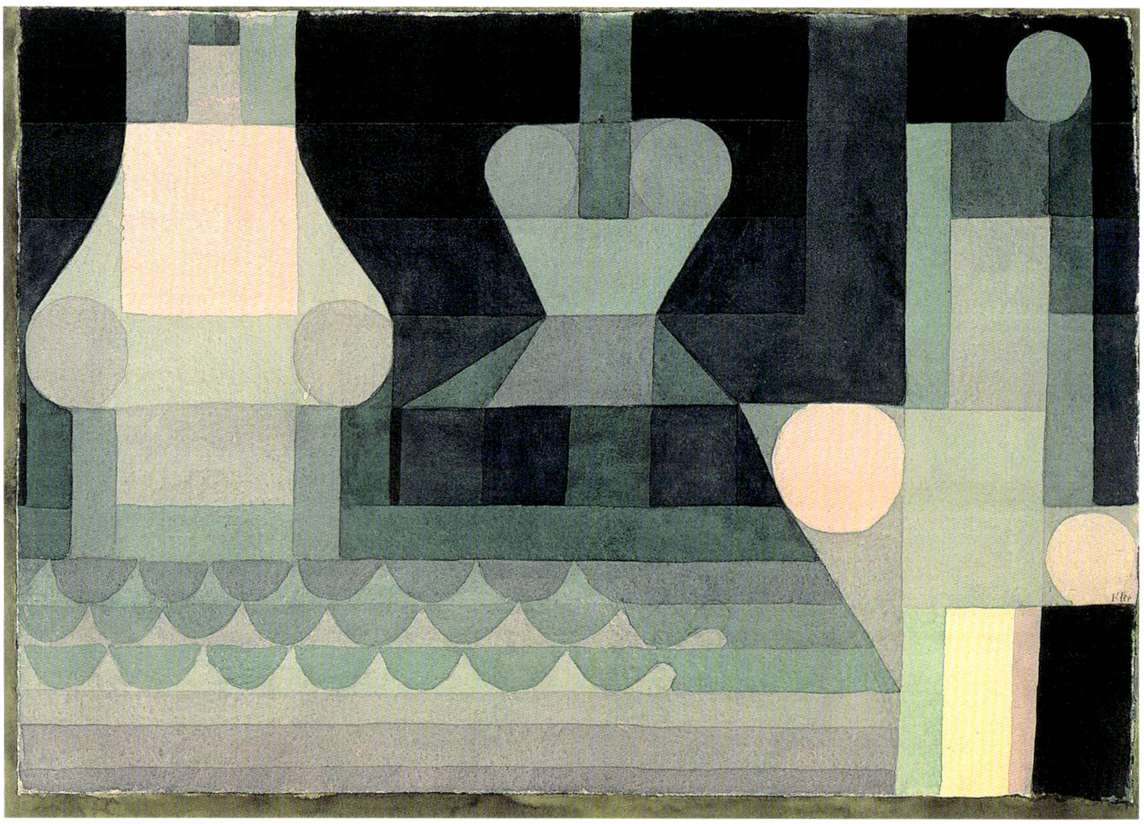

1 *Floodgates / Schleusen, 1922, watercolor and graphite on paper bordered with guache mounted on light cardboard, 20.3 x 30.7 cm (Courtesy of Staatliche Museen zu Berlin, Nationalgalerie, NB MB 119/2000. Photo: Jens Ziehe).*

Her mission to put the Blue Four on the map led the young art lover to America and in her baggage a number of artworks and a joint contract with the artists as well. The Museum Berggruen has four works she once owned, all by Paul Klee.[2] The first one is the watercolor *Floodgates*, painted in 1922 and in her possession between 1925 and 1928. The work was initially part of her first exhibition in the US held at the Daniel Gallery in New York in 1925. *Floodgates* accompanied her on her move to California where she presented it a year later at the Exhibition Park in Los Angeles and the Oakland Art Gallery, in 1927 at the Museum of Art in Portland, Oregon and in 1928 at the Art Association in Spokane, Washington. This was a fruitful period for Galka Scheyer. She

had arrived at the West Coast, became established and made her mark by organizing numerous exhibitions. In 1926, she started a longstanding cooperation with William Clapp, director of the Oakland Art Gallery, where she became its curator for European Art. But her obvious success also revealed that her pioneering achievement was not accompanied by economic prosperity. The exhibition venues were not in the leading centers of modern art, of which there were only a few in California in the 1920s. Oakland, for example, was a boomtown, well known for its expanding car industry and called "Detroit of the West," with a population of 280,000, and a growing center with famous buildings in the latest art deco style. But Oakland was not San Francisco and was overshadowed by the "Paris of the West" with its population of around 600,000 in 1930. Exhibiting art was one thing, selling works of art by modernist European artists another. Galka Scheyer could not sell *Floodgates*. The work was sent back to Paul Klee and stayed in his possession until 1940, returning to the US in the late 1940s thanks to Curt Valentin.[3]

Scene Among Girls, 1923, had a comparable provenance. The paperwork belonged to the stock of works by Paul Klee Scheyer brought to the US in 1924.[4] It was displayed at the Henry Art Gallery, founded in 1927 as the first public museum in the state of Washington based in Seattle and today is part of the University of Washington. Both *Floodgates* and *Scene Among Girls* were returned to Klee unsold in 1928 and went into private possession years later.[5] Both works are examples of Galka Scheyer's enterprises in the 1920s. They show her enthusiasm and engagement but also the meager financial consequence for this type of collaboration on a difficult market.

The third example, the watercolor *Barbarian – Classical – Festive*, painted in 1926, has a choppy provenance history and in regard to Galka Scheyer, also an effective one. The biography of the painting is also interesting from the perspective of the Nationalgalerie Berlin. Before the work came to the US, Bauhaus-teacher and artist Georg Muche, who possessed it on consignment, offered it to the museum in 1927. The offer was turned down.[6] Not until 73 years later, the work came to the Nationalgalerie by acquisition of the Berggruen Collection. After Muche could not sell the work, Galka Scheyer received it on consignment from Klee in 1933. That year, the watercolor was part of a the Blue Four exhibition at the Los Angeles Museum, predecessor of the Los Angeles County Museum of Art (LACMA), curated and accompanied by Scheyer with a lecture on the artists. *Barbarian – Classical – Festive* was displayed in the new Museum of Modern Art

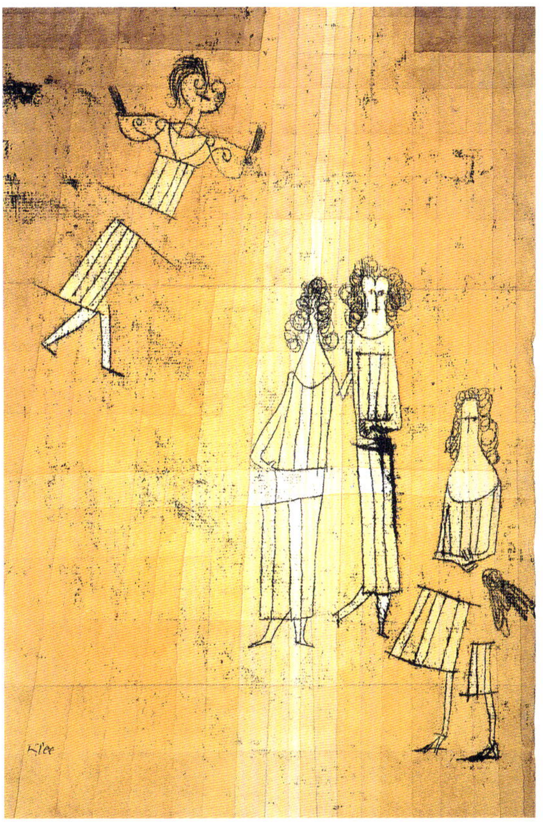

2 Scene among Girls/ Scene unter Mädchen, 1923, transferred printing ink and watercolor on paper mounted on light cardboard, upper and lower border strips in watercolor and ink, 49.5 x 32.1 cm (Courtesy of Staatliche Museen zu Berlin, Nationalgalerie, NG MB 123/2000. Photo: Jens Ziehe).

in San Francisco (SFMOMA) in 1937. There it gained the attention of Charlotte Mack. Two letters from Galka Scheyer to Klee in 1937 reported on long winded negotiations between her and the scion of a benevolent San Francisco based family interested in purchasing the watercolor along with a painting she was bargaining for at a lower price. A not amused Galka Scheyer commented on the offer to Klee: "I hope you answer with a no, because some people just push too hard."[7] But the potential buyer remained adamant: "Mrs. Mack in San Francisco wrote me that she cannot pay more than $700 as she sends three penniless students through university."[8] Similar

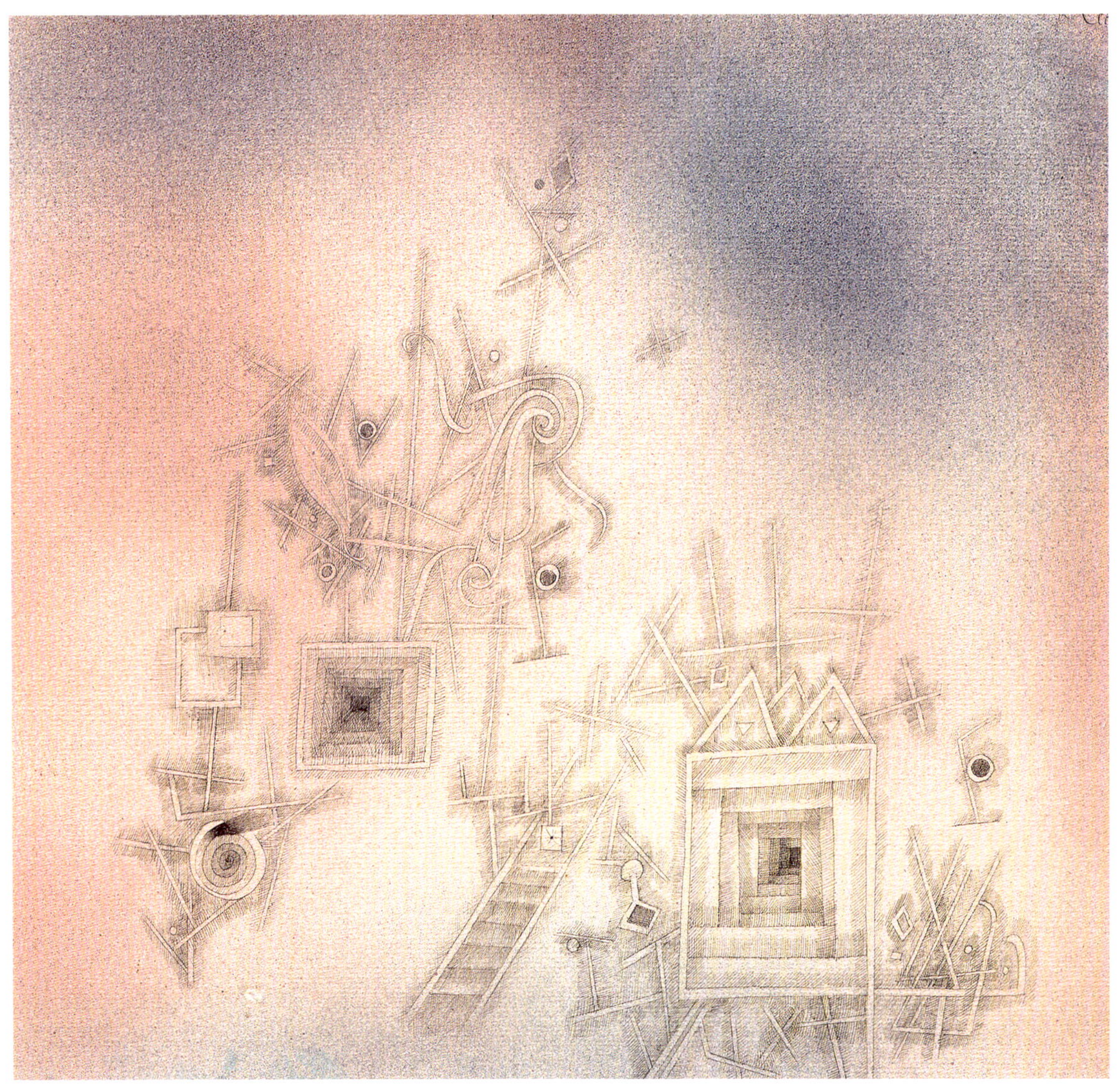

3 Barbarian – Classical – Festive/barbarisch – klassisch – festlich, 1926, pen and watercolor, partially sprayed, on paper mounted on cardboard, 29.3 x 31 cm (Courtesy of Staatliche Museen zu Berlin, Nationalgalerie, NG MB 134/2000. Photo: Jens Ziehe).

to Galka Scheyer, Charlotte Mack was a lover of modern and European art. Her collection contained Gris, Léger, Miró, Kokoschka, and Picasso. His gouache *Man Seated at a Table*, painted in1916, is today also part of the Museum Berggruen, and once belonged to Charlotte Mack. She also collected works by the Blue Four, purchasing them from Galka Scheyer.[9] In the end, *Barbarian*

– Classical – Festive was sold to Charlotte Mack along with a larger painting, for the original price she was willing to pay. In 1940, the watercolor was part of the memorial exhibition for Klee organized at the Buchholz Gallery in New York by Curt Valentin. The catalog lists the work with provenance Charlotte Mack. A sticker on the backside confirmed her as the owner. It is

very likely that the watercolor *Barbarian – Classical – Festive* was one of Mack's the Blue Four acquisitions from Galka Scheyer, even if it is difficult to confirm the transfer with sources in Galka Scheyer papers.[10]

Finally, the fourth instance has a vital provenance history. The list of people who were involved in dealing *Rock Chamber*, painted in 1929, reads like a "Who's Who" of the dealers and traders of Paul Klee's works before 1945: from 1929 to 1933, Alfred Flechtheim had the watercolor in his stock and could have provided it for the sum of 500 Reichsmark. With his emigration from Germany to England, he sent *Rock Chamber* to Daniel Henry Kahnweiler in Paris, who was then Klee's international representative. In 1937, Kahnweiler sold this work of art to New York based Karl Nierendorf for $85. From there it was passed on to Galka Scheyer. While the three other examples came to her on consignment from the individual artists, this was a different construction: *Rock Chamber* had nothing to do with her contract with the Blue Four, but was part of an agreement between herself and Nierendorf. In January 1939, Galka Scheyer received 30 artworks by Klee on consignment, 20 works on paper including *Rock Chamber* and 10 paintings.[11] Since 1938, Nierendorf had been Klee's general representative in the US. Was this an indication that Klee needed a new partner in the US in addition to the enthusiastic but semi-professional Galka Scheyer? The first cooperation between both could have been the beginning of a partnership with representatives on the east and west coast. Above all for Galka Scheyer, this seemed to be a chance to revitalize her own business. But what were Nierendorf's motifs? Since landing in the US in 1936, Nierendorf had become a citizen of the US and successfully established his art gallery. But his situation was also tense and he had to deal with issues. He was Klee's official representative in America but yet not the only dealer to sell the artist's work. His main rival was Curt Valentin. This former em-

ployee of Alfred Flechtheim had become an associate of Berlin based art dealer Karl Buchholz. After leaving Nazi Germany for the US because of his Jewish background, he established a branch of the Buchholz Gallery in Manhattan – a year after Nierendorf's arrival in New York. Whereas Nierendorf exclusively obtained new works directly from Klee, Valentin flooded the market with artworks by German artists, including Klee; these had been confiscated during the "Aktion Entartete Kunst" (degenerate art campaign) in 1937 by museums in Germany or sold off by private owners. The result was that the already existing low prices decreased even more. Nierendorf needed to look for new markets in the West and thus he needed the expertise of Galka Scheyer.

In October 1939, she curated a Klee show with 60 works, including Rock Chamber, at the San Francisco Museum of Modern Art (SFMOMA). Rock Chamber was up for sale for $130 but found no buyer and was returned to Nierendorf. He finally sold the piece after 1942. From 1958 until 1989, it belonged to Hollywood legend Billy Wilder, so that it also had a well know private owner in the provenance chain – along with the noteworthy names of Klee dealers.[12]

These four examples show three different versions of Galka Scheyer-provenance: two unsold works in the 1920s, both were returned to Klee. One sold work and herewith a successful consignment. And a consignment with Karl Nierendorf which ended without sale but was shown at a huge Klee exhibition at SFMOMA, the first museum for 20th-century art in California.

To characterize Galka Scheyer's pioneering achievement in such categories as "successful" or "not successful," in terms of how many works she sold, does not do justice to her mission. Her engagement in popularizing the Blue Four goes beyond this. After she realized that New York was not the right place to achieve this, she did not

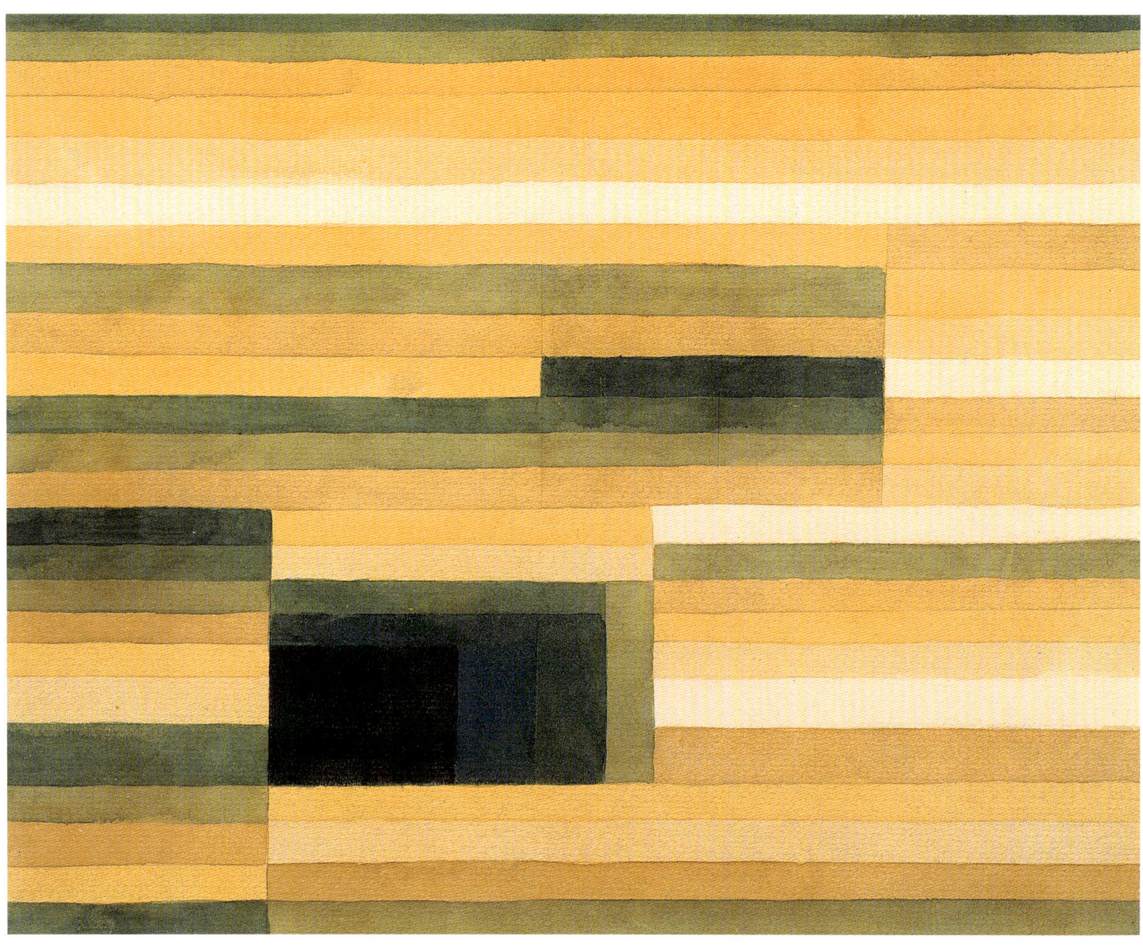

4 Rock Chamber / Felsenkammer, 1929, watercolor and graphite on paper, upper and lower -borders with gouache and pen mounted on cardboard, 25.4 x 31.7 cm (Courtesy of Staatliche Museen zu Berlin, Nationalgalerie, NG MB 139/2000, Photo: Jens Ziehe).

turn her back on America. Instead, she showed frontier spirit, decided to go west and headed out to California. Her achievements dealt more with idealism than in a business sense. She was not an art dealer, she was not a merchant nor a business-woman and never described herself as such. This was not her defined role 1924 in regard to her contract with the Blue Four. She was an agent who wanted to make them known. She curated them in museums, universities and art galler-ies where she kept an eye on their publicity. She showed their art in private circles, such as hotel rooms, flats and from 1933 on, in her house in

Hollywood Hills. Cultural institutions, schools, private and intimate surroundings and the char-acter of art salons were her fields of endeavor, not the art market. She never owned a gallery. For Galka Scheyer, the ideal version of a Klee prov-enance was ownership by herself. In a way she was her own best customer. Her collection as a whole comprised nearly 500 artworks, 350 created by the Blue Four. From the 56 works by Paul Klee in her collection, she received 31 originally desig-nated for selling before she decided to keep them and bought them herself.[13] This worked out while she had several incomes in addition to the selling of art – teaching, curating and financial support from her brothers Paul and Erich Scheyer in Germany, owners of a canning factory. But her situation became difficult in a decade that began with the Great Depression and ended with WWII.

What do the four Klee works introduced here tell us about Galka Scheyer's work? Due to their limited number, the validity of a statement is small. But in combination with other researches, the examples do say something: *First,* there were phases in Galka Scheyer's activities. In the mid-twenties, the Blue Four were a new and exclusive brand: they were a strong group, all worked at the Bauhaus. Galka Scheyer was somewhat of a branch or a display window in the US. Financial pressure was not strong at that time. The Blue Four did not expect many sales. She was a pioneer in California – a unique feature with a small but fine circle of customers. She often spoke about "Moralische Erfolge," about moral success.[14] This situation changed after 1933. She moved to Los Angeles. With the rise of National Socialism, the Bauhaus was closed. The Blue Four were no longer an art collective based at one place. Their art was forbidden in Germany, they went to different places or emigrated and needed the foreign market for the financial income which had come to a halt in their home countries or working environment. Ethical success was not enough anymore. This pressure was also felt by Galka Scheyer. The persecution of Jews hit her brothers hard: they were forced to sell the factory and the family was disassembled. In 1938, they emigrated to the UK and the US. This meant the end of her financial support from them. Matters were further complicated by a weak art market due to the difficult economic situation worldwide as well as an oversupply of modern art coming from Germany. Both were poor preconditions for a move to LA. It meant less exhibitions and more business competition: nationwide with Valentin and Nierendorf, but also with the rising Stendhal Galleries in Los Angeles. A new environment, unfortunate

cooperation and a decreased circle of customers combined with a market in crisis made it hard for her to regain her earlier success. The situation was further aggravated by the fact that Los Angeles at that time was not the glamorous and culturally influenced city we know today. The boom was just beginning and not everyone partook in it. Hollywood Hills could be a lonely place.

Second: There were clusterings within her activity. It all started 1924 with the contract between Scheyer and Paul Klee, Lyonel Feininger, Wassily Kandinsky, and Alexej Jawlensky. The main goal of the cooperation was to spread their artistic ideas through exhibitions, lectures and talks in the US. The artists were the owners of the artworks. Galka Scheyer received new material on consignment from them, but no salary for her engagement. If she sold a work, the artist would get 50% of the sales price. Her share was 30%. 20% went into a checkout fund for expenses. To sell artworks was welcomed, but not her first and foremost task.[15] In the 1930s, she tried to collaborate with other dealers. The cooperation with Nierendorf found no deeper sequel and it would need deeper research to define why. She once described the relationship in general as good.[16] Years later she wrote she never wanted to have anything to do with Nierendorf again on a business level.[17] Another cooperation with Valentin also proceeded without the desired results. Although she was able to sell a Klee for him and he bought some Klees she owned, they lost contact.[18] That her collaboration with the Oakland Art Gallery also came to an end in the 1930s may be another sign that business had become tougher. Some of the letters suggested that she was not satisfied with the cooperation. She also bemoaned her weak position. But this also could reveal that team work was an awkward and tricky task for her.

Third: The examples underline the meaning of provenance research. Maybe the outcome of the examination of the objects is rather thin in the case of the four examples. Neither the back side of the canvases, nor the frames and not even the works on paper contain any signs, stickers or hints to Galka Scheyer. The artworks make the impression that they never were in her possession, that she had nothing to do with them, that they had never met. On consulting archival material, the range of sources widens: lists of artworks, sketches of exhibits and correspondence. Other important sources are catalogues from exhibitions in which she was involved. Provenance research is first of all a discipline to clarify the origin and exclude the context of injustice. Yet it is more than this and can be demonstrated by the four Klees: provenance research sets the artworks in a context of the social history of art. It gives concrete examples for the international reception of art. When we follow the tracks of the artworks with a US-provenance such as the four Klees have, they tell a story about the popularization of European modernism in America and emigration: when and how did modern art come to the States? Who were the people who brought it there? Which role was played by museums and private collectors? What were their motives? What was their taste in art? In the case of Galka Scheyer, we are able to track her activity by the pieces of art which make her business model and passion tangible. Provenance research brings together the artwork with another narrative, such classical exhibition topics as *The Artist* or *The Artwork*. And it helps to rediscover names and biographies of former owners, dealers or collectors which had partly been forgotten. The artworks which they had in their possession are a reminder of these people, who shaped the history of art in many different ways. People like Galka Scheyer.

1 https://www.smb.museum/museen-einrichtungen/museum-berggruen/sammeln-forschen/forschung/biografien-der-bilder-werke-und-provenienzen-im-museum-berggruen/. The project was cofinanced by the Deutsches Zentrum Kulturgutverluste.
2 For provenance information check the documentation of the research project: Petra Winter, Doris Kachel, and Sven Haase, eds., *Biografien der Bilder. Provenienzen im Museum Berggruen* (Berlin, 2018).
3 Winter / Kachel / Haase, *Biografien* (see note 2), p. 177.
4 Norton Simon Museum, Pasadena, CA, Galka Scheyer Archive (henceforth NSM-GSA). List of Klee's works Scheyer took to the US in 1924.
5 Winter/Kachel/Haase, *Biografien der Bilder* (see note 2), p. 178.
6 Zentralarchiv, Staatliche Museen zu Berlin, SMB-ZA, I/ NG 469, 324ff.
7 NSM-GSA, Scheyer to Klee, March 19, 1937: "Ich hoffe Sie antworten mit einem nein, denn manche Leute treiben es gar zu doll."
8 NSM-GSA, Scheyer to Klee, June 15, 1937: "Mrs Mack in San Francisco schrieb mir, dass sie nicht mehr wie $700 zahlen kann, da sie drei unbemittelte Studenten durch die Universität schickt."
9 NSM-GSA, Scheyer to Mack, March 24, 1931.
10 Winter / Kachel / Haase, *Biografien* (see note 2), pp. 183f.
11 NSM-GSA, Nierendorf Galleries. List of Klee's works to Galka Scheyer.
12 Winter/Kachel/Haase, *Biografien der Bilder* (see note 2), p. 186.
13 Vivian Endicott Barnett, *The Blue Four Collection at the Norton Simon Museum*. Catalogue. New Haven, 2020.
14 Vivian Endicott Barnett, "Die letzten Jahre der Blauen Vier 1933–1945," in *Die Blaue Vier. Feininger, Jawlensky, Kandinsky, Klee in der Neuen Welt.* Exhibition catalog. (Cologne, 1997), pp. 263–78, here p. 264.
15 NSM-GSA, Generalvollmacht und Vertrag, March 31, 1924.
16 Scheyer to Kandinsky, June 11, 1939. In: Isabel Wünsche, ed., *Galka Scheyer & The Blue Four. Briefwechsel 1924–1945* (Berlin, 2006), p. 283.
17 NSM-GSA, Scheyer to Lili Klee, September 10, 1945.
18 Anja Tiedemann, "'Klees Tod war für mich der größte Schmerz.' Galka Scheyers und Curt Valentins Engagement für Paul Klee auf dem amerikanischen Kunstmarkt," in Uwe Fleckner, Thomas W. Gaehtgens, Christian Huemer, *Markt und Macht. Der Kunsthandel im Dritten Reich.* (Berlin, 2017), pp. 191–211, here: p. 205.

A Force of Nature –
Galka Scheyer and First Impressions

Gloria Williams Sander

Galka Scheyer stands among the most adventurous female art impresarios of the twentieth century. As a champion of art trends, and as a communicator who energized a broad and diverse constituency to share her passion, she was second to none. The difficulties that Scheyer faced as an agent for the Blue Four in California are often blamed on the negative impacts of the Great Depression (1929–39) and World War II. Although these events undeniably played a role, they tell only part of the story. One obstacle was Scheyer's Sisyphean task of promoting the abstract art of the European modernists in California, where regional narratives and the beauty of the natural landscape remained topical. Another factor was her status as a single Jewish woman working in a man's world without the social and economic connections that favored her more famous East Coast counterparts, who included Katherine Dreier and Hilla Rebay.

First-person recollections of Scheyer, as recounted by the artists, collectors, dealers, and museum directors in her vast network, are peppered with phrases like "dynamo of energy," "fiery enthusiasm," and "unshakable idealism." These traits informed her productiveness in California for some twenty years, 1924 to 1945, as she organized exhibits, lectured, and educated both adults and children in art and art making. And yet, not everyone felt so generous toward Scheyer. She possessed a

temperament that could be difficult. "Aggressive," "rude," and "loud" were some of the adjectives used to describe these troublesome characteristics, which were sometimes on display to the very audiences she was attempting to cultivate. The goal of this brief essay is not to disparage the legacy of this complicated, gifted impresario. It is rather to examine the nature of these grudging reviews and to consider whether, and how, they advanced or subverted her success as an agent of modernism.

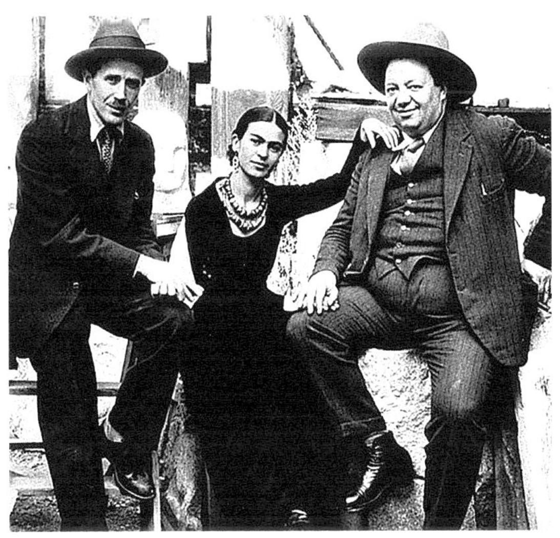

1 Photograph of Ralph Stackpole with Diego Rivera and Frida Kahlo, 1931 (Courtesy of the Archives of American Art, Smithsonian Institution, Emmy Lou Packard Papers, 1900–90).

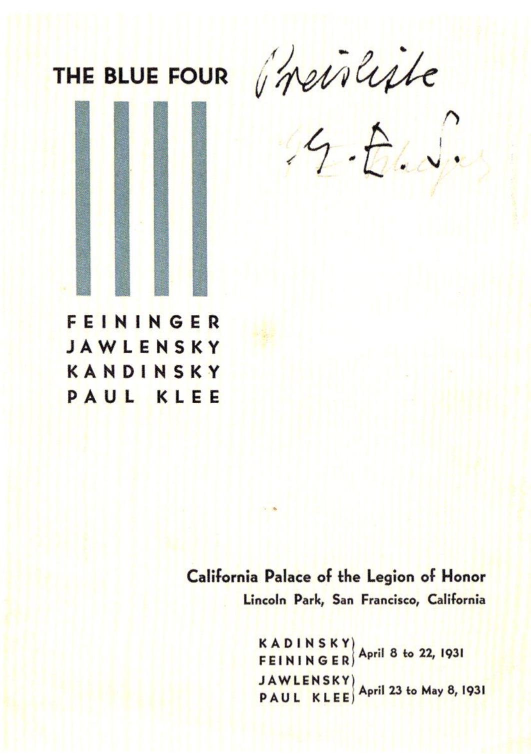

2 *The Blue Four, Exhibition Catalogue (San Francisco, California Palace of the Legion of Honor, 1931).*

Among the campaigns that Scheyer pursued on behalf of the Blue Four was a connection to Diego Rivera and Frieda Kahlo (Fig. 1). Rivera arrived in San Francisco in November 1930, already famous. He had secured two major mural commissions, for the Pacific Stock Exchange Building and for the California School of Fine Arts, and on November 15, a retrospective of his work debuted at the California Palace of the Legion of Honor.

The fearless Scheyer recognized a golden opportunity to introduce herself to Rivera, which she did between February and March of 1931, though the exact date is unknown. Her goal was to acquaint him with her Blue Four artists, and to enlist him in their promotion. Scheyer's timing to establish this connection was perfect, as she had secured April 8 for the opening of her Blue Four exhi-

bition at the California Palace of the Legion of Honor. We know that she gained Rivera's consent to add his name as a sponsor for the Blue Four exhibition and that he wrote an opening statement for it (Fig. 2). It is said that Scheyer even invited his expertise with regard to the installation of her show. Yet, despite what appears to have been a brilliant strategy to flatter and to involve the artist in her affairs, there are no published accounts or memoirs that document this interaction.

One, presumably firsthand, record of the initial meeting between Scheyer and Rivera is preserved in the Archives of American Art in the papers of John M. Weatherwax. A Harvard-trained specialist in the literature of Indigenous peoples, Weatherwax had secured an agreement with the very busy Rivera to create watercolor illustrations for his translation of the Popol Vuh, a mythology and history of the Maya people. For this reason, Weatherwax spent considerable time at the artist's studio in the hopes of capturing moments when the two could work together on this project. To pass the time, and to amuse Rivera and Frida Kahlo, the author wrote clever short stories about their experiences in San Francisco. "Diego, Galka and Toby" is one of them.[2] Although it is not sympathetic to Scheyer, his critical observations about her style as a bold, no-nonsense agent on a mission would be echoed in Scheyer's network throughout her California career.

The following excerpts are from Weatherwax's short story, which begins with Scheyer's unannounced first visit to Rivera, accompanied by her secretary, Toby Edison: After the briefest of introductions, Scheyer declares her purpose: "I've come to see you about the Blue Four."

Rivera respectfully offers her a chair in the main room where Weatherwax is sitting, but Scheyer seizes an available folding chair instead, and brings it close to where Diego is at work. She opens her leather bag and pulls out newspaper clippings and announcements related to her work on behalf of the Blue Four, which "she tosses up onto Diego's draughting table…Even Diego is startled…'Now, Señor Rivera,…I want you to do a favor for me. I want you to sponsor an exhibit in San Francisco of The Blue Four'" (p. 2). According to Weatherwax, Diego's response is relatively passive, he is mainly nodding. But this is enough encouragement for Scheyer to begin a dictation to her secretary. Scheyer begins the press release, "Diego Rivera,…the eminent Mexican Muralist, will sponsor the exhibition of paintings and drawings by The Blue Four…which will be held next Saturday…at The Palace of the Legion of Honour" (p. 3). As the narrative continues, Scheyer presses Rivera for a feature article in the city newspaper highlighting their collaboration (Fig. 3). Rivera's participation in the draft is encouraged, but it is Scheyer who drives the dictation. "Diego murmurs an occasional word," as Weatherwax notes wryly. When the draft is completed, Scheyer places it in her leather bag, declaring to the master, "Of course the article is yours, Diego…I have supplied only the bare facts. It will appear over your signature…in the San Franciscan, the leading feature of the art section" (p. 11).

Weatherwax's account of the first meeting between Rivera and Scheyer is satirical in its exaggeration and absence of generosity. His disrespect for Scheyer is strongly attached to her physical presence as a mature, Jewish woman. It comes in stark contrast to the sympathy he extends to Edison, a recent graduate with an art history diploma. However, Weatherwax's observation of Scheyer as "hard boiled," meaning tough or unsentimental, is not completely inaccurate (p. 4). She was an opportunist, and she acted as the intrepid agent willing to cross the line of decorum and gentility to achieve her goals. Given Weatherwax's description of Scheyer's assertive recruiting style, what motivation did a very busy Rivera have to comply? It so happens that Rivera's high

3 San Francisco Examiner, Sunday, April 19, 1931. Art Section.

Diego Rivera Introduces Blue Four

The group of contemporary artists known as "The Blue Four" whose joint show will continue at the California Palace of the Legion of Honor to May 17, has found an enthusiastic admirer in Diego Rivera, distinguished Mexican artist. The exhibition is held under his auspices as well as those of Mme. Galka E. Scheyer, American representative of the Blue Four. The artist has written the following, in part, appreciation of their art:

By Diego Rivera

There are in Europe, today, expressions of art which are not decadent, but which are, on the contrary, anticipated works destined for a better organized world. The authors of such expressions are pure creators whose work contains all the science of the great masters and all the fresh- of the genius of children. They are beings of the very first quality who progress faster than physical time, and who for this reason are already working in the future reality.

The artists, known in America as "The Blue Four"—Feininger, Jawlenski, Kandinsky and Klee —are men of this order, and for that reason alone, the artist-public of America should be especially interested in the expression of their work.

I am not a critic of art, but a painter who loves his "metier" (work) above all else. I love very much and have infinite esteem for the great artist Klee and his comrades Jewlensky, Feininger and Kandinsky.

The painting of Kandinsky is not an image of life—it is life itself. If there is a painter who merits the name of creator, that painter is Wassily Kandinsky. He organizes his matter as the matter of the Universe was organized, in order that the Universe might exist.

I know of nothing more real than the painting of Kandinsky— nothing more true and nothing more beautiful. The painting of possibility for the dream and for Kandinsky gives the maximum of the enjoyment of matter.

The art of Kandinsky is so human, so universal, that in America it appears American-Indian, and in Russia Russian, while the countries of old times,… the foreign…

status in the city was complicated and closer to that of a cause célèbre. Yes, he was hailed as a great artist whose example might reinvigorate the state of painting in California, but in San Francisco, Rivera became the figurehead of several controversies. First, there was intense indignation because two important mural commissions had not been awarded to local artists.[3] The second objection was problematic because it was widespread among the citizenry: how could the commission to decorate the Pacific Stock Exchange Tower, an institutional symbol of America's financial might, have been awarded to an avowed communist? Perhaps this collaboration with Scheyer offered Rivera an opportunity for positive publicity, at the very least within the arts community? And, Rivera's genuine support for the Blue Four artists and their brand of modernism hopefully softened a public that remained skeptical of their worth. Importantly, it did not preclude Rivera, Kahlo, and Scheyer from becoming friends, an alliance that sparked Scheyer's desire to organize an exhibition of the Blue Four in Mexico City in No-

vember 1931. During her extended, two-month stay in Mexico, at the home of Kahlo and Rivera, Scheyer was introduced to Mexican modernism, examples of which she would add to her personal collection.

Beatrice Wood's relationship with Scheyer affords a more intimate, nuanced understanding of our subject. Affectionately known as the "Mama of Dada," Wood involved herself early on in the American avant-garde movement and affiliated closely with such New York Dada artists as Marcel Duchamp and Francis Picabia. Thanks to her friendship with Duchamp, whom she met in September 1916, Wood gained the confidence to pursue her dream of becoming a visual artist. Importantly, Duchamp introduced Wood to Walter and Louise Arensberg, who count among the first serious collectors of modern art in America. Their collection was notable for the scope of material they acquired from Duchamp, and for the stellar assemblage of French modernist work and pre-Columbian sculpture.[4] In 1927, when the Arens-

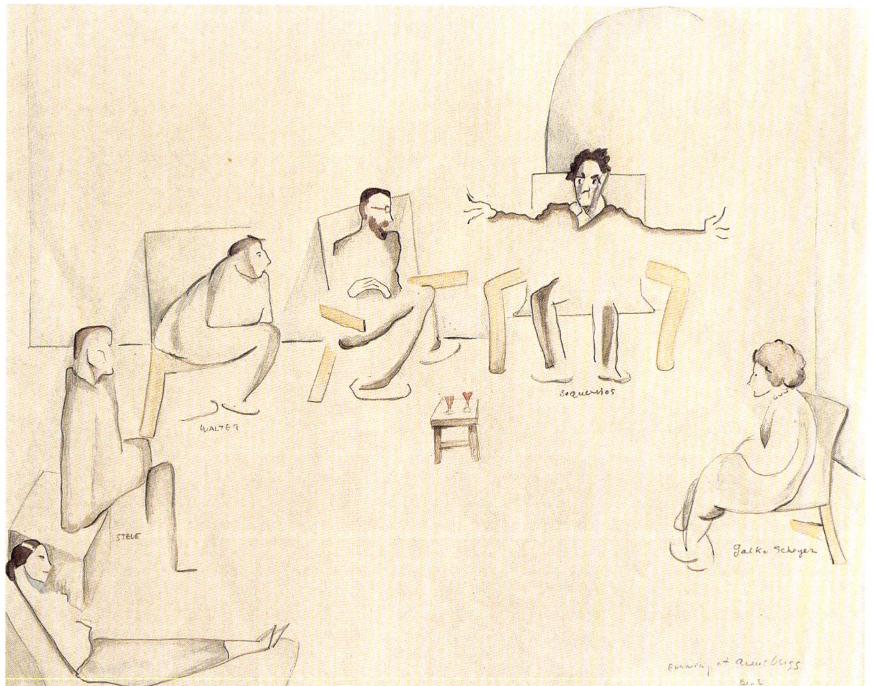

4 Beatrice Wood (American, 1893–1998) Evening at Arensbergs, 1930, Philadelphia (Courtesy of Museum of Art: Gift of the artist, 1978, 1978-98-6 © Beatrice Wood Center for the Arts/Happy Valley Foundation).

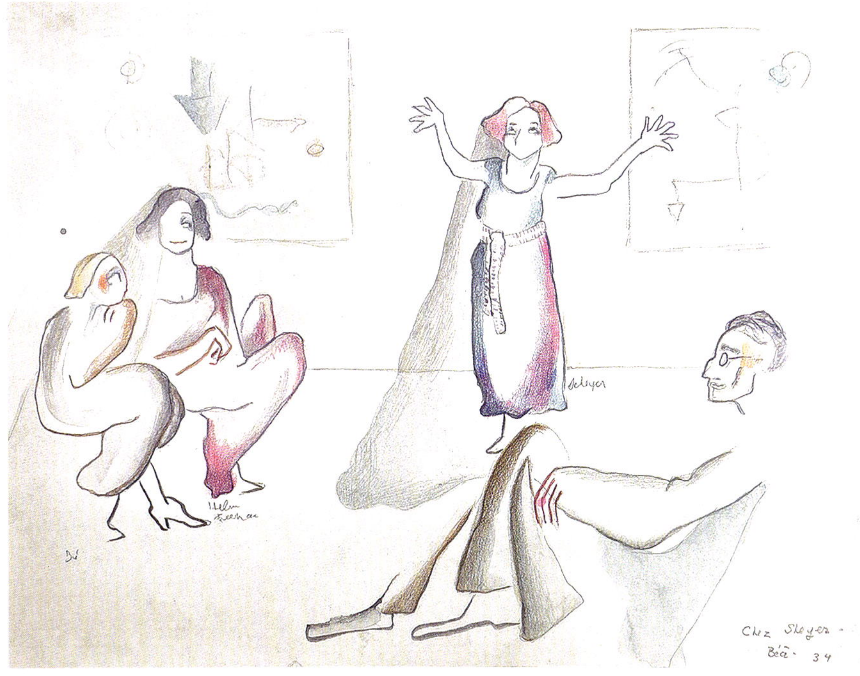

5 Beatrice Wood (American, 1893–1998) Chez Scheyer, 1934 (Courtesy of Philadelphia Museum of Art: Gift of the artist, 1978, 1978-98-5 © Beatrice Wood Center for the Arts/Happy Valley Foundation).

bergs moved permanently to Los Angeles, their home became a social and cultural hub, much as it had been in New York. Wood moved to Los Angeles in 1928. Once settled, she renewed her acquaintance with the Arensbergs and joined the vibrant circle of artists and art lovers who frequented their salons. Occasionally, she recorded the events in the form of evocative pictorial diaries (Fig. 4). Scheyer, too, was a frequent guest at the Arensbergs' Hollywood home for a period of time. She played a pivotal role in arousing in them a passion for the Blue Four. From 1930 forward, they acquired some twenty-seven artworks with her help. In doing so, they developed the most significant collection of Paul Klee on the West Coast. This legendary home is where Scheyer and Wood met.

Wood's first impression of Scheyer was negative:

> When I met Galka Scheyer I wanted to run, for she impressed me as the rudest person I had ever met. Short, with a large head of dyed henna hair

and Semitic features, the unconvetional beauty of her face escaped me. Her voice was stridentand her manner so intense it was abrasive. Yet, she was so alive in a room, and scintillating, that no one else counted. I went home and scolded myself for so readily disliking this woman.[5]

On her next social occasion in Scheyer's company, Wood observed that she

> saw through her rudeness and perceived a person of enormous tolerance and dignity. Galka was like a gourd, rough on the outside, but full of rare delicacy within.[6]

The two became allies in art and spent much time together, as evidenced by Wood's drawing of Scheyer holding court with guests at her Blue Heights Drive home in Los Angeles (Fig. 5).

At this key moment of expansion in Los Angeles's cultural history, during the 1930s, Wood lamented that Scheyer was frequently not invited

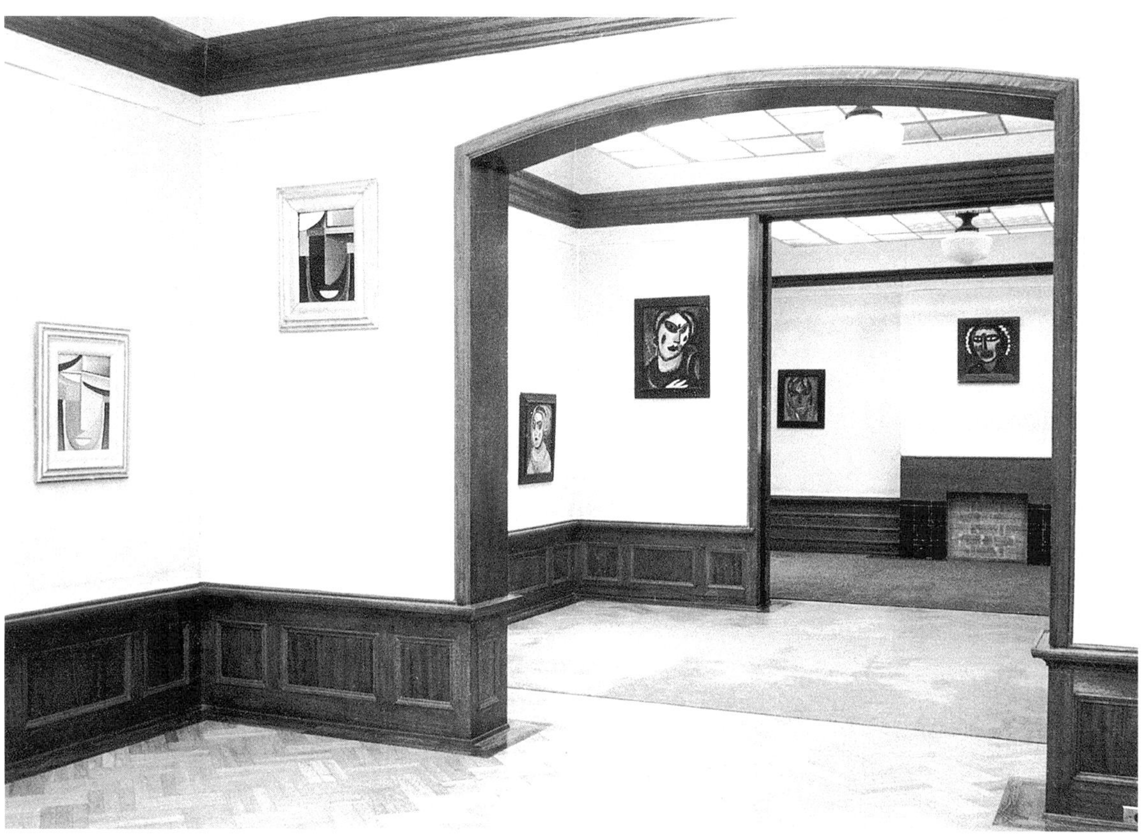

6 Installation photograph: Alexei Jawlensky, Stendahl Gallery, Los Angeles, 1940.

to important affairs where the agendas focused on creating a blueprint for the arts in the city. Bravely, and with good intentions, Wood decided to take up the matter directly with her friend in conversation:

> It was at this time when all the museums in Los Angeles were beginning to talk, were beginning to come of age … Walter (A) was at many of the meetings, Galka was not. I said "Look Galka, if you didn't shriek, maybe they would invite you." She answered: "But I will shriek, I'm more intelligent than they are. Why shouldn't I shriek? What does it matter if I shriek?[7]

Eventually, even Louise Arensberg couldn't sustain her shrill manner, and she severed Scheyer's attendance at their salons.[8] Wood's recollections

of her longtime friend are among the most empathetic and knowing in Scheyer's California network. They remained close friends until Scheyer's death in 1945.

Scheyer's stubborn independence caused sparks with museum professionals and gallerists alike. Marjorie Eaton, an artist whom Scheyer had befriended in San Francisco, and who had advised her with regard to acquiring work by Jawlensky and Klee, provided a vivid description of a run-in with Lloyd LaPage Rollins, director of the Legion of Honor and the de Young Museums in San Francisco, regarding an installation of Blue Four material:

> Galka was in the process of hanging the paintings with the museum attendants and she was

sailing in great form. She hung some of the paintings at eye level, some below eye level, and one way up to the ceiling and so on down the gallery, notes on a musical scale. She conceived it with great style … When Lloyd came in there was a mighty discussion, almost to violence, she protecting her interests and he being firm. He scolded, "I have already broken so many precedents here but this one goes too far!" So he rehung the paintings, so many inches apart, and at eye level, in the conventional way that would be acceptable.[9]

Rollins's protest about breaking precedent is apt for an agent who operated outside convention as a woman and as a professional. An idea of Scheyer's flair for installation design appears in a photograph from the Stendahl Gallery, Los Angeles, that documents a Jawlensky show held there in 1940 (Fig. 6).[10]

Certainly some of Scheyer's difficulties establishing her authority and gaining and maintaining important supporters were of her own making. Her ambition and considerable skills held little merit for dealers hoping to turn a profit, or for museum professionals beset with bureaucracy and deadlines. They saw no benefit in the unorthodox or the unconventional, and that likely included her status as a single, female impresario. Instead, as noted above, she found sympathy if not financial support for herself and her Blue Four artists within the tolerant milieu of artists, architects, and female collectors. They understood and appreciated her expertise and her ability to communicate about art with clarity and empathy, and they found vital support from her for their own artistic endeavors. As Edward Weston said, "She is the ideal 'go-between' for the artist and his public."[11]

Is it any wonder that Lyonel Feininger occasionally addressed Scheyer in his correspondence as "dear little Tornado"? She embodied every characteristic, positive and negative, that defines a force of nature. Only someone with a mind so quick and gifted, and with a missionary zeal akin to that of a prophet, could have succeeded to the degree that she did. She understood that timidity creates nothing. In hindsight, Galka Scheyer conditioned the arts community in California museum officials, gallerists, artists, and collectors to realize they had a responsibility to acquire and exhibit modern, cutting-edge art. Her footprint is measured in the art of the Blue Four that was acquired through her representation and is today conserved in the Oakland Museum of California, San Francisco's Museum of Modern Art, the Los Angeles County Museum of Art, the Long Beach Museum of Art, and the Norton Simon Museum.

1 Scheyer gained notoriety as a curator/dealer before even coming to America, thanks to her vigorous promotion of Alexei Jawlensky's work. Felix Klee recounted a puppet show he presented at the Weimar Bauhaus around 1922, in which Scheyer's aggressive tactics were the subject of comic relief. See Felix Klee, introduction, in Paul Klee, *Puppen, Plastiken, Reliefs, Masken, Theater* (Neuchâtel, 1979), p. 21; and *Bauhaus and Bauhaus People. Personal Opinions and Recollections of Former Bauhaus Members and Their Contemporaries*, ed. by Eckhard Neumann, trans. by Eva Richter and Alba Lorman (New York, NY, 1970), pp. 37ff.

2 John M. Weatherwax, "Diego, Galka and Toby," c. 1930s, typescript, John Weatherwax papers relating to Frida Kahlo and Diego Rivera, 1931–1933, box 1, folder 8, Archives of American Art, Smithsonian Institution, https://edan.si.edu/slideshow/viewer/?damspath=/CollectionsOnline/weatjohn/Box_0001/Folder_008, cited hereafter in the text by page number of the typescript.

3 See Anthony W. Lee, *Painting on the Left. Diego Rivera, Radical Politics, and San Francisco's Public Murals* (Berkeley, CA, 1999), chap. 3.

4 Mark Nelson, William H. Sherman, and Ellen Hoobler, *Hollywood Arensberg. Avant-garde Collecting in Midcentury L.A.* (Los Angeles, CA, 2020).

5 Helen Dixon Hennessey, "Beatrice Wood. Sophisticated Primitive" (PhD diss., Florida State University, 2004), p. 80, https://fsu.digital.flvc.org/islandora/object/fsu%3A182308. American photographer Edward Weston noted, "Galka repelled me at the very start of our acquaintance, but now I find myself wishing she would drop in once more before leaving;" *The Daybooks of Edward Weston*, vol. 2, *California*, ed. by Nancy Newhall (New York, 1973), p. 151.

6 Beatrice Wood, *I Shock Myself. The Autobiography of Beatrice Wood*, ed. by Lindsay Smith, rev. ed. (San Francisco, CA, 1992), pp. 86–87.

7 Ibid., pp. 88–89.

8 Elsa Longhauser and Lisa Melandri, *Beatrice Wood. Career Woman. Drawings, Paintings, Vessels and Objects* (Santa Monica, CA, 2011), p. 105.

9 *Staying Visible. The Importance of Archives. Art and "Saved Stuff" of Eleven 20ᵗʰ Century California Artists*, ed. by Jan Rindfleisch (Cupertino, CA, 1981), pp. 14–17.

10 See April Dammann, *Exhibitionist. Earl Stendahl, Art Dealer as Impresario* (Santa Monica, CA, 2011), pp. 81–82 for the contest of wills that Earl Stendahl had with Scheyer over installations.

11 Newhall, *Daybooks* (see note 5), p. 151.

BIBLIOGRAPHY

Arp, Hans. *Unsern täglichen Traum … Erinnerungen, Dichtungen und Betrachtungen aus den Jahren 1914–1954*. Zürich: Arche, 1955.

Art, Ronnie. "Say what you want but please … don't compare her to Grandma Moses." *California Living*, August 23, 1970.

Baer Smith, Lynne. "The Relationship between Paris, New York and San Francisco." In *From Exposition to Exposition*, ed. Joseph Armstrong Baird, Sacramento: 13–19.

Baird, Joseph Armstrong, Jr., ed. *From Exposition to Exposition. Progressive and Conservative Northern California Painting. 1915–1939*. The development of modern art in northern California 2. Sacramento, CA: Crocker Art Museum, 1981.

Ball, Hugo. *Briefe 1911–1927*. Einsiedeln: Benziger, 1957.

———. *Die Flucht aus der Zeit*. Zürich: Limmat, 1992.

Barnett, Vivian Endicott, and Josef Helfenstein. *Die Blaue Vier. Feininger, Jawlensky, Kandinsky, Klee in der Neuen Welt. Exhibition catalog*. Cologne: DuMont, 1997. Published in conjungtion with the exhibition "Die Blaue Vier. Feininger, Jawlensky, Kandinsky, Klee" shown at the Kunstmuseum Bern and the Kunstsammlung Nordrhein-Westfalen, Düsseldorf.

———. *The Blue Four Collection at the Norton Simon Museum*. New Haven: Yale University Press, 2002.

Bartels, Doris. "Aus der Schule geplaudert—eine Ehemalige berichtet." In *Gymnasium Kleine Burg, Braunschweig. 1863–1988. Festschrift zur 125-Jahr-Feier Gymnasium Kleine Burg*, ed. Brigitte Birkholz. Braunschweig: Bertram, 1988.

Baxter, John. *Von Sternberg*. Lexington, KY: University Press of Kentucky, 2010.

Bein, Reinhard. *Sie lebten in Braunschweig. Biographische Notizen zu den in Braunschweig bestatteten Juden (1797 bis 1983)*. Mitteilungen aus dem Stadtarchiv Braunschweig 1. Braunschweig: Döring, 2009.

———. *Lebensgeschichten von Braunschweiger Juden*. Braunschweig: Döring, 2016.

Belgin, Tayfun, ed. *Alexej von Jawlensky: Reisen, Freunde, Wandlungen*. Published in conjungtion with the exhibition "Alexej von Jawlensky: Reisen, Freunde, Wandlungen" shown at the Museum am Ostwall in Dortmund. Heidelberg: Umschau/Braus, 1998.

Boas, Nancy. *The Society of Six: California Colorists*. Berkeley, CA: University of California Press, 1998.

Borsano, Gabriella, and Harald Szeemann. *Monte Verit, Berg der Wahrheit. Lokale Anthropologie als Beitrag zur Wiederentdeckung einer neuzeitlichen sakralen Topographie*. Milano: Electa Ed., 1978.

Brown, F. W., ed. California Homes Plan Book for 1938. San Francisco, 1938.

Dailey, Victoria, Natalie Shivers, and Michael Dawson. *LA's Early Moderns: Art, Architecture, Photography*. Los Angeles, CA: Balcony Press, 2003.

Dammann, April. *Exhibitionist: Earl Stendahl. Art Dealer as Impresario*. Santa Monica, CA: Angel City Press, 2011.

Dascher, Ottfried. *Es ist was Wahnsinniges mit der Kunst. Alfred Flechtheim: Sammler, Kunsthändler, Verleger*. Wädenswil: Nimbus, 2011.

Denzer, Anthony, and Gregory Ain. *Gregory Ain: The Modern Home as Social Commentary*. New York: Rizzoli International Publications, 2008.

Deshmukh, Marion F. "The Visual Arts and Cultural Migration." *Central European History* 41, no. 4, Imagining Germany from Abroad: The View from Britain and the United States (December, 2008): 569–604.

Deter, Ismene. "Ein Prachtbau in Dornholzhausen. Vom 'Viktoria-Pensionat' zur Notunterkunft." *Mitteilungen des Vereins für Geschichte und Landeskunde zu Bad Homburg vor der Höhe* 50 (2001): 59–89.

Deverell, William. "Introduction." In *LA's Early Moderns : Art, Architecture, Photography*, edited by Victoria Dailey, Natalie Shivers, and Michael Dawson. Los Angeles: Balcony Press, 2003.

Dixon Hennessey, Helen. "Beatrice Wood: Sophisticated Primitive." PhD diss., Florida State University, 2004.

Ehrhardt, Frank, Kirsten Bergemann, and Jonathan Voges. *Zwischen Erfolg und Ablehnung: Jüdische Braunschweiger und ihr Engagement in der Gesellschaft. Eine Spurensuche.* Braunschweig: Arbeitskreis Andere Geschichte, 2013.

Flake, Kolma. "Arrested Moments." *Minicam Photography*, No. 1, September 1945: 50–55.

Fleckner Uwe, Thomas W. Gaehtgens, and Christian Huemer. *Markt und Macht. Der Kunsthandel im "Dritten Reich."* Schriften der Forschungsstelle "Entartete Kunst" 12. Berlin: DeGruyter, 2017.

———. "Zweifelhafte Geschäfte." In idem, Thomas W. Gaehtgens, and Christian Huemer. *Markt und Macht*, pp. 1–26.

Friedman, Alice T. *Women and the Making of the Modern House: A Social and Architectural History.* New York, NY: Abrams, 1998.

Grosz, George. *Ein kleines Ja und ein großes Nein: Sein Leben von ihm selbst erzählt.* Reinbek bei Hamburg: Rowohlt, 1986.

Higgins, Winifred Haines. *Art Collecting in the Los Angeles Area, 1910–1960.* Ann Arbor, 1986.

Hamermesh, Mira, Otto Zarek, and Lette Valeska. "Paintings of the Ghetto." *Zionist Review*, July 31, 1950.

Heuberger, Georg, ed. *Expressionismus und Exil: Die Sammlung Ludwig und Rosy Fischer Frankfurt am Main.* Munich, Prestel: 1990. Published in conjungtion with the exhibition "Expressionismus und Exil" shown at the Jüdisches Museum Frankfurt/Main.

Hines, Thomas S. *Richard Neutra and the Search for Modern Architecture.* New York: Rizzoli, 2005.

Horn, Virginia. "Lette Valeska—Richness of Creativity." *The Los Angeles Times.* August 20, 1965, pt. V.

Jawlensky, Alexej von. "Lebenserinnerungen." In Belgin, *Alexej von Jawlensky*, pp. 104–20.

Jawlensky, Angelica. "Ich habe meine Kunst in Ihre Hände gelegt: Emmy Scheyer und Alexej von Jawlensky—Eine Freundschaft," in Barnett, *Die Blaue Vier.*

Jeuthe, Gesa. *Kunstwerte im Wandel: Die Preisentwicklung der deutschen Moderne im nationalen und internationalen Kunstmarkt 1925 bis 1955.* Berlin: Akad.-Verl., 2011.

Joyner, Flagg Peter. "The Well-Painted Painting: Northern California's Academic Tradition and the Panama-Pacific International Exhibition." In Baird, *From Exposition to Exposition.*

Karlstrom, Paul J., ed. *On the Edge of America: California Modernist Art, 1900–1950.* Berkeley: Univ. of California Press, 1996.

———. *Turning the Tide: Early Los Angeles Modernists 1920–1956.* Santa Barbara, CA: Santa Barbara Museum of Art, 1990, in association with Ehrlich Susan. Published in conjungtion with the exhibition "Exhibition Turning the Tide: Early Los Angeles Modernists 1920–1956" shown at the Laguna Beach Museum of Art Corporation and the Santa Barbara Museum of Art.

Katin, William M. *Hostile Takeovers of Large Jewish Companies, 1933–1935.* Lexington studies in modern Jewish history, historiography, and memory. Lanham: Lexington Books, 2021.

Kirchner, Ernst Ludwig. "In memoriam Ludwig Schames." Including woodcut. *Der Querschnitt* 2, no. 3: *Weihnachtsheft* (1922): 156–57.

Klee, Felix. "Introduction." In *Paul Klee: Puppen, Plastiken, Reliefs, Masken, Theater*. Berne: Klee, 1979.

Koszinowksi, Ingrid. "Wiesbaden 1921–1941. Collectors and Friends," in *Jawlensky. Meine liebe Galka!*, eds. Volker Rattemeyer, Renate Petzinger, Wiesbaden: Museum Wiesbaden, 2004. Published in conjungtion with the exhibition "Expressionismus und Exil" shown at the Jüdisches Museum Frankfurt/Main.

Langsner Jules. "Post-Surrealists and Other Moderns, Hollywood: Stanley Rose Gallery, 1935," in *Pacific Dreams. Currents of Surrealism and Fantasy in California Art, 1934–1957*, ed. Susan Ehrlich. Los Angeles, 1995.

Lasker-Schüler Else. *Werke und Briefe, Kritische Ausgabe*, vol. 7, Briefe 1914-1924. Frankfurt 2004, p. 163.

Lee Anthony W. *Painting on the Left: Diego Rivera, Radical Politics, and San Francisco's Public Murals*. Berkeley, 1999.

Levin Amy K. (, ed.). *Gender, Sexuality and Museums*. A Routledge Reader. London et al., 2010.

Longhauser Elsa, Melandri Lisa. *Beatrice Wood: Career Woman; Drawings, Paintings, Vessels and Objects*. Santa Monica, 2011.

Lufft Peter. "Das Gästebuch Otto Ralfs," in *Arbeitsberichte aus dem Städtischen Museum Braunschweig*, 48. Braunschweig, 1985.

Martersteig Max (, ed.). *Jahrbuch der bildenden Kunst*. Berlin, 1903.

Mayer Bernhard. I*nteressante Zeitgenossen. Interesting Contemporaries. Lebenserinnerungen eines jüdischen Kaufmanns und Weltbürgers. Memoirs of a Jewish merchant and cosmopolitan. 1866-1946*, ed. Erhard Roy Wiehn. Konstanz, 1998.

Millier Arthur. "'Ultra' Gallery Arrives" in *Los Angeles Times*. September 15, 1929.

Nauhaus Julia M. *Die Gemäldesammlung des Städtischen Museums Braunschweig. Vollständiges Bestandsverzeichnis und Verlustdokumentation*. Mit Beiträgen von Justus Lange. Hildesheim, Zürich, New York, 2009.

Nelson Mark, Sherman William H., Hoobler Ellen. *Hollywood Arensberg: Avant-garde Collecting in Mid-century L. A*. Los Angeles, 2020.

Neumann J. B. "Die neue deutsche Kunst in New York", in *Das Kunstblatt*, vol. 11. Potsdam, 1927.

Newhall Nancy. T*he Daybooks of Edward Weston*. New York, 1961.

Pötzsch Hansjörg. "Freunde der Kunst und der Künstler. Galka Scheyer, Otto Ralfs und die Gesellschaft der Freunde Junger Kunst", in *Beiträge zur Kunst der Moderne. Niederdeutsche Beiträge zur Kunstgeschichte*, eds. Rainer Stamm, Gloria Köpnick, new series, vol. 3. Petersberg, 2018.

Rindfleisch Jan (, ed.). Roots and Offshoots: Silicon Valley's Arts Community. Santa Clara, 2017.

Rindfleisch Jan (, ed.). *Staying Visible: The Importance of Archives: Art and "Saved Stuff" of Eleven 20th Century California Artists*. Cupertino, 1981.

Sandback Amy B. Blue Heights Drive, *Artforum*, 28, no. 7. 1990.

Sawelson-Gorse Naomi. "Narrow Circles and Uneasy Alliances: Galka Scheyer and American Collectors of the Blue Four," in *The Blue Four: Feininger, Jawlensky, Kandinsky, Klee in the New World*, eds. Vivian Endicott Barnett, Josef Helfenstein. Cologne, 1997.

Schapire Rosa. *Karl Schmidt-Rottluffs graphisches Werk bis 1923*. Berlin, 1923.

Scheyer Galka E. "Free Imaginative and Creative Work," in *VI. International Congress for Art Education, Drawing and Art Applied to Industry in Prague, 1928: General Report of the Congress*. Prague, 1931.

Schnauber Cornelius. *Spaziergänge durch das Hollywood der Emigranten*. Zürich, 1992.

Schnauber Cornelius. *Hollywood Haven: Homes and Haunts of the European Émigrés*. Riverside, 1997.

Schrott Raoul, *Dada 15/25. Dokumentation und chronologischer Überblick zu TZARA & Co.* Köln, 2004.

Schwitters Kurt, Steinitz Traumann Kate. *Erinnerungen aus den Jahren 1918-1930*. Zurich, 1965.

Stein-Steinfeld Marian, Bekker vom Rath Hanna. *Handelnde für Kunst und Künstler.* Frankfurt am Main, 2018.

Sweeney Robert. "Life in Kings Road: As It Was 1920–1940," in *The Architecture of R. M. Schindler*, eds. Michael Darling and Elizabeth A. T. Smith. New York, 2001.

von Sydow Eckart. "Braunschweig: Klee und Nolde im Landesmuseum", in *Der Cicerone*, vol. 24. Leipzig 1924.

Thau Heyman Therese. "Modernist Photography and the Group f.64," in *On the Edge of America: California Modernist Art, 1900–1950*. Berkeley, 1996.

Ville de Bruxelles, ed. "Liquidation des biens sous séquestre. Catalogue d'une importante et très belle (…) collection Bachrach (…) Salle Delgay (…) Lundi 29 Décembre 1924 (…)", p. 12.

Weiler Clemens. "Galka Scheyer. Bildnis einer Braunschweigerin," in *Brunsvicensia Judaica. Gedenkbuch für die jüdischen Mitbürger der Stadt Braunschweig 1933–1945*. Braunschweig, 1966.

Weston Edward and Newhall Nancy, eds. *The Daybooks of Edward Weston*, vol. 2: California. New York, 1966.

Wilson William. "Mme. Lette Valeska debuts at 85 with paintings, sculpture and woodcuts at La Torture Gallery (1607 Montana Ave, Santa Monica)," in *The Los Angeles Times*. August 17, 1970.

Winter Petra, Kachel Doris, Haase Sven, eds. B*iografien der Bilder. Provenienzen im Museum Berggruen*. Berlin 2018.

Wood Beatrice. *I Shock Myself: The Autobiography of Beatrice Wood*, ed. Lindsay Smith. San Francisco, 1992.

Wünsche Isabel. *Galka E. Scheyer und Die Blaue Vier. Briefwechsel, 1924-1945*. Wabern/Bern, 2006.

Zentrum Paul Klee, Bern, and Stefan Frey, eds. *"In inniger Freundschaft." Alexej Jawlensky, Paul und Lily Klee, Marianne Werefkin. Der Briefwechsel*. Zurich, 2013.

Index of Persons

Volume 5

Aliza Cohen-Mushlin and Harmen H. Thies (Eds.)
**Synagogenarchitektur in Deutschland. Dokumentation zur
Ausstellung „und ich wurde ihnen zu einem kleinen Heiligtum…"**

21 x 26 cm, 272 pages,
298 b/w illustrations,
hardcover, text: German
Petersberg: Michael Imhof Verlag, 2008
ISBN 978-3-86568-344-1

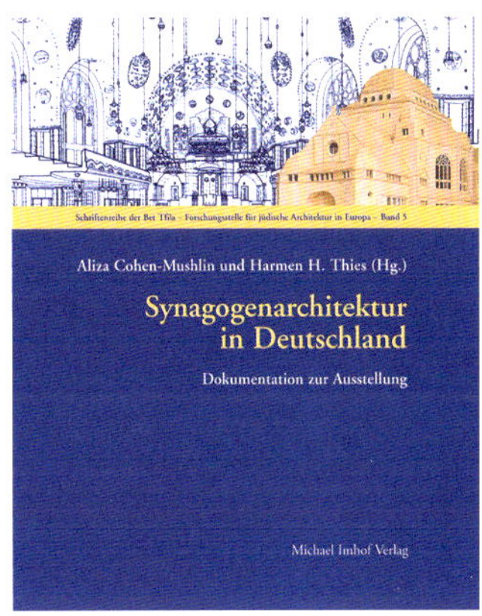

Volume 6

Aliza Cohen-Mushlin and Harmen H. Thies (Eds.)
Jewish Architecture in Europe

21 x 26 cm, 382 pages,
303 b/w illustrations,
hardcover, text: English
Petersberg: Michael Imhof Verlag, 2010
ISBN 978-3-86568-346-5

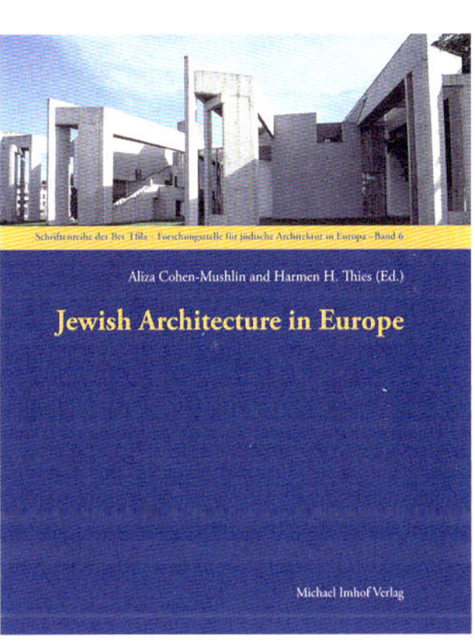

Volume 7

Ole Harck
**Archäologische Studien zum Judentum in der europäischen Antike
und dem zentraleuropäischen Mittelalter**
21 x 26 cm, 656 pages,
b/w illustrations, drawings,
hardcover, text: German
Petersberg: Michael Imhof Verlag, 2014
ISBN 978-3-7319-0078-8

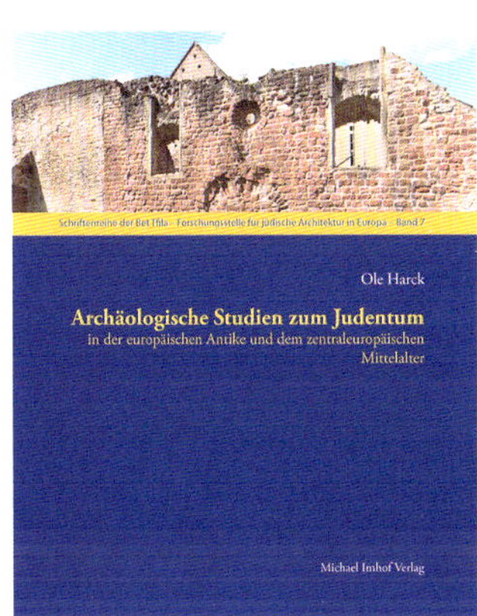

Publications of the Bet Tfila

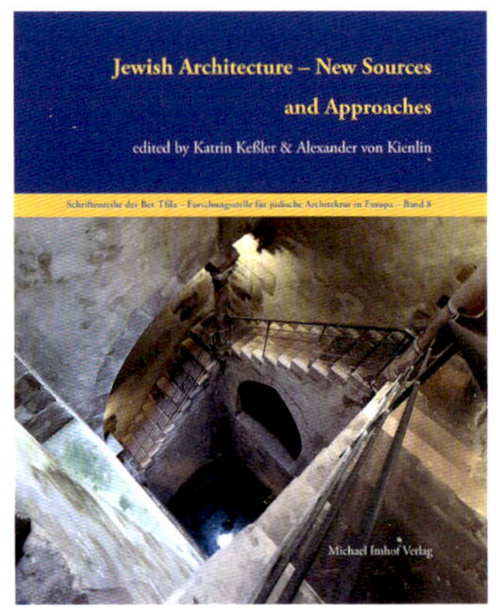

Volume 8

Katrin Keßler, Alexander von Kienin (eds.)
Jewish Architecture – New Sources and Approaches

21 x 26 cm, 159 pages,
colour illustrations,
hardcover, text: English
Petersberg: Michael Imhof Verlag, 2015
ISBN 978-3-7319-0322-2

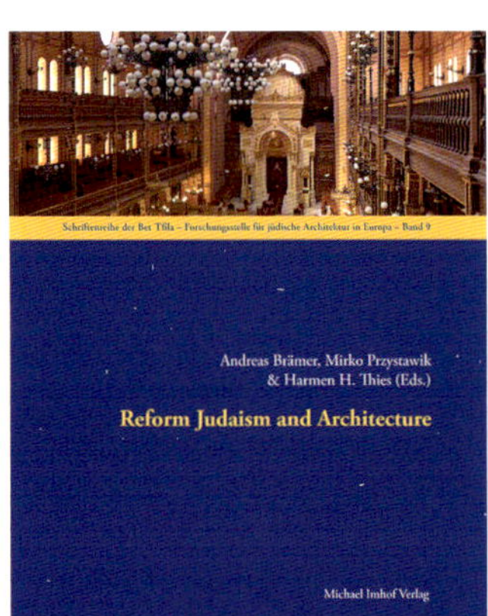

Volume 9

Andreas Brämer, Mirko Przystawik and Harmen H. Thies (Eds.)
Reform Judaism and Architecture

21 x 26 cm, 176 pages,
164 colour and b/w illustrations,
hardcover, text: English
Petersberg: Michael Imhof Verlag, 2016
ISBN 978-3-7319-0307-9

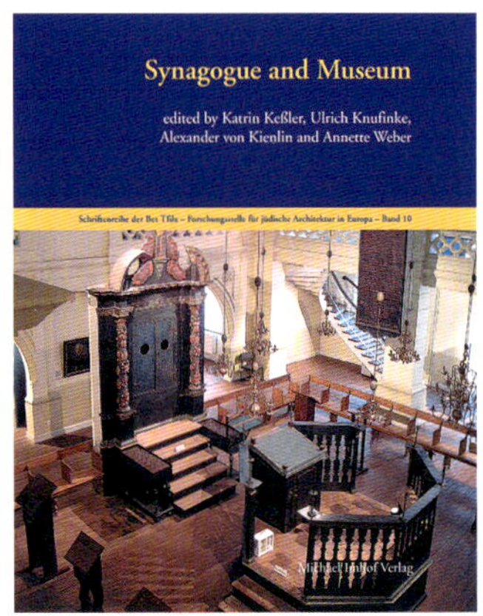

Volume 10

Katrin Keßler, Ulrich Knufinke, Alexander von Kienlin and Annette Weber (Eds.)
Synagogue and Museum

21 x 26 cm, 192 pages,
151 colour and b/w illustrations,
hardcover, text: English
Petersberg: Michael Imhof Verlag, 2018
ISBN 978-3-7319-0794-7

PUBLICATIONS OF THE BET TFILA

Volume 11

Barbara Perlich (Ed.)
Wohnen, beten, handeln. Das hochmittelalterliche jüdische Quartier *ante pontem* **in Erfurt**

21 × 26 cm, 432 pages,
270 illustrations, drawings,
hardcover, text: German
Petersberg: Michael Imhof Verlag, 2019
ISBN 978-3-7319-0835-7

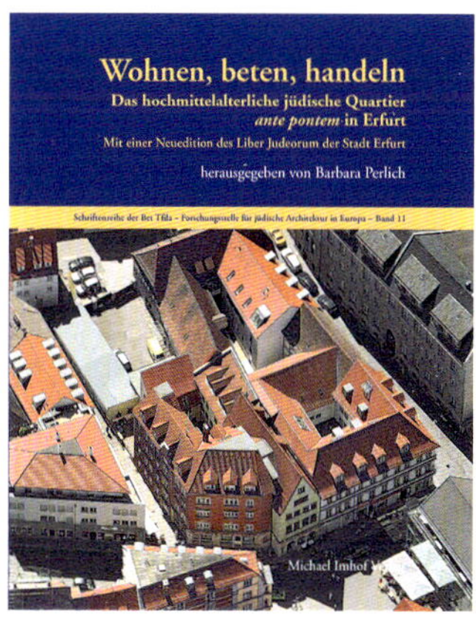

Volume 12

Andreas Brämer, Katrin Keßler,
Ulrich Knufinke & Mirko Przystawik (Eds.)
Jewish Architects – Jewish Architecture?

21 × 26 cm, 216 pages,
108 colour and 70 b/w illustrations,
hardcover, text: English
Petersberg: Michael Imhof Verlag, 2021
ISBN 978-3-7319-0835-7

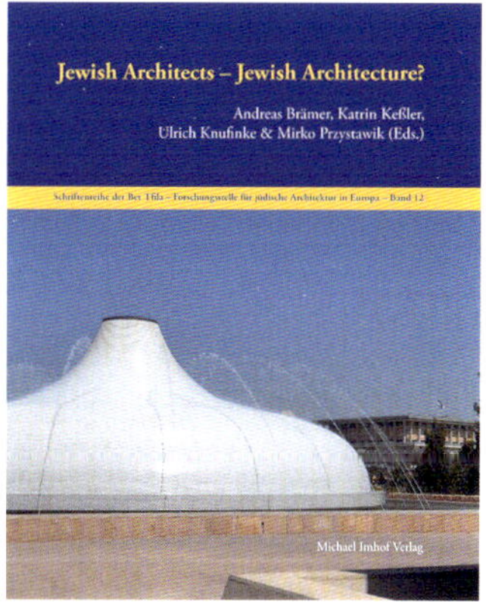

Bet Tfila Studies

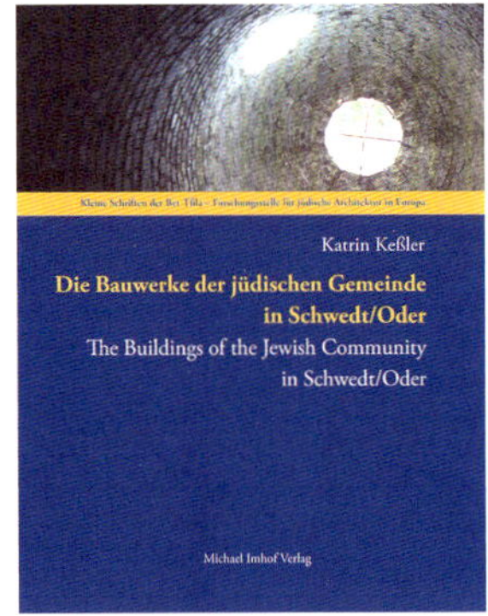

Volume 1

Katrin Keßler
Die Bauwerke der jüdischen Gemeinde in Schwedt/ Oder / The Buildings of the Jewish Community in Schwedt/Oder
21 x 25,5 cm, 64 pages, illustrations and drawings, brochure, text: German/English
Petersberg: Michael Imhof Verlag, 2007
ISBN 978-3-86568-314-4

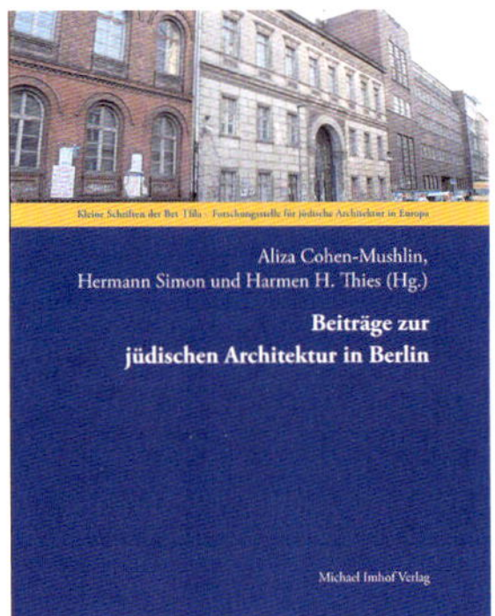

Volume 2

Aliza Cohen-Mushlin, Hermann Simon, Harmen H. Thies (Eds.)
Beiträge zur jüdischen Architektur in Berlin
21 x 25,5 cm, 112 pages, illustrations, brochure, text: English, German summary
Petersberg: Michael Imhof Verlag, 2009
ISBN 978-3-86568-479-0

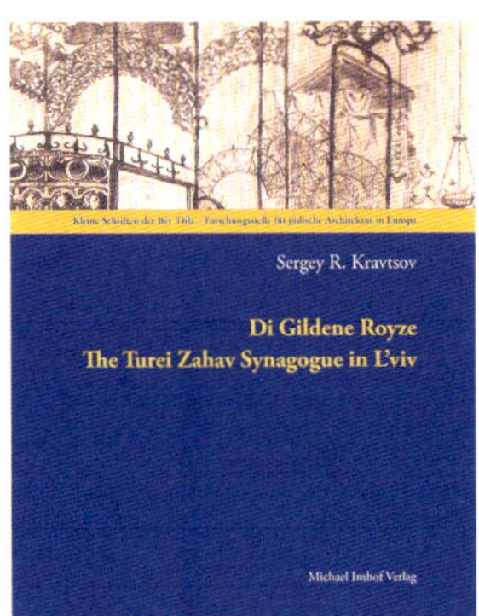

Volume 3

Sergey R. Kravtsov
**Di Gildene Royze –
The Turei Zahav Synagogue in L'viv**
21 x 25,5 cm, 88 pages,
57 b/w illustrations,
brochure, text: English summary
Petersberg: Michael Imhof Verlag, 2011
ISBN 978-3-86568-138-6

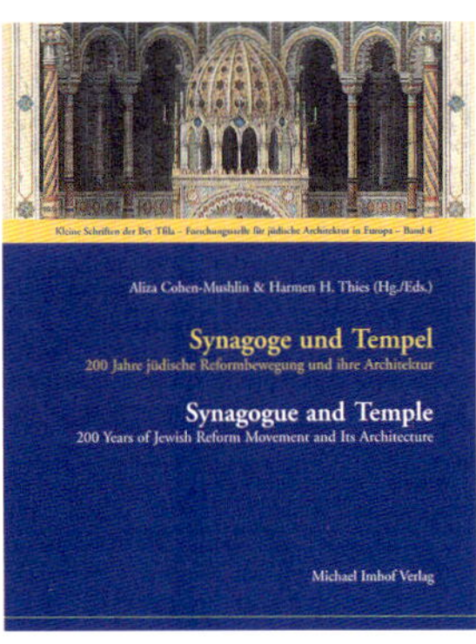

Volume 4

Aliza Cohen-Mushlin, Harmen H. Thies (Eds.)
Synagoge und Tempel – 200 Jahre jüdische Reformbewegung und ihre Architektur
21 x 25,5 cm, 155 pages, illustrations, brochure, text: English, German
Petersberg: Michael Imhof Verlag, 2012
ISBN 978-3-86568-834-7